# Full Stack FastAPI, Re
# and MongoDB

## Fast-paced web app development with the FARM stack

Marko Aleksendrić, Ph.D.

Shrey Batra

Rachelle Palmer

Shubham Ranjan

‹packt›

# Full Stack FastAPI, React, and MongoDB

## Second edition

**Publisher**: Vishal Bodwani

**Product Manager**: Sathya Mohan

**Lead Development Editor**: Afzal Shaikh

**Development Editor**: Rhea Gangavkar

**Copy Editor**: Safis Editing

**Proofreader**: Safis Editing

**Project Coordinator**: Yash Basil

**Production Designer**: Deepak Chavan

**Production reference**: 2230824

Published by Packt Publishing Ltd.

Grosvenor House, 11 St Paul's Square, Birmingham, B3 1RB, UK.

ISBN 978-1-83588-676-2

www.packtpub.com

# Contributors

## About the authors

**Marko Aleksendrić, Ph.D.**, is an analyst, a scientist, and a freelance self-taught web developer with over 20 years of experience. Marko authored the books *Modern Web Development with the FARM Stack* and *Mastering MongoDB 7.0*, published by Packt Publishing. With a keen interest in backend and frontend development, he has been an avid MongoDB user for the last 15 years for various web and data analytics-related projects and has built numerous Python and JavaScript web applications and tools.

**Shrey Batra** is the founder of Cosmocloud, a MongoDB Champion, and a software developer by passion. As a tech start-up founder building a no-code backend with MongoDB, he combines his passion for both MongoDB and building applications at scale. Working in the industry for over eight years, he is also an active contributor to the technical community, speaks at various world conferences and meetups, and writes his own newsletter, *System Design and Architecture*, which has 50K+ subscribers. He is also a distributed algorithm patent holder for his work at LinkedIn on its Search and Discovery platform.

**Rachelle Palmer** is the Product Leader for Developer Database Experience and Developer Education at MongoDB, overseeing the driver client libraries, documentation, framework integrations, and MongoDB University. She has built sample applications for MongoDB in Java, PHP, Rust, Python, Node.js, and Ruby. Rachelle joined MongoDB in 2013 and was previously the Director of the Technical Services Engineering team, creating and managing the team that provided support and CloudOps to MongoDB Atlas.

**Shubham Ranjan** is a Product Manager at MongoDB for Python and a core contributing member to AI initiatives at MongoDB. He is also a Python developer and has published over 700 technical articles on topics ranging from data science and machine learning to competitive programming. Since joining MongoDB in 2019, Shubham has held several roles, progressing from software engineer to product manager for multiple products.

# About the reviewer

**Rea Rustagi** is a technical writer who is interested in developer productivity and educational tools. She maintains technical documentation for the client libraries of MongoDB, as well as language frameworks, tools, and integrations. She writes tutorials, reference materials, and sample applications in a variety of languages, including Rust, PHP, Go, and JVM languages. She is passionate about using different methodologies to help developers adapt to and learn about new technologies. Rea also has experience as the editor of a literary journal and as an academic researcher in physical oceanography. Some of her other interests include environmental health, literature, and sustainability.

# Note from Author

As someone who began their journey through web development in what were considered the early days of yore, I first learned pure HTML. I remember using tables for layouts and animated GIF banners popping up everywhere. My own development career started with Java and C at university. Like many, I found these languages to be complex, unwieldy, and difficult to be excited about. Later, I made half-hearted attempts at learning Ruby and JavaScript. I resigned myself to *not* being a software engineer because I hated writing code.

And then I discovered Python.

I watched a single course on YouTube, plunking along with each lesson, and it just made sense. I fell headlong in love with how easy, simple, and *fast* everything was. It was fast to learn and fast to write and flexible enough to use with sysadmin tasks, and excel at analysis and web development. As my confidence grew, I jumped head-first into Bash and Linux networking, distributed systems, and tracing. Even now, years later, having tried Rust, C#, and PHP, there is no programming language as fun as Python was in those early years. Because of that experience, and all the years after, I have been able to easily acclimate to the new world of AI/ML, building generative AI applications. Due to that, I owe Python and its community a great debt. My career as it is would not have been the same without Python.

In 2022, my team and I conducted a survey of MongoDB users. We asked them the basics, such as their role, their preferred programming language, and what tasks they conducted. The results astounded me, particularly when I learned that 83% of MongoDB users were developers, followed by 10% being DevOps engineers. Just 5% were database administrators. We also learned that of all the programming language cohorts, the engineers who took on the most jobs were Python developers.

**72% of Python developers who consider themselves software engineers take on tasks that are not software development, such as data science, sysadmin, data cleansing, data migrations, and, of course, web development.**

This was not true for any other language, and it speaks to the versatility of the programming language itself that it can enable its users to do so many different things. Those survey results were not a surprise, at least not to me, because I'd already lived that experience.

If you are reading this book, I imagine that you are in the beginning stages of this journey. You're somewhat new, perhaps, to web development with Python. It is (maybe) the start of your own career, your own adventure. This book will teach you the simplest and fastest way to build a modern web application with Python, which, in my opinion, is the FARM stack. You'll learn about FastAPI, React, and MongoDB as you go along, and by the end, you'll have your own working application. I hope that you will be just as thrilled to build as we were to write this book.

I'm excited for you to turn the page and begin.


**Rachelle Palmer**

Director, Product Management

MongoDB, Inc.

# Table of Contents

# 3

## Python Type Hints and Pydantic                                                    43

# 4

## Getting Started with FastAPI                                                       69

# 5

## Setting Up a React Workflow                                                97

# 6

## Authentication and Authorization                                         119

# 10

## Web Development with Next.js 14                                    247

# 11

## Useful Resources and Project Ideas                                 277

# Preface

*Full Stack FastAPI, React, and MongoDB, Second Edition*, is a fast-paced, concise, and hands-on beginner's guide that aims to boost the potential of web developers and help them stay ahead in the rapidly evolving web development and AI fields with the flexibility, adaptability, and robustness of the FARM stack. This book introduces each element of the stack and then explains how to make them work together to build a medium-sized web application.

It demonstrates, with hands-on examples and real-world use cases, how to set up a document store with MongoDB, build a simple API with FastAPI, and create an application with React. Furthermore, it delves into using Next.js, ensuring data integrity and security with MongoDB, and integrating third-party services with applications.

## How this book will help you

This book takes a hands-on approach to demonstrating web application development with real-world examples using the FARM stack. By the end of the book, you will have the confidence to use the FARM stack to develop fully functional web applications at a fast pace.

## Who this book is for

This book is for intermediate web developers with basic JavaScript and Python knowledge who want to enhance their developer skills, master a powerful and flexible stack, and write better applications faster.

## What this book covers

*Chapter 1, Web Development and the FARM Stack*, provides a deep understanding of the web development landscape by giving you a quick walk-through of the widely used technologies available. It introduces the most popular option—the FARM stack. It highlights the benefits of FARM stack components, how they relate to each other, and why this particular set of technologies is a great fit for web apps.

*Chapter 2, Setting Up the Database with MongoDB*, provides an overview of MongoDB, and then shows how to set up the data storage layer for a FARM application. It helps with exploring the basics of creating, updating, and deleting documents. Furthermore, this chapter details the aggregation pipeline framework—a strong analytic tool.

*Chapter 3, Python Type Hints and Pydantic*, includes examples that teach you about more web-specific aspects of FastAPI and how to blend data seamlessly between MongoDB, Python data structures, and JSON.

*Chapter 4, Getting Started with FastAPI*, focuses on introducing the FastAPI framework, along with the standard REST API practices and how they are implemented in FastAPI. It covers very simple examples of how FastAPI achieves the most common REST API tasks and the way it can help you by leveraging modern Python features and libraries such as Pydantic.

*Chapter 5, Setting Up a React Workflow*, shows how to design a simple application with a few components using the React framework. It discusses the tools needed to be able to explore React and its various functionalities.

*Chapter 6, Authentication and Authorization*, details a simple yet robust and extensible setup for your FastAPI backend, based on **JSON Web Tokens (JWTs)**. It demonstrates the integration of JWT-based authentication methods into React, leveraging some of React's powerful features—namely, Hooks, Context, and React Router.

*Chapter 7, Building a Backend with FastAPI*, helps in working on a simple business requirement and turning it into a fully functional API deployed on the internet. It shows how to define the Pydantic models, perform CRUD operations, build your FastAPI backend, and connect to MongoDB.

*Chapter 8, Building the Frontend of the Application*, illustrates the steps for building the frontend of a full stack FARM application. It shows how to create a React application using a modern Vite setup and implement the basic functionalities.

*Chapter 9, Third-Party Services Integration with FastAPI and Beanie*, gives the basics of Beanie, a popular ODM library for MongoDB, built on top of Motor and Pydantic. It shows how to define models and Beanie documents that map to MongoDB collections. You'll see how to build another FastAPI application and integrate third-party services with the help of background tasks.

*Chapter 10, Web Development with Next.js 14*, gives a walk-through of important Next.js concepts, such as Server Actions, form handling, and cookies to help in creating a new Next.js project. You'll also learn how to deploy your Next.js application on Netlify.

*Chapter 11, Useful Resources and Project Ideas*, provides some practical advice when working with the FARM stack, along with project ideas where the FARM stack, or very similar stacks, could be applicable and helpful.

# To get the most out of this book

You need to know the basics of JavaScript and Python. Having prior knowledge of MongoDB is preferable but not essential. You will require the following software:

| Software/hardware covered in the book | Operating system requirements |
|---|---|
| MongoDB version 7.0 or later | Windows, macOS, or Linux |
| MongoDB Atlas Search | Windows, macOS, or Linux |
| MongoDB Shell 2.2.15 or later | Windows, macOS, or Linux |
| Node.js version 18.17 or later | Windows, macOS, or Linux |
| Python 3.11.7 or later | Windows, macOS, or Linux |
| Next.js 14 or later | Windows, macOS, or Linux |
| FastAPI 0.111.1 | Windows, macOS, or Linux |
| React 18 or later | Windows, macOS, or Linux |

If you are using the digital version of this book, we advise you to type the code yourself or access the code from the book's GitHub repository (a link is available in the next section). Doing so will help you avoid any potential errors related to the copying and pasting of code.

# Download the example code files

You can download the example code files for this book from GitHub at `https://github.com/PacktPublishing/Full-Stack-FastAPI-React-and-MongoDB-2nd-Edition`. If there's an update to the code, it will be updated in the GitHub repository.

We also have other code bundles from our rich catalog of books and videos available at `https://github.com/PacktPublishing/`. Check them out!

# Download the color images

We also provide a PDF file that has color images of the screenshots and diagrams used in this book. You can download it here: `http://www.packtpub.com/sites/default/files/downloads/Bookname_ColorImages.pdf`.

# Conventions used

There are a number of text conventions used throughout this book.

`Code in text`: Indicates code words in text, database table names, folder names, filenames, file extensions, pathnames, dummy URLs, user input, and Twitter handles. Here is an example: "Optionally, you can create a `middleware.js` function that will contain middleware that will be applied on every (or only selected) request."

A block of code is set as follows:

```
const Cars = () => {
    return (
        <div>Cars</div>
    )
}
export default Cars
```

When we wish to draw your attention to a particular part of a code block, the relevant lines or items are set in bold:

```
<body>
    <Navbar />
    {children}
</body>
```

Any command-line input or output is written as follows:

```
git push -u origin main
```

**Bold**: Indicates a new term, an important word, or words that you see onscreen. For instance, words in menus or dialog boxes appear in **bold**. Here is an example: "Select the Windows version and click on **Download**."

> **Tips or important notes**
> Appear like this.

# Get in touch

Feedback from our readers is always welcome.

**General feedback**: If you have questions about any aspect of this book, email us at customercare@packtpub.com and mention the book title in the subject of your message.

**Errata**: Although we have taken every care to ensure the accuracy of our content, mistakes do happen. If you have found a mistake in this book, we would be grateful if you would report this to us. Please visit www.packtpub.com/support/errata and fill in the form.

**Piracy**: If you come across any illegal copies of our works in any form on the internet, we would be grateful if you would provide us with the location address or website name. Please contact us at copyright@packt.com with a link to the material.

**If you are interested in becoming an author**: If there is a topic that you have expertise in and you are interested in either writing or contributing to a book, please visit authors.packtpub.com.

# Download a free PDF copy of this book

Thanks for purchasing this book!

Do you like to read on the go but are unable to carry your print books everywhere?

Is your eBook purchase not compatible with the device of your choice?

Don't worry, now with every Packt book you get a DRM-free PDF version of that book at no cost.

Read anywhere, any place, on any device. Search, copy, and paste code from your favorite technical books directly into your application.

The perks don't stop there, you can get exclusive access to discounts, newsletters, and great free content in your inbox daily

Follow these simple steps to get the benefits:

1.  Scan the QR code or visit the link below

https://packt.link/free-ebook/9781835886762

2.  Submit your proof of purchase

3.  That's it! We'll send your free PDF and other benefits to your email directly

# 1

# Web Development and the FARM Stack

Websites are built using a set of technology that is often called a **stack**. Every component of the stack is responsible for one layer of the application. While in theory, you could combine any type of frontend technology with any type of backend technology and, thus, end up with a custom stack, some have proven their worth in terms of agility and reduced development time. If you are a web developer or an analyst who must put some data online from time to time, or you just want to broaden your developer horizons, this chapter should give you some perspective on this set of tools, and how they compare to alternative technologies.

This chapter provides an overview of today's web development landscape in terms of the available technologies and demands, and at the end of this chapter, we will make a case for using the **FARM** stack—a combination of **FastAPI** for the REST API layer, **React** for the frontend, and **MongoDB** as the database.

This book focuses on the high-level concepts of the technologies that constitute the FARM stack. By learning these concepts, you will be able to develop your next web development project at a fast pace and with modern capabilities. For now, we will not go into details or concrete examples, but rather compare the selected stack components (MongoDB, FastAPI, and React) with their possible counterparts.

By the end of this chapter, you will have a good understanding of the benefits that individual FARM stack components bring to a development project, how they relate to each other, and why this particular set of technologies is a great fit for web apps that have fluid specifications—both in terms of the data handled and desired functionalities.

This chapter will cover the following topics:

- What is the FARM stack and how do the components fit together?
- Why use MongoDB for data storage?
- What is FastAPI?
- The frontend—React

## Technical requirements

For this book, you'll need a few things to aid you in your journey. The following are recommendations:

- The latest version of Python
- FastAPI (`https://pypi.org/project/fastapi/`)
- A local development environment on your laptop/desktop for your application server
- A MongoDB Atlas cloud account to host your database (`https://www.mongodb.com/cloud/atlas/register`)
- Visual Studio Code or the IDE of your choice

Let's begin with a very basic understanding of what the FARM stack is.

## What is the FARM stack?

Stacks are sets of technologies that cover different parts of a modern web app, blended and well integrated. The right stack will enable you to satisfy certain criteria while building a web application, with considerably less effort and in less time than building it from scratch.

First, let's see what you need to build a functional web application:

- **An operating system**: Usually, this is Unix/Linux-based.
- **A storage layer**: A SQL or NoSQL database. In this book, we'll use MongoDB.
- **A web server**: Apache and NGINX are quite popular, but we will talk about Python solutions for FastAPI, such as Uvicorn or Hypercorn.
- **A development environment**: Node.js/JavaScript, .NET, Java, or Python.

Optionally, and often, you could also add a frontend library or framework (such as Vue.js, Angular, React, or Svelte) since the vast majority of web development companies benefit from adopting one in terms of consistency, development speed, and compliance with standards. In addition, user expectations have shifted over time. There are unsaid standards for what logins, buttons, menus, and other website elements should look like, and how they function. Using a framework will make your application more consistent with the modern web and go a long way toward user satisfaction.

The most famous stacks are as follows:

- **MERN**: **MongoDB + Express.js + React + Node.js (MERN)** is probably one of the most popular stacks today. Developers can be comfortable and never leave JavaScript, except when they need to write some style sheets. With the addition of React Native for mobile apps and something such as Electron.js for desktop apps, a product can encompass virtually every platform while relying solely on JavaScript.

- **MEAN**: **MongoDB + Express.js + Angular.js + Node.js (MEAN)** is similar to the previously mentioned MERN, with Angular.js managing the frontend in a more structured **Model–View–Controller (MVC)** way.

- **LAMP**: **Linux + Apache + MySQL + PHP (LAMP)** is probably the first stack acronym to gain popularity and one of the most widely used in the past 20 years. It is still quite popular today.

The first two stacks run on the Node.js platform (a server-run JavaScript V8 engine) and have a web framework in common. Although Express.js is the most popular, there are excellent alternatives in the Node.js universe, such as Koa.js, Fastify.js, or some more structured ones such as Nest.js.

Since this is a Python book, we will also go through some important Python frameworks. The top three most popular frameworks for Python developers are **Django**, **Flask**, and **FastAPI**. Using the Django web framework and the excellent **Django REST Framework (DRF)** for building REST APIs in a modern and logical way is very popular. Django itself is very mature and well known among Python developers. It also has an admin site, the possibility of customizing and serializing REST responses, the option to choose between functional and class-based views, and more.

FastAPI, on the other hand, is a relative newcomer. First released in December 2018, this alternative, lightweight framework was fast to gain advocates. Almost immediately, these advocates had created a new acronym for FastAPI within the tech stack—**FARM**.

Let's understand what FARM stands for:

- **FA** stands for FastAPI—in technology years, a brand-new Python web framework

- **R** stands for React, the most popular UI library

- **M** denotes the data layer—MongoDB, which is the most popular NoSQL database available today

*Figure 1.1* provides a high-level overview of the integrations between the constituent parts involved in the FARM stack:

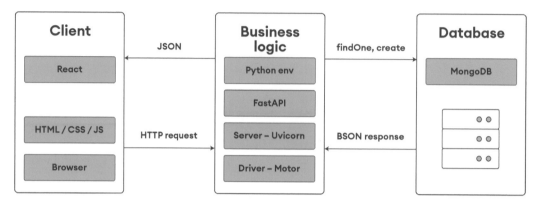

Figure 1.1: FARM stack with its components

As you can see in the preceding diagram, the FARM stack is composed of three layers:

1. The user performs an action using the client, which, in our case, will be based on React—this ultimately creates a bundle of HTML, Cascading Style Sheets (CSS), and JavaScript.

2. This user action (a mouse click, a form submit, or some other event) then triggers an HTTP request (such as GET, POST, PUT, or another HTTP verb with a payload).

3. Finally, this request gets processed by the REST API service (FastAPI).

The Python part is centered around FastAPI and optional dependencies and is served by **Uvicorn**—a fast Python-based server. The backend is responsible for dispatching the appropriate database calls to MongoDB using various commands and queries (such as findOne, find, create, update, and more) and using the MongoDB aggregation framework. The results obtained from the database are interpreted by FastAPI through the Python driver of choice (Motor), converted from BSON into appropriate Python data structures, and finally, output from the REST API server in the form of plain JSON. If you use **Motor**, which is an asynchronous Python driver for MongoDB, these calls will be handled asynchronously.

Finally, returning to the diagram in *Figure 1.1* and the arrow labeled **JSON**, the data is fed to the UI where it is handled by React and used to update the interface, render the necessary components, and synchronize the UI with React's virtual DOM tree.

The next few sections will talk about the motivations behind the birth of the FARM stack. Why these technologies and, more importantly, why these technologies together? You will get a detailed introduction to each component and the features that make it a good fit in more detail. After a brief introduction to the benefits of the stack as a whole, the sections will provide a high-level overview of each choice and underline the benefits that it can provide to a modern web development workflow.

# Why the FARM stack?

The flexibility and simplicity of the stack, along with its components, give a real boost in terms of development speed, extensibility, and maintainability while allowing scalability (due to the distributed nature of MongoDB on the one hand and the async nature of FastAPI on the other hand) down the road. This might be crucial if your product needs to evolve and become bigger than it was initially supposed to be. The ideal scenario would probably be a small-to-medium-scale web app that you can experiment with.

Developers and analysts alike could greatly benefit from Python's ecosystem and extensibility through a rich ecosystem of modules that encompasses virtually every human activity that includes some type of computing.

# Why use MongoDB?

MongoDB is a free, fast, and scalable database with a JSON format and simple syntax. It enables flexible schemas and, thus, iterative and rapid development. MongoDB is able to accommodate data structures of varying complexities. Additionally, its querying and aggregation methods make it an excellent choice for a flexible REST API framework such as FastAPI, coupled with an official Python driver such as Motor. It has a high level of adoption and maturity and is one of the pillars of the NoSQL data storage movement that took the web development world by storm a decade ago.

The following are some other features that will be detailed for use in this book:

- **Complex nested structures**: MongoDB documents allow other documents and arrays of documents to be embedded, which naturally translates into the data flow of a modern data web app (for example, you can embed all comments into the blog post they respond to). Denormalization is encouraged.

- **Simple, intuitive syntax**: The methods for performing basic **create, read, update, delete (CRUD)** operations, coupled with powerful aggregation frameworks and projections, allow you to achieve almost all data reads quite easily through the use of drivers. The commands should be intuitive for anyone with a bit of SQL experience.

- **Community and documentation**: MongoDB is backed by a mature company and a strong community, and it offers various tools to facilitate the development and prototyping process. For instance, **Compass** is a desktop application that enables users to manage and administer databases. The framework of the serverless functions is constantly being updated and upgraded, and there are excellent drivers for virtually every programming language.

Of course, MongoDB is not a silver bullet, and some challenges are worth noticing upfront. On the one hand, the schema-less design and the ability to insert any type of data into your database might be a bit panic-inducing but translates to the need for stronger data integrity validation on the backend side. You will see how **Pydantic**—an excellent Python validation and type-enforcement library—can help you with stronger data integrity. The absence of complex joins, which are present in the SQL world, might be a dealbreaker for some types of applications.

Now that you understand what MongoDB brings to the table in terms of scalability and flexibility, with its schema-less approach, take a look at the REST API framework of choice, FastAPI, and learn how it can help you implement that schema-less approach and simplify your interactions with the data.

## Why use FastAPI?

FastAPI is a modern and performant web framework for building APIs. Built by Sebastian Ramirez, it uses the newest features of the Python programming language, such as type hinting and annotations, the *async – await* syntax, Pydantic models, web socket support, and more.

If you are not familiar with APIs, let's get into it in more depth by understanding what an API is. An **application programming interface** (**API**) is used to enable some kind of interaction between different pieces of software, and they communicate using **Hypertext Transfer Protocol** (**HTTP**) through a cycle of requests and responses. Therefore, an API is, as its name suggests, an interface. Via this interface, humans or machines interact with an application or a service. Every API provider should have an interface that is well suited for the type of data that they provide; for instance, a weather forecasting station provides an API that lists the temperatures and humidity levels for a certain location. Sports sites provide statistical data about the games that are being played. A pizza delivery API will provide you with the selected ingredients, the price, and the estimated time of arrival.

APIs touch every aspect of your life, for example, transmitting medical data, enabling fast communications between applications, and even used in tractors in fields. APIs are what make today's web run and, put simply, are the best form of information exchange.

This chapter will not go over the rigorous definitions of REST APIs, but just list some of their most important features:

- **Statelessness**: REST APIs are said to be stateless, which means that neither the client nor the server stores any states in between. All the requests and responses are handled by the API server in isolation and without information about the session itself.

- **Layered structure**: To keep the API scalable and understandable, a RESTful architecture implies a layered structure. The different layers form a hierarchy and communicate with each other but not with every component, thus improving overall security.

- **Client-server architecture**: APIs should be able to connect different systems/pieces of software without limiting their own functionalities—the server and the client have to stay separate and independent from each other.

There are numerous reasons why MongoDB chose FastAPI for their REST API layer, even though it's new compared to other Python frameworks. Here are some of the reasons:

- **High performance**: FastAPI can achieve very high performance, especially compared to other Python-based solutions. By using Starlette under the hood, FastAPI's performance reaches levels that are usually reserved for Node.js and Go.

- **Data validation and simplicity**: Being heavily based on Python types and Pydantic brings numerous benefits. Since Pydantic structures are just instances of classes the developers define, you can use complex data validations, deeply nested JSON objects, and hierarchical models (using Python lists and dictionaries), and this relates very well with the nature of MongoDB.

- **Faster development**: Development becomes more intuitive, with strong **integrated development environment (IDE)** support, which leads to faster development time and fewer bugs.

- **Standards compliance**: FastAPI is standard-based and fully compatible with open standards for building APIs—such as OpenAPI and JSON schema.

- **Logical structuring of apps**: The framework allows the structuring of APIs and apps into multiple routers and allows granular request and response customization, and easy access to every part of the HTTP cycle.

- **Async support**: FastAPI uses an **asynchronous server gateway interface (ASGI)** and, with the use of an ASGI-compatible server, such as Uvicorn or Hypercorn, is able to provide a truly asynchronous workflow without actually having to import the `asyncio` module into Python.

- **Dependency injection**: The dependency injection system in FastAPI is one of its biggest selling points. It enables the creation of complex functionalities that are easily reusable across your API. This is a pretty big deal and probably the feature that makes FastAPI ideal for hybrid web apps—it gives developers the opportunity to easily attach different functionalities to the REST endpoints.

- **Great documentation**: The documentation of the framework itself is excellent and second to none. It is both easy to follow and extensive.

- **Automatic documentation**: Being based on OpenAPI, FastAPI enables automatic documentation creation, which essentially means that you get your API documented for free with Swagger.

Also, getting started is relatively simple:

```
pip install fastapi
```

In order to get at least a basic idea of what coding with FastAPI looks like, let's take a look at a minimal API:

```
# main.py
from fastapi import FastAPI

app = FastAPI()

@app.get("/")

async def root():
    return {"message": "Hello World"}
```

The preceding few lines of code define a minimal API with a single endpoint (/) that responds to a GET request with the message Hello world. You can instantiate a FastAPI class and use decorators to tell the server which HTTP methods should trigger which function for a response.

## Python and REST APIs

Python has been used to build REST APIs for a very long time. While there are many options and solutions, **DRF** and **Flask** seem to be the most popular ones, at least until recently. If you are feeling adventurous, you can Google less popular or older frameworks such as **bottle.py** and **CherryPy**.

DRF is a plugin system for the Django web framework and enables a Django system to create highly customized REST API responses and generate endpoints based on the defined models. DRF is a very mature and battle-tested system. It is regularly updated, and its documentation is very detailed.

Flask, Python's lightweight microframework, is a real gem among the web-building Python tools and can create REST APIs in a lot of different ways. You can use pure Flask and just output the appropriate format (i.e., JSON instead of HTML) or use some of the extensions developed to make the creation of REST APIs as straightforward as possible. Both of these solutions are fundamentally synchronous, although there seems to be active development in the direction of enabling async support.

There are also some very robust and mature tools, such as Tornado, which is an asynchronous networking library (and a server) that is able to scale to tens of thousands of open connections. Finally, in the last couple of years, several new Python-based solutions have been created.

One of these solutions, and arguably the fastest, is Starlette. Dubbed as a lightweight ASGI framework/ toolkit, it is ideal for building high-performance async services.

Sebastian Ramirez built FastAPI on top of Starlette and Pydantic, while also adding numerous features and goodies by using the latest Python features, such as type hinting and async support. According to some recent developer surveys[1], FastAPI is quickly becoming one of the most popular and most loved web frameworks.

In later chapters of this book, you'll go over the most important features of FastAPI, but at this point, we'll stress the significance of having a truly async Python framework as the glue for the most diverse components of a system. In fact, besides doing the usual web framework stuff, such as communicating with a database, spitting out data to a frontend, and managing authentication and authorization, this Python pipeline enables you to quickly integrate and easily carry out frequently required tasks such as background jobs, header and body manipulation, response and request validation, and more through the dependency injection system.

The book will try to cover the absolute minimum necessary for you to be able to build a simple FastAPI system, but along the way it will consider various web server solutions and deployment options (such as Deta, Heroku, and DigitalOcean) for your FastAPI Python-based backend, while trying to opt for free solutions.

---

1   https://www.jetbrains.com/lp/devecosystem-2023/python/#python_web_libs_two_years

So, to cut a long story short, you should consider choosing FastAPI because you ideally want the ability and speed to handle requests asynchronously as if you were using a Node.js server while having access to the Python ecosystem. Additionally, you want the simplicity and development speed of a framework that automatically generates documentation for you.

After reviewing the backend components, it is time to finalize your stack and work on the frontend. The next section gives you a brief introduction to React and discusses what distinguishes it from other (also valid) solutions.

# The frontend – React

The changes in the world of the web are most visible when talking about the frontend—the part of the website that is facing the users. Tim Berners-Lee made the first HTML specification public in 1991, and it consisted of text and under 20 tags. In 1994, CSS was introduced and the web started looking a little nicer. Legend has it that the new browser scripting language called Mocha was created in just 10 days—that was in 1995. Later, this language went through numerous changes and became what we know today as JavaScript—a powerful and fast language that, with the advent of Node.js, was able to conquer the servers, too.

In May 2013, React was presented in the US and the web development world was able to witness virtual DOM, one-way data flow, the Flux pattern, and more.

This is a bit of history to just try and provide some context and continuity because web development, like any other creative human activity, rarely moves in quantum leaps. Usually, it moves in steps that enable users to resolve the issues that they are facing. It would be unfair not to mention Vue.js, which is an excellent choice for building frontends that also sports an entire ecosystem of libraries, and Svelte.js, which offers a radical shift in building UIs in the sense that the UI is compiled, and the bundled size is significantly smaller.

## Why use React?

Interactive, attractive, fast, and intuitive UIs are a necessity for any public-facing web application. It is possible, though very difficult, to achieve most or every functionality that even a simple web application is expected to provide using just plain JavaScript. FastAPI is more than capable of serving HTML (and static files, such as JavaScript or CSS) using any compatible templating engine (the most widely used in the Python world is probably Jinja2), but we and the users want more.

Compared to other frameworks, React is small. It isn't even considered a framework, but a library—actually, a couple of libraries. Still, it is a mature product with over 10 years of development behind it, created for the needs of Facebook and utilized by the biggest companies such as Uber, X (formally known as Twitter), and Airbnb.

This book does not explore React in depth because we want to focus on how all the different parts of the FARM stack connect and fit within the bigger picture. Additionally, 81% of developers already use React[2] and are familiar with its features, so we assume our readers have a level of familiarity with this framework already.

Most developers want a streamlined and structured way of building UIs. React enables developers to create dynamic applications in a much easier way by relying on JSX—a mix of JavaScript and XML that has an intuitive tag-based syntax and provides developers with a way to think of the application in terms of components that go on to form other, more complex, components, thus breaking the process of crafting complex UI and interactions into smaller, more manageable steps.

The main benefits of using React as a frontend solution can be summarized as follows:

- **Performance**: By using the React virtual DOM, which operates in memory, React apps provide smooth and fast performance.

- **Reusability**: Since the app is built by using components that have their own properties and logic, you can write out components once and then reuse them as many times as needed, cutting down development time and complexity.

- **Ease of use**: This is always a bit subjective but React is easy to get started. Advanced concepts and patterns require some level of proficiency, but even novice developers can reap immediate benefits just from the possibility of splitting the application frontend into components and then using them like LEGO bricks.

React and frameworks based on React empower you, as a developer, to create single-page applications that have a desktop-like look and feel, but also server-side rendering that is beneficial for search engine optimization. Knowing your way around React enables you to benefit from some of today's most powerful frontend web frameworks such as Next.js, static site generators (such as Gatsby.js), or exciting and promising newcomers (such as React Remix).

In *version 16.8*, the React library introduced **Hooks**, which enable developers to use and manipulate the state of the components, along with some other features of React, without the need to use classes. This is a big change that successfully tackles different issues—it enables the reusability of stateful logic between components and simplifies the understanding and management of complex components.

The simplest React Hook is probably the useState Hook. This Hook enables you to have and maintain a stateful value (such as an object, array, or variable) throughout the life cycle of the component, without having to resort to old-school class-based components.

For instance, a very simple component that could be used to filter search results when a user is trying to find the right car might contain the desired brand, model, and a production year range. This functionality would be a great candidate for a separate component—a search component that would need to maintain the state of different input controls, probably implemented as a series of dropdowns. Let's just see the simplest possible version of this implementation.

---

2   https://2022.stateofjs.com/en-US/libraries/front-end-frameworks/

The following block of code creates a simple functional component with a single stateful string value—an HTML `select` element that will update the stateful variable named `brand`:

```
import { useState } from "react";

const Search = () => {
const [brand, setBrand] = useState("");
return (
<div>
<div>Selected brand: {brand}</div>
<select onChange={(ev) => setBrand(ev.target.value)}>
<option value="">All brands</option>
<option value="Fiat">Fiat</option>
<option value="Ford">Ford</option>
<option value="Renault">Renault</option>
<option value="Opel">Opel</option>
</select>
</div>
);
};
export default Search;
```

The bold line is where the Hook magic happens, and it must be within the body of a function. The statement simply creates a new state variable, called `brand`, and provides you with a setter function that can be used inside the component to set the desired value.

There are many Hooks that solve different problems, and this book will go over the following fundamental ones:

- **Declarative views**: In React, you do not have to worry about transitions or mutations of the DOM. React handles everything, and the only thing you have to do is declare how the view looks and reacts.

- **No templating language**: React practically uses JavaScript as a templating language (through JSX), so all you have to know in order to be able to use it effectively is some JavaScript, such as array manipulation and iteration.

- **Rich ecosystem**: There are numerous excellent libraries that complement React's basic functionality—from routers to custom Hooks, external library integrations, CSS framework adaptations, and more.

Ultimately, Hooks provide React with a new way of adding and sharing stateful logic across components and can even replace (in simpler cases) the need for Redux or other external state management libraries. Most of the examples shown in this book make use of the Context API—a React feature that enables passing objects and functions down the component tree without the need to pass props through components that do not need it. Coupled with a Hook—the useContext Hook—it provides a straightforward way of passing and maintaining stateful values in every part of the app.

React uses (although it is not imperative) the newest features of functional JavaScript, ES6, and ES7, particularly when it comes to arrays. Working with React improves understanding of JavaScript, and a similar thing could be said of FastAPI and modern Python.

The final piece of the puzzle will be the choice of a CSS library or framework. Currently, in 2024, there are dozens of CSS libraries that play nice with React, including Bootstrap, Material UI, Bulma, and more. Many of these libraries merge with React to become meaningful frameworks of prebuilt customizable and parameterized components. We will use Tailwind CSS as it is simple to set up—and it is intuitive once you get the hang of it.

Keeping the React part to a bare minimum should allow you to focus more on the true protagonists of the story—FastAPI and MongoDB. You can easily replace React, should you wish to do so, be it Svelte.js, Vue.js, or vanilla handcrafted ECMAScript. However, by learning the basics of React (and Hooks), you are embarking on a wonderful web development adventure that will enable you to use and understand many tools and frameworks built on top of React.

Arguably, Next.js is the feature-richest server-side rendering React framework that enables fast development, filesystem-based routing, and more.

## Summary

This chapter laid the background for the FARM stack, from describing the role of each component to their strengths. Now, you will be confident in choosing the FARM stack and you know how to implement it within the context of a flexible and fluid web development project. Since you're reading this, I'll assume that my case was compelling—that you're still interested and ready to explore the FARM stack.

The next chapter will provide a fast-paced, concise, and actionable overview of MongoDB, and then set up your data storage layer for your FARM application. As you go along, we are confident that you will find the combination of FastAPI, React, and MongoDB to be the best choice for your next web application.

# 2

# Setting Up the Database with MongoDB

In this chapter, you will explore some of the main features of MongoDB through several simple yet illustrative examples. You will learn about the basic commands of the MongoDB Query API to start interacting with your data stored in a MongoDB database. You will learn the essential commands and methods that will enable you to insert, manage, query, and update your data.

The aim of this chapter is to help you understand how easy it is to set up a MongoDB database on your local machine or in the cloud and perform the operations that might be needed in a fast-paced web development process.

Querying, through MongoDB methods and aggregation, is best learned by experimenting with data. This chapter utilizes real-world sample datasets provided by MongoDB Atlas that are loaded into your cloud database. You will learn to execute CRUD and aggregation queries against them.

This chapter will cover the following topics:

- The structure of a MongoDB database
- Installing MongoDB Community Server and tools
- Creating an Atlas cluster
- MongoDB querying and CRUD operations
- Aggregation framework

# Technical requirements

For this chapter, you will require MongoDB version 7.0.7 and Windows 11 (and Ubuntu 22.04 LTS). MongoDB version 7.0 is compatible with the following:

- Windows 11, Windows Server 2019, or Windows Server 2022 (64-bit versions)
- Ubuntu 20.04 LTS (Focal) and Ubuntu 22.04 LTS (Jammy) for Linux (64-bit releases)

The following are recommended system configurations:

- A desktop or laptop with at least 8 GB of RAM.
- There are no CPU requirements specified as such but make sure it's modern (a multi-core processor) to ensure efficient performance.

# The structure of a MongoDB database

MongoDB is widely regarded as the leading NoSQL database in terms of popularity and usage—its power, ease of use, and versatility make it an excellent choice for large- and small-scale projects. Its scalability and performance enable the data layer of your app to have a very solid foundation.

In the following sections, you will take a deeper look into the basic concepts and building blocks of MongoDB: the document, the collection, and the database. Since this book takes a bottom-up approach, you will start from the very bottom and see an overview of the simplest data structures available in MongoDB and then take it up from there into documents, collections, and so on.

## Documents

MongoDB is a document-oriented database. But what does that actually mean?

In MongoDB, documents serve a similar purpose to rows in a traditional relational database. Each document in MongoDB is a data structure that consists of key-value pairs, representing a single record. Data stored in MongoDB offers great flexibility to application developers to model their data as per their needs and allows them to easily evolve the schema as their application requirements change in the future. MongoDB has a flexible schema model, which essentially means that you can have different fields in different documents within a collection. You can also have different data types for fields across documents based on your needs.

However, if your application requires a more consistent structure of the data throughout the documents in a collection, you can use schema validation rules in MongoDB to enforce consistency. MongoDB empowers you to store data in a way that makes the most sense for your application needs.

Documents in MongoDB are just an ordered set of key-value pairs. In this book, the terms **key** and **field** are used interchangeably as they represent the same thing. This structure, as you will explore later, corresponds with data structures in every programming language; in Python, you will see that this structure is a dictionary and lends itself perfectly to the flow of data of a web app or a desktop application.

The rules for creating documents are pretty simple: the key/field name must be a string, with a few exception that you can read more about in the docs, and a document cannot contain duplicate key names. Remember that MongoDB is case sensitive.

In this chapter, you will load a sample dataset into your MongoDB Atlas cluster called `sample_mflix`. The dataset has many collections, but one that is of interest to us in this chapter is the `movies` collection, which contains documents that describe movies. The following document could be in this collection:

```
{
  _id: ObjectId("573a1390f29313caabcd42e8"),
  plot: 'A group of bandits stage a brazen train hold-up, only to find a
determined posse hot on their heels.',
  genres: [ 'Short', 'Western' ],
  runtime: 11,
  cast: [
    'A.C. Abadie',
    "Gilbert M. 'Broncho Billy' Anderson",
    'George Barnes',
    'Justus D. Barnes'
  ],
  poster: 'https://m.media-amazon.com/images/M/MV5BMTU3NjE5NzYtYTYyNS00MDVmL
WIwYjgtMmYwYWIxZDYyNzU2XkEyXkFqcGdeQXVyNzQzNzQxNzI@._V1_SY1000_SX677_AL_.
jpg',
  title: 'The Great Train Robbery',
  fullplot: "Among the earliest existing films in American cinema - notable
as the first film that presented a narrative story to tell - it depicts a
group of cowboy outlaws who hold up a train and rob the passengers. They
are then pursued by a Sheriff's posse. Several scenes have color included -
all hand tinted.",
  languages: [ 'English' ],
  released: ISODate("1903-12-01T00:00:00.000Z"),
  directors: [ 'Edwin S. Porter' ],
  rated: 'TV-G',
  awards: { wins: 1, nominations: 0, text: '1 win.' },
  lastupdated: '2015-08-13 00:27:59.177000000',
  year: 1903,
  imdb: { rating: 7.4, votes: 9847, id: 439 },
  countries: [ 'USA' ],
  type: 'movie',
  tomatoes: {
    viewer: { rating: 3.7, numReviews: 2559, meter: 75 },
    fresh: 6,
    critic: { rating: 7.6, numReviews: 6, meter: 100 },
    rotten: 0,
    lastUpdated: ISODate("2015-08-08T19:16:10.000Z")
  },
  num_mflix_comments: 0
}
```

> **Note**
>
> When it comes to nesting documents within documents, MongoDB supports 100 levels of nesting, which is a limit you probably won't reach in most applications.

## Supported data types in MongoDB

MongoDB allows you to store any of the BSON data types as field values. BSON is very closely related to JSON and it stands for "Binary JSON." BSON's binary structure makes it faster and adds native support for more data types than JSON. One of the first important decisions when designing any type of application is the choice of data types. As a developer, you would never want to use the wrong tools for the job at hand.

> **Note**
>
> The full list of supported data types in MongoDB can be found in the official documentation: `https://www.mongodb.com/docs/mongodb-shell/reference/data-types/`.

Some of the most important data types supported by MongoDB are:

- **Strings**: These are probably the most basic and universal data type in MongoDB, and they are used to represent all text fields in a document.

- **Numbers**: MongoDB supports different types of numbers, including:

  - **int**: 32-bit integer

  - **long**: 64-bit integer

  - **double**: 64-bit floating point

  - **decimal**: 128-bit decimal-based floating point

- **Booleans**: This is the standard Boolean `true` or `false` value; they are written without quotes since you do not want them to be interpreted as strings.

- **Objects or embedded documents**: In MongoDB, fields within a document can contain embedded documents, allowing for complex data structuring within a single document. This capability supports the deep nesting of JSON-like structures, facilitating flexible and hierarchical data modeling.

- **Arrays**: Arrays can contain zero or more values in a list-like structure. The elements of the array can be any MongoDB data type, including other documents and arrays. They are zero-based and particularly suited for making **embedded relationships**. For instance, you could store all of the post comments inside the blog post document itself, along with a timestamp and the user that made the comment. Arrays can benefit from the standard JavaScript array methods for fast editing, pushing, and other methods.

- **ObjectId**: Every document in MongoDB has a unique field called `_id` that acts as the primary key. If an inserted document omits the `_id` field, MongoDB automatically generates an ObjectId for the `_id` field that is used to uniquely identify a document in the collection. ObjectId values are 12 bytes in length. They are small, likely unique, fast to generate, and ordered. These ObjectIds are extensively used as keys for traditional relationships – ObjectIds are automatically indexed.

- **Dates**: Though JSON does not support date types and stores them as plain strings, MongoDB's BSON format supports date types explicitly. They represent the 64-bit number of milliseconds since the Unix epoch (January 1, 1970). All dates are stored in UTC and have no time zone associated. A BSON date type is signed. Negative values represent dates before 1970.

- **Binary data**: Binary data fields can store arbitrary binary data and are the only way to save non-UTF-8 strings to a database. These fields can be used in conjunction with MongoDB's GridFS filesystem to store images, for example.

- **Null**: This can represent a null value or a nonexistent field, and we can even store JavaScript functions as a different data type.

Now that you have an idea of what types of fields are available in MongoDB and how you can map your business logic to a (flexible) schema, it is time to get introduced to collections—groups of documents and a counterpart to a table in the relational database world.

## Collections and databases

Even though you can store multiple schemas in the same collection, there are many reasons to store your data in multiple databases and multiple collections:

- **Data separation**: Collections allow you to logically separate different types of data. For example, you can have a collection for user data, another collection for product data, and yet another collection for order data. This separation makes it easier to manage and query specific types of data.

- **Performance optimization**: By separating data into different collections, you can optimize performance by indexing and querying specific collections more efficiently. This can improve query performance and reduce the amount of data that needs to be scanned.

- **Data locality**: Grouping documents of the same type in a collection will require less disk seek time, and considering that indexing is defined by collection, the querying is much more efficient.

Although a single instance of MongoDB can host several databases at once, it is considered good practice to keep all the document collections used in an application inside a single database.

> **Note**
>
> When you install MongoDB, there will be three databases created and their names cannot be used for your application database: `admin`, `local`, and `config`. They are built-in databases that shouldn't be replaced, so avoid accidentally naming your database the same way or making any changes to these databases.

### Options to install the MongoDB database

After reviewing the basic terms, concepts, and structure of the MongoDB database, it is time to learn how to set up a MongoDB database server locally and in the cloud.

The local database setup is convenient for quick prototyping that doesn't even require an internet connection. However, we recommend that you use a cloud-hosted database in MongoDB Atlas when you're setting up a database to use as the backend in future chapters.

MongoDB Atlas offers many benefits over the local installation. First, it is easy to set up, and, as you will see, you can get it up and running literally in minutes with a generous free-tier database ready for work. MongoDB handles all the operational aspects of the database, such as provisioning, scaling, backup, and monitoring.

Atlas takes away much of the manual setup and guarantees availability. Other benefits include the involvement of the MongoDB team (which tries to implement best practices), high security by default with access control, firewalls and granular access control, automated backups (depending on the tier), and the possibility to be productive right away.

# Installing MongoDB and related tools

MongoDB is not just a database service provider, but a full-fledged developer data platform that has a set of technologies built around the core database to meet all your data needs and improve your productivity as a developer. Let's examine the following components that you will be installing or using in the following sections:

- **MongoDB Community Edition**: A free version of MongoDB that runs on all major operating systems. It is what you are going to use to play around with data locally.

- **MongoDB Compass**: A **graphical user interface** (**GUI**) for managing, querying, aggregating, and analyzing MongoDB data in a visual environment. Compass is a mature and useful tool that you'll be using throughout your initial querying and aggregation explorations.

- **MongoDB Atlas**: The database-as-a-service solution from MongoDB. This offering is one of the main reasons MongoDB is a central part of the FARM stack. It is relatively easy to set up and it relieves you from manually administering the database.

- **MongoDB Shell** (`mongosh`): A command-line shell that not only performs simple **create**, **read**, **update**, and **delete** (**CRUD**) operations on your database but also enables administrative tasks such as creating and deleting databases, starting and stopping services, and similar jobs.

- **MongoDB Database Tools**: Several command-line utilities that allow administrators and developers to export or import data to and from a database, provide diagnostics, or enable manipulation of large files stored in MongoDB's GridFS system.

This chapter will focus on the procedure to have a fully functional installation. Check the installation instructions that correspond to your operating system. This chapter includes instructions for Windows, Linux, and macOS.

# Installing MongoDB and Compass on Windows

In this section, you will learn how to install the latest version of MongoDB Community Edition, which at the time of writing is 7.0. MongoDB Community is only supported on 64-bit versions of Windows on x86_64 architecture. Windows versions supported are Windows 11, Windows Server 2019, and Windows Server 2022. To install MongoDB and Compass, you can refer to the following steps.

> **Note**
>
> We strongly advise you to check the instructions on the MongoDB website (`https://www.mongodb.com/docs/manual/tutorial/install-mongodb-on-windows/`) to ensure you have access to the latest information, as they might slightly change.

1. To download the installer, head over to the MongoDB Download Center at `https://www.mongodb.com/try/download/community`, select the Windows version, and click on **Download** as follows:

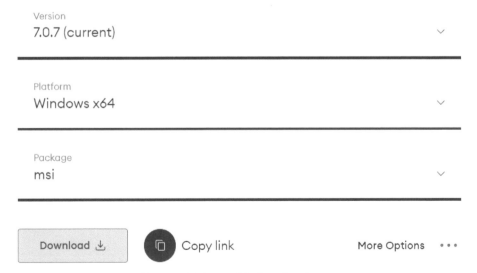

Figure 2.1: MongoDB download page

2.  Next, execute it. If a security prompt displays **Open Executable File**, select **Yes** and proceed to the MongoDB setup wizard.

3.  Read the license agreement, select the checkbox, and then click on **Next**.

4.  This is an important screen. When asked which type of setup to choose, select **Complete**, as follows:

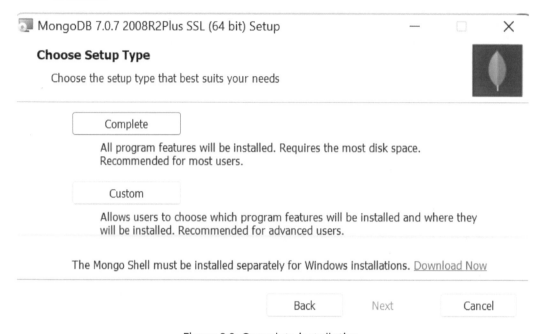

Figure 2.2: Complete installation

5.  The next wizard will ask you whether you want MongoDB to run as a Windows network service (that's what you should prefer) or as a local and domain service. Leave the default values selected and proceed to the next step without making any changes.

6.  Another wizard will appear prompting whether you want to install Compass, MongoDB's GUI tool for database management. Select the checkbox and proceed to install it:

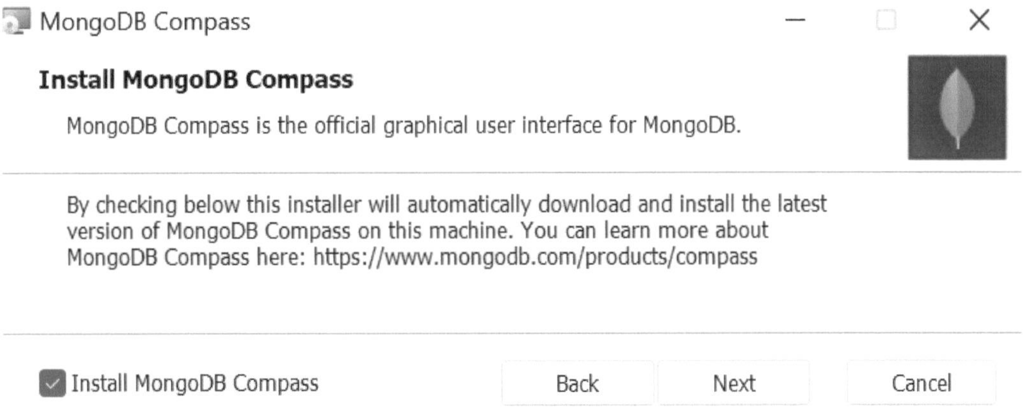

Figure 2.3: Install Compass

7.  Finally, the **User Account Control** (**UAC**) Windows warning screen will pop up, and you should select **Yes**.

Now that you have installed MongoDB Community Server on your local machine, the next section will show you how to install other necessary tools that you will be using throughout this book.

# Installing the MongoDB Shell (mongosh)

After installing MongoDB Community Server and Compass on your computer, you will next install mongosh, the MongoDB Shell.

> **Note**
>
> For instructions on other operating systems, please visit the MongoDB documentation: https://www.mongodb.com/docs/mongodb-shell/install/.

Here's how you can do it for Windows:

1.  Navigate to the MongoDB Download Center (https://www.mongodb.com/try/download/shell) and, in the **Tools** section, select **MongoDB Shell**.

2.  From the dropdowns, select the Windows version and the **msi** package and click on **Download**.

Figure 2.4: Download the MongoDB Shell

3.  Next, locate the **msi** package on your computer and execute it. If a security prompt asks **Open Executable File**, select **Yes** and proceed to the MongoDB setup wizard. The wizard will open the following page. Click on **Next**:

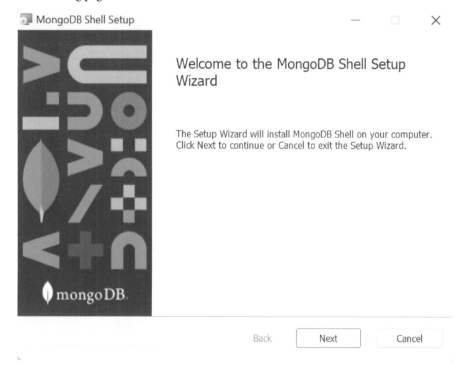

Figure 2.5: The MongoDB Shell Setup Wizard

4.  In the prompt, select the destination folder for installing `mongosh`, or leave the default option as it is if it looks good to you, and then finish the installation.

5.  At this point, you should be able to test whether MongoDB is running (as a service). Enter the following command in the command prompt of your choice (preferably, use **cmder**, available at `https://cmder.app`):

    ```
    mongosh
    ```

6.  You should see various notifications and a tiny prompt denoted with >. Try typing the following:

    ```
    Show dbs
    ```

    If you see the automatically generated `admin`, `config`, and `locals` databases, you should be good to go.

7.  Now, check the installation of Compass. On Windows, you should be able to find it in your start menu under **MongoDBCompass** (no spacing).

8.  If you just click the **Connect** button, without pasting or typing in any connection string, Compass will connect to the local MongoDB service running on port `27017` and you should be able to see all of the databases that you saw when you used the command line with MongoDB: `admin`, `config`, and `local`.

# MongoDB Database Tools

The MongoDB Database Tools are a collection of command-line utilities for working with a MongoDB deployment. Some of the common database tools are as follows:

- `mongoimport`: Imports content from an extended JSON, CSV, or TSV export file
- `mongoexport`: Produces a JSON or CSV export of data stored in a `mongod` instance
- `mongodump`: Creates a binary export of the contents of a `mongod` database

There are some other tools, such as `mongorestore`, `bsondump`, `mongostat`, `mongotop`, and `mongofiles`. The MongoDB Database Tools can be installed with an MSI installer (or downloaded as a ZIP archive).

> **Note**
>
> The `msi` package can be downloaded from the MongoDB Download Center (`https://www.mongodb.com/try/download/database-tools`).
>
> After downloading, you can follow the installation instructions provided in the MongoDB documentation (`https://www.mongodb.com/docs/database-tools/installation/installation-windows/`).

The next section provides a walk-through of the process of installing MongoDB on a standard Linux distribution.

# Installing MongoDB and Compass on Linux: Ubuntu

Linux offers numerous benefits for the development and management of local servers, but most importantly, should you decide that the database-as-a-service of MongoDB isn't what you want to use anymore, you will probably want to work on a Linux-based server.

In this book, we will go over the installation process on Ubuntu version 22.04 LTS (Jammy), while the MongoDB version also supports Ubuntu 20.04 LTS (Focal) on x86_64 architecture. The necessary steps to install MongoDB Ubuntu will be listed here, but you should always check the MongoDB Ubuntu installation page (`https://www.mongodb.com/docs/manual/tutorial/install-mongodb-on-ubuntu/`) for recent changes. The process, however, shouldn't change.

The following actions are to be performed in a Bash shell. Download the public key that will allow you to install MongoDB, then you will create a list file and reload the package manager. Similar steps are required for other Linux distributions, so be sure to check the documentation on the website of your chosen distribution. Finally, you will perform the actual installation of MongoDB through the package manager and start the service.

It is always preferable to skip the packages provided by the Linux distribution as they are often not updated to the latest version. Perform the following steps to install MongoDB on Ubuntu:

1.  Import the public key used by the package management system as follows.

    You need to have `gnupg` and `curl` installed on your system. If you don't already have them, you can install them by running the following command:

    ```
    sudo apt-get install gnupg curl
    ```

    To import the MongoDB public GPG key, run the following command:

    ```
    curl -fsSL https://www.mongodb.org/static/pgp/server-7.0.asc | \
        sudo gpg -o /usr/share/keyrings/mongodb-server-7.0.gpg \
        --dearmor
    ```

    Create the `/etc/apt/sources.list.d/mongodb-org-7.0.list` file for Ubuntu 22.04 (Jammy) by running the following command:

    ```
    echo "deb [ arch=amd64,arm64 signed-by=/usr/share/keyrings/mongodb-
    server-7.0.gpg ] https://repo.mongodb.org/apt/ubuntu jammy/mongodb-
    org/7.0 multiverse" | sudo tee /etc/apt/sources.list.d/mongodb-org-
    7.0.list
    ```

2.  Reload the local package database with:

    ```
    sudo apt-get update
    ```

3.  Install the MongoDB package. To install the latest stable version, issue the following command:

    ```
    sudo apt-get install -y mongodb-org
    ```

4.   Run MongoDB Community Edition. If you follow these instructions and install MongoDB through the package manager, the `/var/lib/mongodb` data directory and the `/var/log/mongodb` log directory will be created during the installation.

5.   You can start the `mongod` process with:

```
sudo systemctl start mongod
```

If you receive an error similar to the following on initiating `mongod`:

```
Failed to start mongod.service: Unit mongod.service not found.
```

Run the following command first:

```
sudo systemctl daemon-reload
```

Then run the `start` command (shown in *step 5*) again.

6.   You should be able to start using the MongoDB Shell (`mongosh`) by simply typing:

```
mongosh
```

MongoDB isn't particularly different than any other Linux software when it comes to installation and process management. However, if you have any issues with the installation, the first recommendation would be to visit the MongoDB Linux installation page.

# Setting up Atlas

MongoDB Atlas—a cloud database service provided by MongoDB—is one of the strongest selling points of MongoDB.

MongoDB Atlas is a fully managed database service, which means that MongoDB handles the infrastructure management, database setup, configuration, and maintenance tasks for you. This allows you to focus on developing your applications instead of managing the underlying infrastructure.

> **Note**
> The processes of signing up and setting up a MongoDB Atlas instance are well documented at `https://www.mongodb.com/docs/atlas/getting-started/`.

There are two ways in which you can set up your Atlas account:

- Atlas UI (website)
- Atlas CLI (command line)

The Atlas CLI provides a dedicated CLI for MongoDB Atlas, allowing you to manage your Atlas database deployments and Atlas Search directly from your terminal. In this book, you will see how to do it from the UI.

Head over to `https://www.mongodb.com/cloud/atlas/register` to create an Atlas account if you don't already have it. You can use either your Google account, GitHub account, or email account to sign up for this service.

> **Note**
>
> The Atlas UI and cluster creation steps may change as more features are introduced. It is highly recommended that you refer to the documentation while setting up the cluster for the latest instructions (`https://www.mongodb.com/docs/atlas/getting-started/`).

After setting up the account (here, a Gmail address is used, so you can log in with a Google account for faster access), you will be prompted to create a cluster. You will create an M0 cluster, which is free, and you should select a **Cloud Provider & Region** option that is as close to your physical location as possible to minimize latency.

## Creating an Atlas cluster

To set up an Atlas cluster, perform the following steps:

1. On your Atlas dashboard, you will see the **Create a deployment** option. Click on **Create** to start the process of creating your first Atlas cluster.

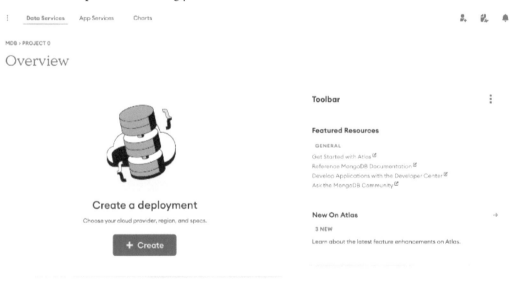

Figure 2.6: The Atlas dashboard

In this step, you need to do multiple things:

I.   Select a free **M0 sandbox** option.

II.  Give your cluster a meaningful name, such as `farm-stack`. You can choose any other name of your choice.

III. Make sure that both the **Automate security setup** and **Add sample dataset** options are checked. This will come in very handy later.

IV.  Select the cloud service provider of your choice (by default, it's AWS)

V.   Choose the region that is nearest to your location to minimize latency, and click on **Create Deployment**.

> **Note**
>
> Creating an Atlas user and setting up IP is an important step that you must complete before you start using the Atlas cluster.

2.  On the next screen, you will be asked to create a database user that will have a username and password. Both the fields are auto-populated for you to simplify the process. Feel free to change the username and password according to your preference. **Make sure that you save the password somewhere as you will require it later when you connect to your cluster.**

3.  By default, your current IP address is added to enable local connectivity. MongoDB Atlas provides many layers of security and restricted IP address access is one of them. If you are going to use your cluster from any other IP address, you can add that later, or you also have the option to enable access from anywhere (`0.0.0.0/0`), which will allow you to connect from anywhere, but this is not the recommended option for security reasons.

After you complete these steps, you have successfully created your first Atlas cluster!

## Getting the connection string of your Atlas Cluster

Next, you'll look at the sample dataset that is automatically loaded for you. In this section, you will connect the dataset to your Atlas cluster from Compass and explore the same dataset using it:

1.  On the Atlas dashboard, click on the **Browse collections** button, as shown in *Figure 2.7*.

Figure 2.7: The Atlas dashboard

2.  You can see that the `sample_mflix` dataset has already been loaded in your cluster. You'll have a database named `sample_mflix` and six collections created under it: `comments`, `embedded_movies`, `movies`, `sessions`, `theatres`, and `users`.

3.  Now, go to your Atlas dashboard and get the connection string to connect to your Atlas cluster from Compass.

4.  On the Atlas dashboard, click on the green **Connect** button.

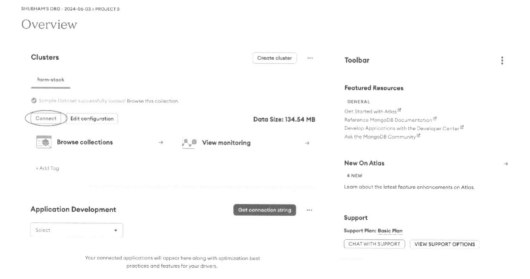

Figure 2.8: Connect to your cluster

5.  Then, select **Compass**:

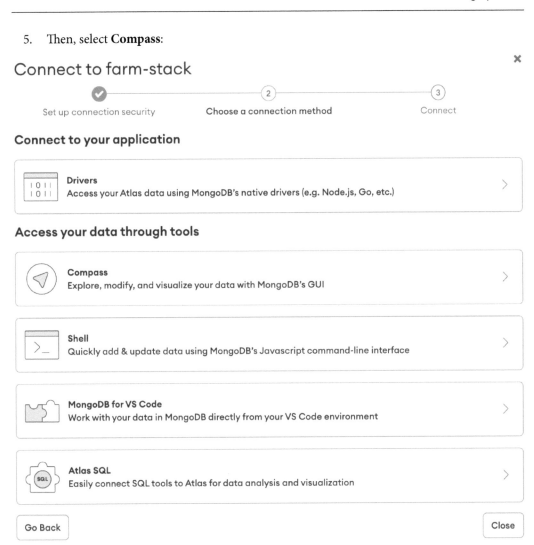

Figure 2.9: Connect to your cluster

6.  In the next wizard, copy the connection string shown in the box:

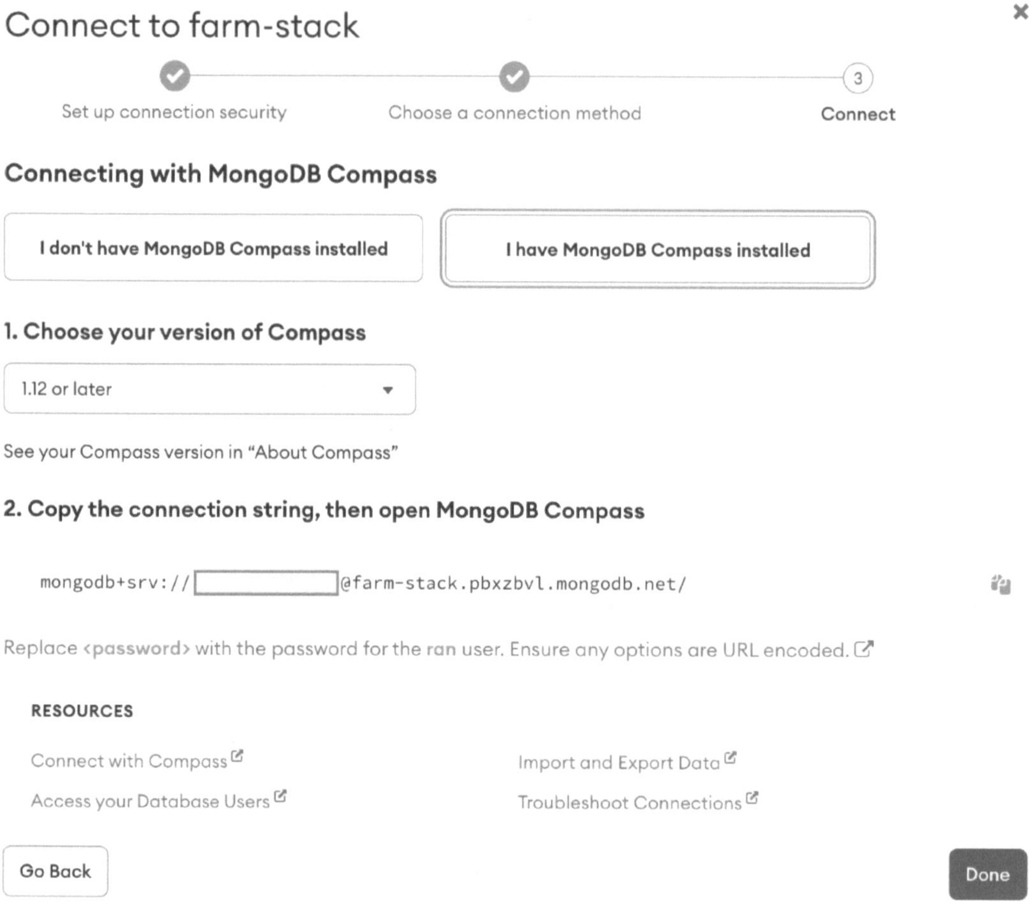

## Connect to farm-stack

Set up connection security — Choose a connection method — Connect

### Connecting with MongoDB Compass

| I don't have MongoDB Compass installed | I have MongoDB Compass installed |

**1. Choose your version of Compass**

1.12 or later ▼

See your Compass version in "About Compass"

**2. Copy the connection string, then open MongoDB Compass**

```
mongodb+srv://[          ]@farm-stack.pbxzbvl.mongodb.net/
```

Replace <password> with the password for the ran user. Ensure any options are URL encoded.

**RESOURCES**

Connect with Compass      Import and Export Data

Access your Database Users      Troubleshoot Connections

Go Back      Done

Figure 2.10: Get the connection string

Great! Now, you have the connection string for your Atlas cluster. You can go to Compass and use this connection string to connect to your Atlas cluster from Compass. Don't forget to replace <password> with your Atlas user password before connecting to your cluster.

## Connecting to the Atlas cluster from Compass

Perform the following steps to connect to your Atlas Cluster from Compass:

1. Launch Compass if it's not already running on your computer. In the **URI** box, paste the connection string you copied from the previous step and add your password to it. Next, click on **Connect**:

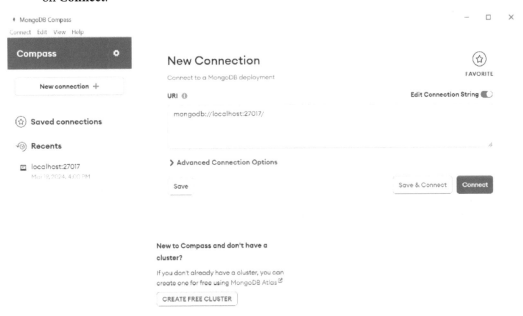

Figure 2.11: MongoDB Compass

2. After successfully connecting to your Atlas cluster, you will see something similar to *Figure 2.12*:

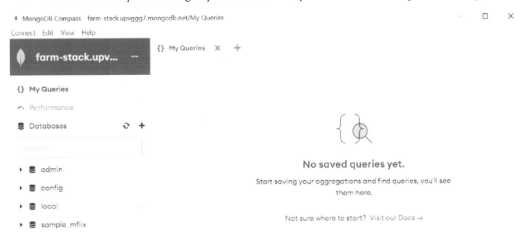

Figure 2.12: The My Queries tab in MongoDB Compass

3.   You can see the list of databases in your cluster in the left panel. Click on **sample_mflix** to expand the dropdown and expose the list of collections. Then, click on **movies** to see the documents stored in that collection:

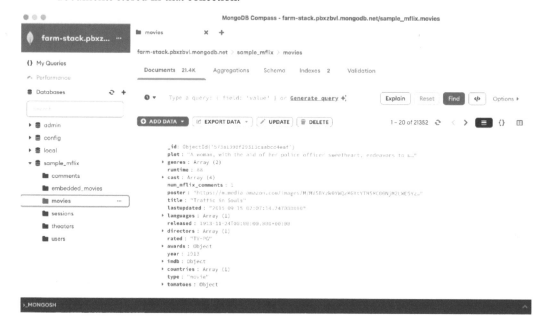

Figure 2.13: List of documents in collections

*Figure 2.13* shows that you have 21.4k documents in your `sample_mflix.movies` collection.

Now you should have a fully functional instance of the world's most popular NoSQL database on your machine. You have also created an online account and managed to create your very own cluster, ready to take on most data challenges and power your web app.

# MongoDB querying and CRUD operations

Let's see MongoDB in action and experience firsthand the power of the most popular NoSQL database. This section will show you the most essential MongoDB commands, through simple examples. These methods will enable you, as a developer, to take control of your data, create new documents, query documents by using different criteria and conditions, perform simple and more complex aggregations, and output data in various forms.

Although you will be talking to MongoDB through the Python drivers (Motor and PyMongo), it is helpful to learn how to write queries directly at first. You'll begin by querying the `sample_mflix.movies` dataset that was imported into your cluster at the time of cluster creation, then you'll go through the process of creating new data—inserting, updating, and so on.

Let's first define the two options for executing MongoDB commands, as follows:

- Compass GUI
- MongoDB Shell (mongosh)

Connect to your MongoDB Atlas cluster from mongosh and perform CRUD operations on your data:

1. To connect to your Atlas cluster from mongosh (MongoDB Shell), navigate to your Atlas cluster dashboard and fetch the connection string for mongosh. The steps will be the same as for Compass, except for the connecting tool. For this, you'll need the MongoDB Shell and not Compass.

   *Figure 2.14* shows the connection string for mongosh:

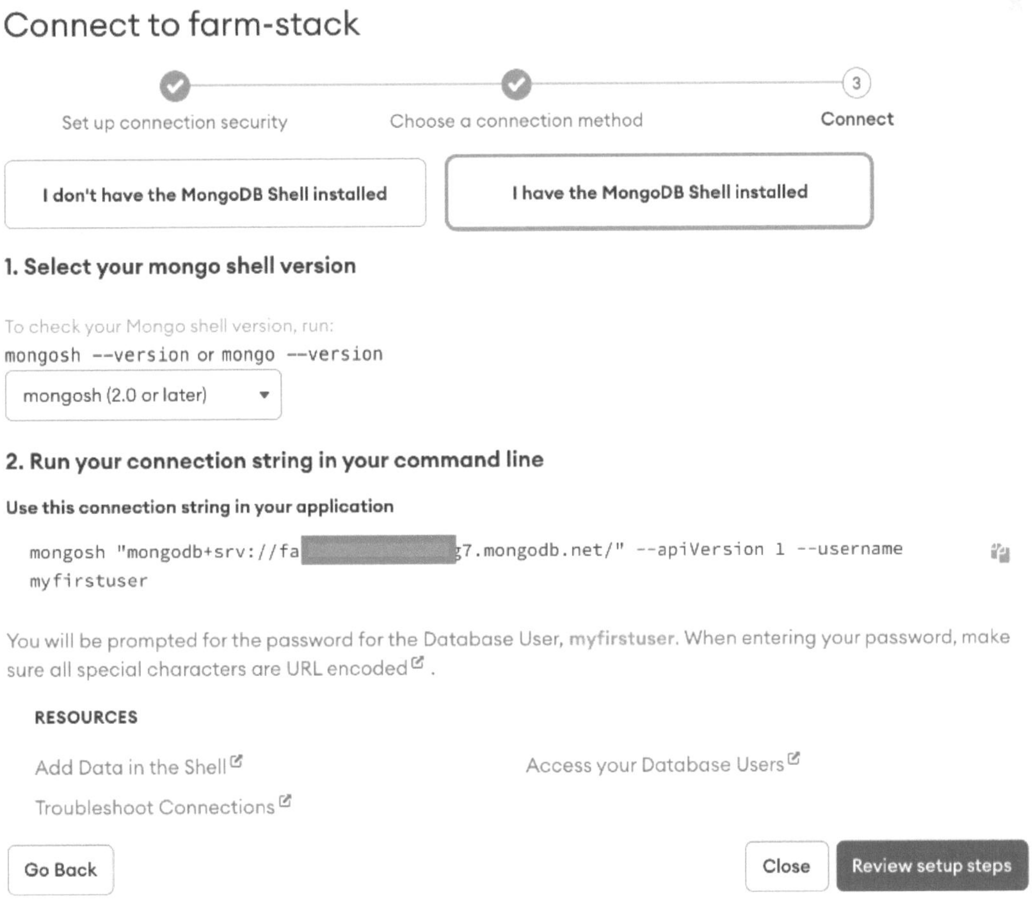

Figure 2.14: Connect to mongosh (MongoDB Shell)

2.  Copy the connection string and navigate to the CLI on your computer.

3.  Now, to set up the options for working with and executing commands in our cloud database in Atlas, perform the following steps:

    I.   In a shell session (Command Prompt on Windows or Bash on Linux), paste the connection string in the prompt, and hit *Enter*. Then, provide the password and hit *Enter*.

        You can also explicitly pass the password in the connection string by using the `--password` option followed by your password. To avoid any typos/errors in typing the password, you can use this option.

    II.  On successfully connecting to your Atlas cluster, you should see something like this:

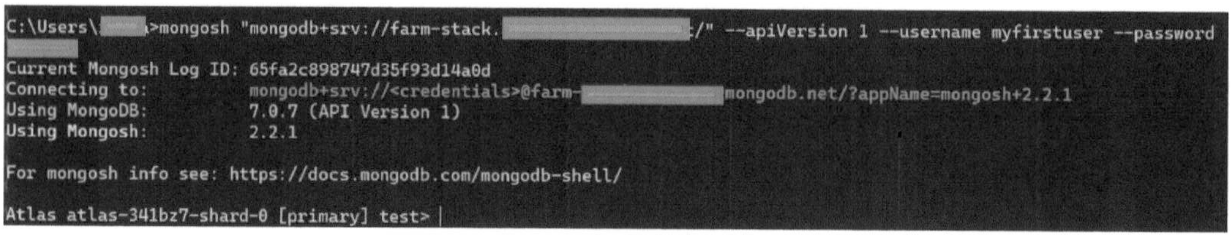

Figure 2.15: Connecting to a MongoDB database successfully

    III. Next, use the `show dbs` command to list all the databases present in your cluster:

        show dbs

        This command should lists all of the available databases: `admin`, `local`, and `sample_mflix` (your database).

    IV.  In order to use your database, type the following code:

        use sample_mflix

        The console will respond with `switched to db sample_mflix`, which means that now you can query and work on your database.

    V.   To see the available collections inside `sample_mflix`, try the following code:

        show collections

You should be able to view all six collections that we saw in the Atlas UI and Compass, that is, `comments`, `embedded_movies`, `movies`, `sessions`, `theatres`, and `users`. Now that you have your database and collection available, you can proceed and use some querying options.

# Querying in MongoDB

This section will show the use of the `sample_mflix.movies` collection as an example for demonstration. Working with real data with some expected query results helps reinforce the acquired notions and makes understanding the underlying processes easier and more thorough.

The most frequent MongoDB query language commands—and the ones that this chapter will be covering—are as follows:

- `find()`: Finds and selects documents matching simple or complex criteria

- `insertOne()`: Inserts a new document into the collection

- `insertMany()`: Inserts an array of documents into the collection

- `updateOne()` and `updateMany()`: Update one or more documents according to some criteria

- `deleteOne()` and `deleteMany()`: Delete one or more documents from the collection

There are 21,349 documents in the `sample_mflix.movies` collection. To query for all the documents, type the following command in the MongoDB Shell:

```
db.movies.find()
```

The preceding command will print several documents, as follows:

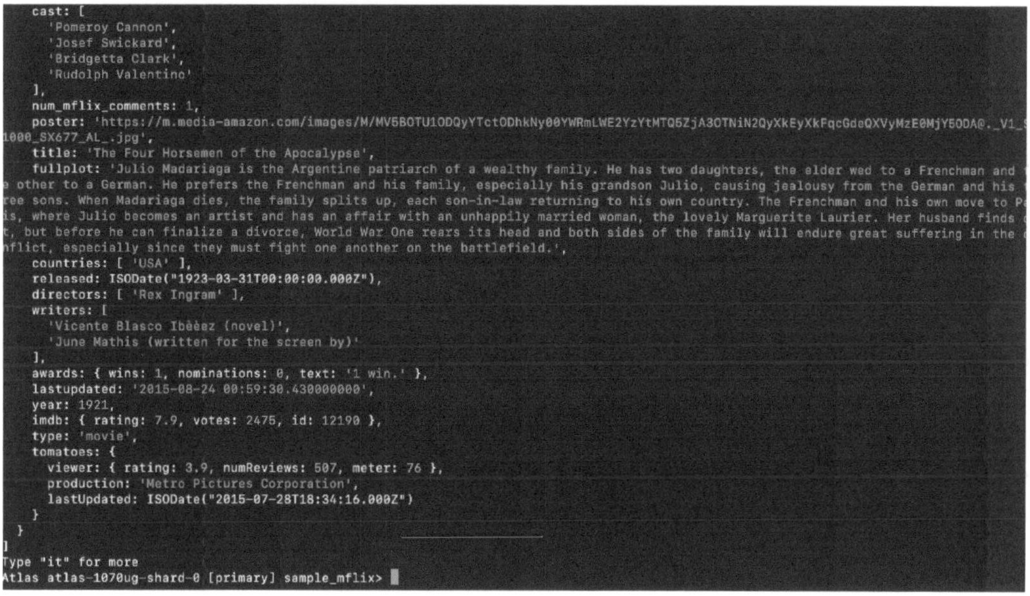

Figure 2.16: find() query output

The console will print the message `Type "it" for more`, as the console prints out only 20 documents at a time. This statement could be interpreted as a classic `SELECT * FROM TABLE` in the SQL world.

> **Note**
>
> The `find()` method returns a cursor and not the actual results. The cursor enables performing some standard database operations on the returned documents, such as limiting the number of results, ordering by one or more keys (ascending or descending), and skipping records.

You can also apply some filters and only return those documents that satisfy the specified criteria. The `movies` collection has the `years` field, which represents the year in which the movie was released. For instance, you can write a query to only return movies that were released in 1969.

In the command prompt, enter the following command:

```
db.movies.find({"year": 1969}).limit(5)
```

Here, you used the `limit()` method on the cursor to specify the maximum number of documents the cursor should return, in this case 5.

The preceding command will return the search results:

```
Atlas atlas-1070ug-shard-0 [primary] sample_mflix> db.movies.find({"year":  1969}).limit(5)
[
  {
    _id: ObjectId("573a1396f29313caabce344e"),
    plot: "During the rehearsals for the production of the tragedy Andromaque, the leading actress and her director, a couple behind
the scenes, can't find a way to leave their personal problems at ...",
    genres: [ 'Drama', 'Romance' ],
    runtime: 252,
    cast: [
      'Bulle Ogier',
      'Jean-Pierre Kalfon',
      'André S. Labarthe',
      'Josée Destoop'
    ],
    title: "L'amour fou",
    fullplot: "During the rehearsals for the production of the tragedy Andromaque, the leading actress and her director, a couple beh
ind the scenes, can't find a way to leave their personal problems at home. And life imitates fiction, creating a real tragedy for thi
s couple when the man finds comfort with other women while the actress prefers to stay focused on her work, as if nothing is happenin
g with her partner.",
    languages: [ 'French' ],
    released: ISODate("1969-01-15T00:00:00.000Z"),
    directors: [ 'Jacques Rivette' ],
    writers: [ 'Marilè Parolini', 'Jacques Rivette (dialogue)' ],
    awards: { wins: 2, nominations: 0, text: '2 wins.' },
    lastupdated: '2015-07-28 00:00:08.310000000',
    year: 1969,
    imdb: { rating: 8.1, votes: 335, id: 62663 },
    countries: [ 'France' ],
    type: 'movie',
    tomatoes: {
```

Figure 2.17: find() operation with a filter criteria

The results should now contain only documents that satisfy the condition that the `year` key is equal to 1969. Looking at the results, it seems like there are many documents. You can also do a count operation on a query by using the `db.collection.countDocuments()` method. For example:

```
db.movies.countDocuments({"year": 1969})
```

The preceding command returns `107`, which means you have 107 documents in your collection that matched your search criteria; that is, 107 movies were released in the year `1969`.

The JSON syntax that you used in the previous query is a **filter**, and it can have numerous key-value pairs with which you define your query method. MongoDB has many operators that enable you to query fields with more complex conditions than plain equality, and their updated documentation is available on the MongoDB site at `https://docs.mongodb.com/manual/reference/ operator/query/`.

You can visit the page and look around some of the operators as they can give you an idea of how you might be able to structure your queries.

For instance, suppose you want to find all the `Comedy` (genre) movies that were released in `USA` after the year `1945`. The following query will do the job:

```
db.movies.find({"year": {$gt: 1945}, "countries": "USA", "genres":
"Comedy"})
```

After running the query, you should see a bunch of documents returned by the cursor.

You can also use the `countDocuments` method to find out the exact number of documents that match the filter criteria:

```
db.movies.countDocuments({"year": {$gt: 1945}, "countries": "USA",
"genres": "Comedy"})
```

You will find that there are `3521` documents in the collection that match your search criteria.

The `$gt` operator is used to specify that the year should be greater than `1945`, ensuring the movies selected were released after this year. The conditions on country and genre are straightforward, requiring the `countries` array to include `USA` and the `genres` array to contain `Comedy`.

Remember that the `find()` method implies an **AND** operation, so only documents satisfying all three conditions will be returned.

Some of the most widely used query operators are as follows:

- `$gt`: Greater than
- `$lt`: Less than
- `$in`: Providing a list of values

However, you can see on the MongoDB documentation (`https://www.mongodb.com/docs/ manual/reference/operator/query/`) that there are many more—logical *and*, *or*, and *nor*; *geospatial* operators for finding the nearest points on a map; and so on. It is time to explore other methods that allow you to perform queries and operations.

`findOne()` is similar to `find()`; it also takes an optional filter parameter but returns only the first document that satisfies the criteria.

Before you dive into the process of creating, deleting, and updating existing documents, it's important to mention a very useful feature called **projection**.

## Projection

Projection allows you to specify which fields should be included or excluded in the documents returned from query results. This is achieved by providing an additional argument to the `find()` and `findOne()` methods. This argument is an object that specifies which fields to include or exclude, effectively tailoring the query results to only contain the information that is needed.

Building projections is easy; a projection query is just a JSON object in which the keys are the names of the fields, while the values are 0 if you want to exclude a field from the output or 1 if we want to include it. The `ObjectId` type is included by default, so if you want to remove it from the output, you have to set it to 0 explicitly. Also, if you have not included the name of any field in the projection, it is assumed to have a 0 value and is not projected.

Suppose in your previous query you only want to project the movie title, country released, and year. To do that, execute the following command:

```
db.movies.find({"year": {$gt: 1945}, "countries": "USA", "genres":
"Comedy"}, {"_id":0, "title": 1, "countries": 1, "year": 1}).sort({"year":
1}).limit(5)
```

The sort and limit operations first sort the returned documents by the `year` field in ascending order and then restrict the result to five documents, as specified by the `limit` parameter. In the projection part, the `_id` field is suppressed by setting it to 0, and the `title`, `countries`, and `year` fields are included by setting them to 1. Since the `genres` field and all other fields in the projection are omitted, they are automatically excluded from the returned documents.

## Creating new documents

The method used to create new documents in MongoDB is `insertOne()`. You can try inserting the following fictitious movie into your database:

```
db.movies.insertOne({"title": "Once upon a time on Moon",
"genres":["Test"], year: 2024})
```

The preceding command will print the following message:

```
{
  acknowledged: true,
  insertedId: ObjectId("66b25f48b959c3fb3a4e56ed")
}
```

The first part means that MongoDB acknowledged the insertion operation, whereas the second property prints out the `ObjectId` key, which is the primary key that MongoDB uses and assigns automatically to the newly inserted documents if not provided manually.

MongoDB, naturally, also supports inserting many documents at once with the `insertMany()` method. Instead of providing a single document, the method accepts an array of documents. You could, for example, insert another couple of sample movies as follows:

```
db.movies.insertMany([{"title": "Once upon a time on Moon",
"genres":["Test"], year: 2024}, {"title": "Once upon a time on Mars",
"genres":["Test"], year: 2023}, {"title": "Tiger Force in Paradise",
"genres":["Test"], year: 2019, rating: "G"}])
```

Here, you inserted three fictitious movies and the third one has a new property, rating (which is set to G), which does not exist in any other movies, just to highlight MongoDB's schema flexibility. The shell acknowledges this and prints out the `ObjectId` key of the newly inserted documents.

## Updating documents

Updating documents in MongoDB is possible through several different methods that are suited for different scenarios that might arise in your business logic.

The `updateOne()` method updates the first encountered document with the data provided in the fields. For example, let's update the first movie whose `genres` field has `Test` in it and set it to `PlaceHolder` genre, as follows:

```
db.movies.updateOne({genres: "Test"}, {$set: {"genres.$": "PlaceHolder"}})
```

You can also update existing properties of the document as long as you use the `$set` operator. Let's say that you want to make similar updates to all documents in your collection (i.e., set the `genres` field value to the `placeHolder` genre) that match the passed filter criteria and also increase the year value by 1 in all matched documents. You could try it with the following command:

```
db.movies.updateMany( { "genres": "Test" }, { $set: { "genres.$":
"PlaceHolder" }, $inc: { "year": 1 } } )
```

The preceding command updates many documents, namely all movies that satisfy the simple requirement of having `Test` in the `genres` field.

Updating documents is an atomic operation—if two or more updates are issued at the same time, the one that reaches the server first will be applied.

`mongosh` also provides a `replaceOne()` method that takes a filter, like your earlier methods, but also expects an entire document that will take the place of the preceding one. You can get more information on the collection methods in the following documentation: https://www.mongodb.com/docs/manual/reference/method/db.collection.updateOne/.

## Deleting documents

Deleting documents works in a similar way to the `find` methods—you can provide a filter specifying the documents to be deleted and use the `deleteOne` or `deleteMany` method to execute the operation.

Let's delete all the fake movies that you inserted in your collection by using the following command:

```
db.movies.deleteMany({genres: "PlaceHolder"})
```

The shell will acknowledge this operation with a `deletedCount` variable equal to 4—the number of deleted documents. The `deleteOne` method operates in a very similar way by deleting the first document that matches the filter criteria.

To drop an entire collection in MongoDB, you can use the `db.collection.drop()` command. However, it is not recommended to drop an entire collection without careful consideration as it will delete all the data and related indexes. It is advised that you don't run this command for the movies dataset as we need it for the rest of this chapter.

> **Note**
> Make sure to import the data again in Atlas (you should see an option on the Atlas dashboard) if you deleted all the documents.

### Aggregation framework

The MongoDB aggregation framework is an extremely useful tool that enables offloading some (or most) of the computing burden of making calculations and aggregations of varying complexity to the MongoDB server and sparing your client side, as well as the (Python-based) backend, of some workload.

Centered around the concept of a **pipeline** (something that you might be familiar with if you have done some analytics or you have ever connected a few commands in Linux), the aggregation framework is, at its simplest, an alternative way to retrieve sets of documents from a collection. It is similar to the `find` method that you already used extensively but with the additional benefit of data processing in different stages or steps.

The MongoDB documentation site (`https://www.mongodb.com/docs/manual/reference/method/db.collection.aggregate/`) is the best place to start if you want to get acquainted with all the possibilities. However, we'll start with a couple of simple examples.

The syntax for the aggregation is similar to other methods that you used earlier, such as `find()` and `findOne()`. We use the `aggregate()` method, which takes a list of stages as a parameter.

Probably the best aggregation, to begin with, would be to mimic the `find` method.

Write an aggregation query to select all movies where the `genres` field includes `Comedy`:

```
db.movies.aggregate([{$match: {"genres": "Comedy"}}])
```

This is probably the simplest possible aggregation, and it consists of just one stage, the `$match` stage, which tells MongoDB that you only want comedy movies, so the output of the first stage is exactly that.

In your collection, you have both `series` and `movies` data. Let's write an aggregation pipeline to filter out films that are of the movie type and have `Comedy` as the genre. Then, group them together to find out the average runtime of comedy movies:

```
db.movies.aggregate([ {$match: {type: "movie", genres: "Comedy" } },
{$group: {_id: null, averageRuntime: { $avg: "$runtime" } } } ])
```

The preceding code will return the following output:

```
[ { _id: null, averageRuntime: 98.86438291881745 } ]
```

Here is a more detailed explanation of the preceding aggregation query:

- **$match stage**: This is an aggregation stage that filters documents to pass only those that match the given criteria to the next stage. Think of it as a filter that screens out documents not meeting specific conditions. The parameters to `$match` define the criteria for filtering documents. In this case, `{type: "movie", genres: "Comedy"}` specifies that documents must have the type equal to `movie` and must include `Comedy` in their `genres` array to pass through.

- **$group stage**: This stage is used to aggregate documents. Documents that meet the criteria from previous stages are grouped based on a specified identifier and can be processed collectively, often to perform operations such as summing or averaging values.

  The `$group` stage takes parameters that define how to group the documents and what calculations to perform on the grouped data.

- **_id: null**: In the `$group` stage, `_id` specifies the grouping criteria. Setting `_id` to null means all documents passed from the previous stage will be aggregated into a single group, rather than being divided into multiple groups based on distinct field values.

- **averageRuntime: { $avg: "$runtime" }**: This part calculates the average of the runtime values of all documents in the group. `$avg` is an accumulator operator used here to compute the average. `$runtime` specifies that the runtime field from each document should be used in the calculation.

Once the data is grouped and aggregated the way you want it, you can apply other simpler operations, such as sorting, ordering, and limiting.

# Summary

This chapter detailed the basic building blocks that define MongoDB and its structure. You have seen how to set up a database in the cloud using MongoDB Atlas and explored the basics of creating, updating, and deleting documents. Further, this chapter detailed the aggregation pipeline framework—a strong analytic tool.

The next chapter will show how to create APIs with FastAPI—an exciting and new Python framework. We will provide a minimal yet complete guide of the main concepts and features, which should hopefully convince you that building APIs can be fast, efficient, and fun.

# 3

# Python Type Hints
# and Pydantic

Before exploring FastAPI, it is useful to explore some Python concepts that will be heavily used throughout your journey with FastAPI.

Python type hinting is a very important and relatively new feature of the language that facilitates the work of developers, bringing greater robustness and maintainability to the development workflow. Types make your code more readable and understandable, and most importantly, they promote good practices.

FastAPI is heavily based on Python type hints. So, before diving into the framework, it is useful to review the basic concepts of type hinting, what they are, how they are implemented, and what their purpose is. This foundational knowledge will help you create robust, maintainable, and scalable APIs with FastAPI.

By the end of this chapter, you will have a deep understanding of the role of type annotations in Python with FastAPI and Pydantic. Pydantic is a modern Python library that enforces type hints at runtime, provides customizable and user-friendly errors when data is invalid, and allows definition of data structures using Python type annotations.

You will be able to model your data with precision, leveraging the advanced features of Pydantic to make you a better and more productive FastAPI developer.

This chapter will cover the following topics:

- Python type hints and their usage
- A general overview of Pydantic and its main functions, including parsing and validating data
- Data deserialization and serialization, including advanced and special cases
- Validation and data transformation, aliases, and field and model-level validation
- Advanced Pydantic usage such as nested models, fields, and model settings

## Technical requirements

To run the sample application in this chapter, you should have Python version 3.11.7 (`https://www.python.org/downloads/`) or higher installed on your local computer, a virtual environment, and a couple of packages. As the examples in this chapter will not make use of FastAPI, if you wish, you can create a pristine virtual environment and install Pydantic with the following:

```
pip install pydantic==2.7.1 pydantic_settings==2.2.1
```

In this chapter, you will be working with Pydantic and some Pydantic-related packages, such as `pydantic_settings`.

## Python types

The different types present in a programming language define the language itself—they define its boundaries and set some ground rules for what is possible and, more importantly, what the recommended way of achieving something is. Different types of variables have completely different sets of methods and properties available. For example, while capitalizing a string makes perfect sense, capitalizing a floating number or a list of integers doesn't.

If you have used Python for a while, even for the most mundane tasks, you already know that, like every programming language, it supports different types of data—strings and different numerical types such as integers and floats. It also features a rather rich data structure library: from dictionaries to lists, from sets to tuples, and so on.

Python is a **dynamically typed language**. This means that the type of a variable is not determined at compile time, but at runtime. This feature gives the language itself a lot of flexibility and enables you to declare a variable as a string, use it, and then later on reassign it to a list. However, the ease of changing the variable type can make larger and more complex codebases more prone to errors. Dynamic typing implies that the type of a variable is embedded with the variable itself and is easily modifiable.

On the other end of the spectrum lie the so-called statically typed languages: C, C++, Java, Rust, Go, and so on. In these languages, the type of the variable is known at compile time, and it cannot change over time. The type-checking is performed at compile time (so before runtime) and errors are caught before runtime, as the compiler will prevent the program from being compiled.

Programming languages are divided into different categories along another, different axis: strongly typed languages and weakly typed languages. This characteristic tells us how much a language restricts its types to operations inherent to those specific types and how easy it is to coerce, or change, a variable from one to another type. Unlike JavaScript, for instance, Python is considered to be on the stronger side of the spectrum, and the interpreter sends strong messages when you try to perform an illegal operation, such as typing the following in a Python interpreter to add a `dict` type to a number:

```
>>>{}+3
Traceback (most recent call last):
File "<stdin>", line 1, in <module>
TypeError: unsupported operand type(s) for +: 'dict' and 'int'
```

So, while Python does complain when you attempt to perform unsupported operations, it only does so at runtime, not before executing the code. In fact, there is no indication to you—the developer—that you are writing code that violates the Python type system.

# Type hinting

As you have seen in the previous section, Python is a dynamically typed language, and types aren't known until runtime. Since variable types are embedded in the value of the variable itself, as a developer, you cannot know the type of a variable that you encounter in a codebase just by looking at it or inspecting it with your IDE of choice. Fortunately, Python introduced a very sought-out feature starting from version 3.5—type annotations (https://peps.python.org/pep-0484/).

Type annotations or hints in Python are an additional syntax that notifies you, the developer, of the expected type of a variable. They are not used by the Python language at runtime, and they do not modify or affect the behavior of your program in any way. You might be wondering what the use of these hints is if the Python interpreter cannot even see them.

As it turns out, several important benefits will make almost any codebase much more robust, more maintainable, and future-proof:

- **Faster code development**: Any developer reading your code will know exactly the type of any annotated variable—whether it is an integer or a floating point, a list or a set, allowing for faster development.

- **Knowledge of methods and properties**: You will know exactly which methods or properties are available for any given variable. Inadvertently changing the type of a variable in a larger codebase will be picked up immediately.

- **Simplified code development**: Code editors and IDE (such as Visual Studio Code) will provide excellent support and auto-completion (IntelliSense), further simplifying development and reducing the cognitive load on the developer.

- **Automatic code generation**: FastAPI provides automatic and interactive (as in a fully functional REST API) documentation that is entirely based on Python type hints.

- **Type checkers**: This is the most important benefit. These are programs that run in the background and perform static analysis of your code, spotting potential problems and informing you immediately.

- **Easier to read and smaller cognitive load**: Annotated code is much easier to read and puts much less cognitive load on you as a developer when you have to work on a piece of code and are trying to figure out what it is supposed to do.

- **Strongly typed and flexible**: Preserves the language's strongly typed nature and dynamic typing flexibility, while allowing for imposing the necessary safety requirements and constraints. While recommended for larger codebases, Python type hints are ingrained into FastAPI and Pydantic, so even the smallest projects will require you to at least know your way around types and how to work with them.

Type hinting is at the very base of FastAPI. Coupled with MongoDB's flexible document schema, it is the backbone of FARM stack development. Type hinting ensures that your application data flow maintains the right data types going in and out of the system at every moment. While this might seem trivial for simpler endpoints—quantities should be integers, names should be strings, and so on—when your data structure becomes more complex, debugging type errors can become very cumbersome.

Type hints can also be defined as a formalism—a formal solution to statically (before runtime) indicate the type of a value to a type checker (**Mypy**, in your case), which will ensure that when the Python runtime encounters your program the types will not be problematic.

The next section will detail the syntax of type hints, how to annotate functions, and how to check your code with Mypy.

## Implementing type hints

Let's see how you can implement type hinting. Create a directory named Chapter3 and create a virtual environment inside it, as shown earlier. Inside, add a requirements.txt file with the following contents if you want to be able to recreate the examples in the chapter exactly:

```
mypy==1.10.0
pydantic==2.7.4
```

Install the packages with requirements.txt:

```
pip install -r requirements.txt
```

Now you are ready to explore the world of Python type hints.

While there are many Python type checkers—basically tools that perform static analysis of the source code without running it—we will use mypy as it is easily installable. Later, you will have tools such as Black or Ruff at your disposal. These perform different actions on your source code, including type checking.

In order to showcase the Python type annotation syntax, a simple function, such as the following will suffice:

1.  Create a file called `chapter3_01.py` and define a simple function:

    ```
    def print_name_x_times(name: str, times: int) -> None:
        for _ in range(times):
            print(name)
    ```

    The previous function accepts two parameters, `name` (a string) and `times` (an integer), and returns `None`, while the function prints the given name for a given number of times in the console. If you try to call the function in your code and start typing the arguments, Visual Studio Code (or any IDE with Python type-checking support) will immediately suggest a string as the first positional argument and an integer as the second.

2.  You can try to input the wrong argument types, for instance, an integer first and then a string afterward, save the file, and run `mypy` on the command line:

    ```
    mypy chapter3_01.py
    ```

3.  Mypy will inform you that there are two errors:

    ```
    types_testing.py:8: error: Argument 1 to "print_name_x_times" has
    incompatible type "int"; expected "str"   [arg-type]
    types_testing.py:8: error: Argument 2 to "print_name_x_times" has
    incompatible type "str"; expected "int"   [arg-type]
    Found 2 errors in 1 file (checked 1 source file)
    ```

This example was simple enough, but take a look again at what **Python Enhancement Proposal 8 (PEP 8)** recommends when it comes to the type-hinting syntax with another example:

1.  Insert a simple variable that has a value:

    ```
    text: str = "John"
    ```

    The colon is attached to the variable (no spaces), there is one space after the colon, and, in cases where you do provide a value, there are spaces around the equal sign.

2.  When annotating the output of a function, the "arrow," which is made up of a dash and greater than sign (`->`), should be surrounded by one space, like this:

    ```
    def count_users(users: list[str]) -> int:
        return len(users)
    ```

So far, you have seen simple annotations that constrain a variable to some Python primitive types including integers and strings. Typing annotations can be more flexible: you might want to allow a variable to accept several variable types, such as an integer and a string.

3.  You can achieve this with the use of the `Union` package from the `typing` module:

```
from typing import Union
x: Union(str, int)
```

4.  The previously defined x variable can take a string or an integer value. The more modern and concise way of achieving the same functionality is the following:

```
x: str | int
```

These annotations mean that the variable x can be an integer or it can take a value of `string`, which is a different type from an integer.

The `typing` module contains several types of so-called generics, including the following:

- `List`: For variables that should be of the list type

- `Dict`: For dictionaries

- `Sequence`: For any type of sequence of values

- `Callable`: For callables, such as functions

- `Iterator`: Indicates that a function or variable accepts an iterator object (an object that implements the iterator protocol and can be used in a `for` loop)

> **Note**
>
> You are encouraged to explore the `typing` module but bear in mind that the types from the module are gradually being imported into Python's code functionality.

For instance, the `List` type is very useful in working with FastAPI as it allows you to serialize a list of items or resources quickly and efficiently into a JSON output.

An example of a `List` type is the following, in a new file called `chapter3_02.py`:

```
from typing import List

def square_numbers(numbers: List[int]) -> List[int]:
    return [number ** 2 for number in numbers]

# Example usage
input_numbers = [1, 2, 3, 4, 5]
squared_numbers = square_numbers(input_numbers)
print(squared_numbers)  # Output: [1, 4, 9, 16, 25]
```

Another useful type is `Literal`, which restricts the possible values of a variable to a few admissible states:

```
from typing import Literal
account_type: Literal["personal", "business"]
account_type = "name"
```

The preceding lines showcase the power of type hints. There is nothing inherently wrong with assigning the `account_type` variable to a string, but that string is not part of the admissible state set and thus Mypy complains and returns an `Incompatible types in assignment` error.

Now, look at an example that includes a `datetime` argument. Create a new file called `chapter3_03.py`:

```
from datetime import datetime
def format_datetime(dt: datetime) -> str:
    return dt.strftime("%Y-%m-%d %H:%M:%S")


now = datetime.now()
print(format_datetime(now))
```

The previously defined function accepts one parameter—a datetime object—and outputs a string: a nicely formatted date and time, useful for displaying on websites. If you try to type *dt* and then a dot in your Visual Studio Code editor, you will be prompted by the autocompletion system, offering all the methods and properties related to the datetime object.

To declare a structure as a list of dictionaries (something very familiar to anyone working with a JSON-based API), you could use something like this, in a file named `chapter3_04.py`:

```
def get_users(id: int) -> list[dict]:
    return [
        {"id": 1, "name": "Alice"},
        {"id": 2, "name": "Bob"},
        {"id": 3, "name": "Charlie"},
    ]
```

After having covered the basic annotation types in Python, the next few sections will look at some more advanced types that are very useful when working with FastAPI and Pydantic.

## Advanced annotations

The annotations you have seen so far are very simple and convey basic information related only to the specific desired type of a variable, function, class argument, or output. Python's typing system is capable of much more and it can be used to restrict the allowable variables' state further and prevent you, the developer, from creating impossible or illegal states in your code.

The most frequently used types are the following:

- The `Optional` type is used for handling optional values and `None` values in an explicit and developer-friendly way.

- The `Union` type allows you to define a union of possible types, such as integers and strings. Modern Python uses the pipe operator ( | ), as shown in the previous example.

- The `self` type is used to indicate that the value will be an instance of a certain class, useful in Pydantic model validators as we will see later.

- The `New` type allows developers to define completely new types based on existing types.

This section detailed Python type hints, their purpose, and how they are implemented. The next section will take a deeper look at Pydantic, the workhorse of FastAPI data validation.

# Pydantic

Pydantic is a data validation library labeled on its website as the most widely used data validation library for Python. It allows you to model your data in a granular way and perform various types of validation while being firmly rooted in the Python type hinting system. The actual version, V2, has critical parts of the code rewritten in **Rust** for speed and allows for an excellent developer experience. The following list describes some of the benefits of using Pydantic:

- **Based on type hints that are part of the standard library**: Instead of needing to learn contrived new systems or terminologies, you just need to learn pure Python types.

- **Excellent speed**: Everything about FastAPI and MongoDB revolves around speed—fast and responsive applications delivered in record time—so having a fast validation and parsing library is mandatory. The core of Pydantic is written in Rust, which ensures high-speed operations on data.

- **Huge community support and wide adoption**: Learning your way around Pydantic will prove useful when working with popular packages such as Django Ninja, SQLModel, LangChain, and more.

- **The possibility of emitting JSON schema**: It facilitates integration with other systems.

- **More flexibility**: Pydantic supports different modes (strict and lax when it comes to coercion) and nearly unlimited customization options and flexibility.

- **Popular among developers**: It has been downloaded more than 70 million times and over 8,000 packages on PyPI depend on Pydantic (as of July 2024).

> **Note**
> You can take a look at Pydantic in detail in its documentation: `https://docs.pydantic.dev/latest/`.

Broadly speaking, Pydantic tackles many important problems in a modern web development workflow. It ensures that the data that is ingested into your application is properly formed and formatted, falls within the desired range, is of the appropriate type and dimensions, and reaches your document store safely and without errors.

Pydantic also ensures that your application outputs the data exactly as intended and according to the specification, omitting fields that should not be exposed (such as user passwords) and even more complex tasks, including interfacing with other incompatible systems.

FastAPI is standing on the shoulders of two powerful Python libraries—Starlette and Pydantic. While Starlette takes care of the web-related aspects of the framework, often through thin wrappers and utility functions and classes provided by FastAPI, Pydantic is responsible for FastAPI's phenomenal developer experience. Pydantic is fundamental to FastAPI, and leveraging its powerful capabilities opens up the playing field for all FARM stack developers.

While type checking is performed statically (without running the code), the role of Pydantic is apparent during runtime and performs the role of a guardian of inbound data. Your FastAPI application will receive data from users, from a flexible MongoDB database schema, and from other systems via APIs—and Pydantic will facilitate the parsing and data validation. Instead of crafting complex validation logic for every possible invalid case, you will simply create Pydantic models of desired complexity, matching your application's needs as closely as possible.

In the following sections, you will explore most of functionality of Pydantic through examples with increasing complexity and demands as we feel that it is the best and most effective way of familiarizing yourself with the library.

## Pydantic basics

Unlike some other libraries that provide similar functionality (such as `dataclasses`), Pydantic provides a base model (aptly named `BaseModel`) that enables the parsing and validation functionality through inheritance. Since you will be building a user model in the coming sections, you can start by jotting down the most basic data that needs to be associated with your user. At the minimum, you will need the following:

- A username
- An email address
- An ID (keep it as an integer for now)
- A date of birth

In Pydantic, a user model that would be associated with this specification could look like the following, in a file called chapter3_05.py:

```python
from datetime import datetime
from pydantic import BaseModel


class User(BaseModel):
    id: int
    username: str
    email: str
    dob: datetime
```

The User class already handled a lot of work for you—there is no need to perform validation checks as the instantiation of the class performs the validation and parsing immediately.

The process of constructing the class is pretty straightforward: each field has a type declaration, and Pydantic is ready to inform you of any erroneous types it might encounter.

If you try and create a user, you shouldn't see any errors:

```python
Pu = User(id=1, username="freethrow", email="email@gmail.com",
dob=datetime(1975, 5, 13))
```

Say however, you create a user with the wrong data, and conveniently import the Pydantic ValidationError:

```python
from pydantic import BaseModel, ValidationError
try:
    u = User(
        id="one",
        username="freethrow",
        email="email@gmail.com",
        dob=datetime(1975, 5, 13),
    )

    print(u)
except ValidationError as e:
    print(e)
```

Pydantic will inform you that the data cannot be validated when you run the program:

```
1 validation error for User
id
  Input should be a valid integer, unable to parse string as an integer
[type=int_parsing, input_value='one', input_type=str]
```

The error messages of Pydantic, derived from `ValidationError`, are deliberately informative and precise. The field with an error is called `id` and the type of error is described. The first useful aspect that comes to mind is that if there were several errors—for instance, you might provide an invalid `datetime`—Pydantic will not stop at the first error. It will continue parsing the entire instance and outputting the list of errors that can easily be output in JSON format. That is actually the desired behavior when working with APIs; you want to be able to list all the errors, for instance, to a user that has sent the wrong data to the backend. The exception contains a list of all the encountered errors.

The model guarantees that the instance, once validation is passed, will have the required fields and that they are of the correct type.

You can also provide defaults and nullable types, according to the type hinting conventions:

```
class User(BaseModel):
    id: int = 2
    username: str
    email: str
    dob: datetime
    fav_colors: list[str] | None = ["red", "blue"]
```

The previous model has a default `id` value (which is not something that you would want to do in practice) and a list of favorite colors as strings, which can also be `None`.

When you create and print a model (or more precisely, when you invoke its representation via the `print` function), you get a nice output:

```
id=2 username='marko' email='email@gmail.com' dob=datetime.datetime(1975,
5, 13, 0, 0) fav_colors=None
```

Pydantic by default operates in a lax mode, which means that it will try to coerce the provided types to the ones that are declared in the model. For instance, if you pass the user ID as a string `"2"` to the model, there will not be any errors, as Pydantic automatically converts the ID to an integer.

Although fields are available through the dot notation (`user.id`) and they can be easily modified, this is not recommended as the validation rules will not be applied. You could instantiate a user with an `id` value of 5, access `user.id`, and set it to a string `"five"`, but that is probably not something you would want.

Besides pure data validation, Pydantic provides other important functionalities to your application. Some of the most widely used operations with Pydantic models are the following:

- **Data deserialization**: Ingesting data into the model
- **Data serialization**: Outputting validated data from the model into Python data structures or JSON
- **Data modification**: Sanitizing or modifying data on the fly

The next few sections will look at each of these operations in more detail.

## Deserialization

Deserialization refers to the process of providing data to the model, which is the input phase, as opposed to the process of serialization, which means outputting model data in a desired form. Deserialization is tightly coupled with validation as the processes of validation and parsing are performed when instantiating the model, although this can be overridden.

In Pydantic, the term **validation** refers to the process of instantiating a model (or other type) that adheres to specified types and constraints. Pydantic guarantees the types and constraints of the output, not the input data. This distinction becomes apparent when you consider the `ValidationError` type of Pydantic that is raised when data cannot be successfully parsed into a model instance.

While you have already performed a couple of validations through instantiating the Pydantic-based user models, the data to be validated is often passed in the form of a dictionary. The following is an example of passing data as a dictionary, in a file named `chapter3_06.py`:

Create another version of your user model and pass it a dictionary of data:

```
class User(BaseModel):
    id: int
    username: str
    email: str
    password: str


user = User.model_validate(
    {
        "id": 1,
        "username": "freethrow",
        "email": "email@gmail.com",
        "password": "somesecret",
    }
)


print(user)
```

The `.model_validate()` method is a helper that accepts a Python dictionary and performs the class instantiation and thus validation. This method creates your `user` instance and validates the data types in one step.

Similarly, `model_validate_json()` accepts a JSON string (useful when working with APIs).

There is also a method for constructing a model instance without validation with `model_construct()` but this has very specific user cases and is not recommended in most cases.

You have learned how to pass data to your simple Pydantic model. The next section will take a closer look at the model fields and their properties.

## Model fields

Pydantic fields are based on Python types and setting them to be required or nullable and providing default values is intuitive. For instance, to create a default value for a field, it is enough to provide it in the model as a value, while the nullable field follows the same conventions that you saw in the *Python types* sections—by using the older union syntax from the `typing` module, or the newer syntax with the pipe operator.

The following is an example of another user model in a file named `chapter3_07.py`:

1.  Insert some default values:

    ```python
    from pydantic import BaseModel
    from typing import Literal


    class UserModel(BaseModel):
        id: int
        username: str
        email: str
        account: Literal["personal", "business"] | None = None
        nickname: str | None = None
    ```

    The previously defined `UserModel` class defines a couple of standard string-type fields: an account that can have exactly two values or be equal to `None` and a nickname that can be a string or `None`.

2.  You may use the `model_fields` property to inspect the model as follows:

    ```python
    print(UserModel.model_fields)
    ```

    You will get a handy list of all the fields belonging to the model with information about them including their types and whether they are required:

    ```
    {'id': FieldInfo(annotation=int, required=True), 'username':
    FieldInfo(annotation=str, required=True), 'email':
    FieldInfo(annotation=str, required=True), 'account':
    FieldInfo(annotation=Union[Literal['personal', 'business'],
    NoneType], required=False, default=None), 'nickname':
    FieldInfo(annotation=Union[str, NoneType], required=False,
    default=None)}
    ```

The next section will detail Pydantic-specific types that make working with the library easier and faster.

## Pydantic types

While Pydantic is based on standard Python types such as strings, integers, dictionaries, and sets, which makes it very intuitive and straightforward for starting, the library also provides a plethora of customizations and solutions for common cases. In this section, you will get to know the most useful ones.

Strict types such as `StrictBool`, `StrictInt`, `StrictStr`, and other Pydantic-specific types are types that will pass validation only if the validated value belongs to these types, without any coercion: a `StrictInt` must be of type `Integer` and not `"1"` or `1.0`, for example.

Constrained types provide additional constraints for existing types. For instance, `condate()` is a date type with greater than, greater than or equal, less than, and less than or equal constraints. `conlist()` wraps the list type and adds length validation or can impose a rule that the items contained must be unique.

Pydantic is not limited to the validation of primitive types such as strings and integers. Many additional validators cover the vast majority of uses that you might run into while modeling your business logic. For instance, the `email` validator validates email addresses and, since it is not part of the core Pydantic package, it needs to be installed separately by using the following command:

```
pip install pydantic[email]
```

The Pydantic website (`https://docs.pydantic.dev/latest/api/types/`) provides a comprehensive list of additional validation types that extend the functionalities—lists can have a minimum and maximum length, uniqueness can be required, integers can be positive or negative, and many more, including CSS color codes, for instance.

## Pydantic fields

While the simple Python type annotations might suffice in many cases, the real power of Pydantic starts to show when you begin to use the `Field` class for the fields. The `Field` class is used to customize models and add metadata to the model fields.

Let's see how you can use the `Field` class for the `UserModel` explored in the previous section. Create a file and name it `chapter3_08.py`.

First, rewrite your previous `UserModel` with the help of the `Field` class:

```python
from typing import Literal
from pydantic import BaseModel, Field


class UserModelFields(BaseModel):
    id: int = Field(...)
    username: str = Field(...)
    email: str = Field(...)
    account: Literal["personal", "business"] | None = Field(default=None)
    nickname: str | None = Field(default=None)
```

This model is equivalent to the one previously defined without fields. The first syntactic difference can be seen in the way default values are provided—the Field class accepts a default value that is defined explicitly.

Fields also provide additional model flexibility, through the use of aliases, as you will see in the next section.

### Field aliases

Fields allow you to create and use aliases, which is very useful when dealing with different systems that need to be compatible with your Pydantic-based data definition. Create a file named chapter3_09.py. Assume that your application uses the UserModelFields model for users, but also needs to be able to ingest data from another system, maybe through a JSON-based API, and this other system sends the data in the following JSON format:

```
external_api_data = {
    "user_id": 234,
    "name": "Marko",
    "email": "email@gmail.com",
    "account_type": "personal",
    "nick": "freethrow",
}
```

This format clearly doesn't conform to your UserModelFields model and aliases provide an elegant way of dealing with this incompatibility:

```
class UserModelFields(BaseModel):
    id: int = Field(alias="user_id")
    username: str = Field(alias="name")
    email: str = Field()
    account: Literal["personal", "business"] | None = Field(
        default=None, alias="account_type"
    )
    nickname: str | None = Field(default=None, alias="nick")
```

This updated model provides aliases for all the fields that have different names, so it is possible to validate your external data:

```
user = UserModelFields.model_validate(external_api_data)
```

In this case, you have used the simple alias parameter, but there are other options for aliases for serialization or for validation only.

Additionally, the Field class enables numeric values to be constrained in different ways, which is a feature heavily used in FastAPI. Create a file called chapter3_10.py and start populating it.

Suppose you need to model a chess event that has the following fields:

```
from datetime import datetime
from uuid import uuid4
from pydantic import BaseModel, Field


class ChessTournament(BaseModel):
    id: int = Field(strict=True)
    dt: datetime = Field(default_factory=datetime.now)
    name: str = Field(min_length=10, max_length=30)
    num_players: int = Field(ge=4, le=16, multiple_of=2)
    code: str = Field(default_factory=uuid4)
```

In this relatively simple class, Pydantic fields introduce some complex validation rules that would otherwise be very verbose and cumbersome to write:

- dt: The datetime object of the tournament uses a default_factory parameter, a function invoked at instantiation time that provides the default value. In this case, the value is equal to datetime.now.

- name: This field has some length constraints, such as the minimum and maximum length.

- **The number of enlisted players is constrained**: It must be greater than or equal to 4, less than or equal to 16, and additionally, it must be an even number—a multiple of 2—to allow for all players to play in each round.

- **The code of the tournament**: This is another string generated by a default factory, in this case the uuid library.

- id: This field is an integer, but this time you apply the strict flag, which means you override the default behavior of Pydantic and do not allow strings like "3" to pass validation, even though they could be cast to integers.

---

**Note**

A useful page in the Pydantic documentation is dedicated to Fields: https://docs.pydantic.dev/latest/concepts/fields/. There are numerous validation options available through the Field class, and you are encouraged to skim through them before you start your modeling process.

---

The next section will detail how to get the data out of the model through the process of deserialization.

## Serialization

The most important task of any parsing and validation library is data serialization (or data dumping). It is the process of converting and outputting a model instance to a Python dictionary or a JSON-encoded string. The method for generating a Python dictionary is `model_dump()`, as demonstrated by the following user model example, in a new file called `chapter3_11.py`.

To be able to use email validation in Pydantic, add the following line to the `requirements.txt` file:

```
email_validator==2.1.1
```

And then, re-run the user model:

```
pip install -r requirements.txt
class UserModel(BaseModel):
    id: int = Field()
    username: str = Field(min_length=5, max_length=20)
    email: EmailStr = Field()
    password: str = Field(min_length=5, max_length=20, pattern="^[a-
zA-Z0-9]+$")
```

The user model that you are using is a fairly standard one, and, with your knowledge of Pydantic fields, you can already understand it. There are a couple of new validations, but they are intuitive: the `EmailStr` object imported from Pydantic is a string that validates email addresses, while the `password` field contains an additional regular expression to ensure that the field contains only alphanumeric characters and no spaces. Here's another example:

1.  Create an instance of the model and serialize it to a Python dictionary:

    ```
    u = UserModel(
        id=1,
        username="freethrow",
        email="email@gmail.com",
        password="password123",
    )
    print(u.model_dump())
    ```

    The result is a simple Python dictionary:

    ```
    {'id': 1, 'username': 'freethrow', 'email': 'email@gmail.com',
    'password': 'password123'}
    ```

2.  Try to dump the model to a JSON representation and omit the password for security reasons:

    ```
    print(u.model_dump_json(exclude=set("password")))
    ```

    The result is a JSON string with the password omitted:

    ```
    {"id":1,"username":"freethrow","email":"email@gmail.com"}
    ```

Serialization uses the field names and not the aliases by default, but that is another setting that can be easily overridden by setting the `by_alias` flag to `True`.

An example of an alias used when working with FastAPI and MongoDB is MongoDB's `ObjectId` field, which is mostly serialized as a string. Another useful method is `model_json_schema()`, which generates the JSON schema for a model.

Models can be additionally configured through the `ConfigDict` object, and the special field called `model_config`—the name is reserved and mandatory. In the following file, called `chapter3_12.py`, you are using the `model_config` field to allow populating the model by name and prevent passing additional data to the model:

```
from pydantic import BaseModel, Field, ConfigDict, EmailStr
class UserModel(BaseModel):
    id: int = Field()
    username: str = Field(min_length=5, max_length=20, alias="name")
    email: EmailStr = Field()
    password: str = Field(min_length=5, max_length=20, pattern="^[a-
zA-Z0-9]+$")

    model_config = ConfigDict(extra="forbid", populate_by_name=True)
```

The `model_config` field allows for additional configuration of the model. For instance, the `extra` keyword refers to additional data fields that are passed to the deserialization process: the default behavior is just to ignore this data.

In this example, we set `extra` to `forbid`, so any additional data passed and not declared in the model will throw a validation error. `populate_by_name` is another useful setting as it allows us to populate a model by using field names and not only aliases, practically mixing and matching. You will see that this feature is handy when crafting APIs that have to talk to different systems.

### Custom serializers

Pydantic can provide you with virtually unlimited capabilities when it comes to serialization and also provides different serialization methods for Python and JSON outputs with the use of the `@field_serializer` decorator.

> **Note**
>
> Python decorators are a powerful and elegant feature that allow you to modify or extend the behavior of functions or methods without changing their actual code.
>
> Decorators are higher-order functions that take a function as input, add some functionality, and return a new, decorated function. This approach promotes the reusability, modularity, and separation of concerns in your Python programs.

In the following example, you are going to create a very simple bank account model and use different serializers depending on the type of serialization. Your requirement is to round the balance to exactly two decimals and, only when serializing to JSON, to format the updated field according to the ISO format:

1. Create a new file named chapter3_13.py and add a simple model for a bank account that contains only two fields, the balance and the time of the last account update:

```python
from datetime import datetime
from pydantic import BaseModel, field_serializer

class Account(BaseModel):
    balance: float
    updated: datetime

    @field_serializer("balance", when_used="always")
    def serialize_balance(self, value: float) -> float:
        return round(value, 2)

    @field_serializer("updated", when_used="json")
    def serialize_updated(self, value: datetime) -> str:
        return value.isoformat()
```

You have added two custom serializers. The first is the balance serializer (as denoted by the string "balance"), which will always be used. This serializer simply rounds the balance to two decimals. The second serializer is used only for JSON serialization and returns the date as an ISO-formatted datetime string.

2. If you try to populate the model and inspect the serializations, you will see how the serializers modified the initial default output:

```python
account_data = {
    "balance": 123.45545,
    "updated": datetime.now(),
}

account = Account.model_validate(account_data)

print("Python dictionary:", account.model_dump())
print("JSON:", account.model_dump_json())
```

You will get a similar output:

```
Python dictionary: {'balance': 123.46, 'updated': datetime.
datetime(2024, 5, 2, 21, 34, 11, 917378)}
JSON: {"balance":123.46,"updated":"2024-05-02T21:34:11.917378"}
```

Earlier in this chapter, you saw basic validation provided by Pydantic through the mere instantiation of the model class. The next section will discuss the various custom validation methods of Pydantic with the help of Pydantic decorators and how they can be leveraged to move beyond serialization and provide powerful custom validation functionality.

## Custom data validation

Similar to custom field serializers, custom field validators are implemented as decorators, with the @field_validator decorator.

Field validators are class methods, so they must receive the entire class as the first argument, not the instance, while the second value is the name of the field to be validated (or a list of fields, or the * symbol for all fields).

Field validators should return either the parsed value or a ValueError response (or AssertionError) in case the data passed to the validator doesn't conform to the validation rules. As with other Pydantic features, it is much easier to start with an example. Create a new file called chapter3_14.py and insert the following code:

```
from pydantic import BaseModel, field_validator
class Article(BaseModel):
    id: int
    title: str
    content: str
    published: bool

    @field_validator("title")
    @classmethod
    def check_title(cls, v: str) -> str:
        if "FARM stack" not in v:
            raise ValueError('Title must contain "FARM stack"')
        return v.title()
```

The validator is run before the class instantiation and accepts the class and the name of the validated field as arguments. The `check_title` validator checks that the title contains the string `"FARM stack"` and if it doesn't, it throws `ValueError`. Additionally, the validator returns the string in title case, so we can perform data transformation as well, at the field level.

While field validators provide great flexibility, they do not consider field interactions and the combinations of field values. That is where model validators come into play, as the next section will outline.

## Model validators

Another useful feature when performing validation of web-related data is model validation—the possibility to write validation functions at the model level, allowing for complex interactions between various fields.

The model validators can run before or after instantiating the model class. Again, we will take a look at a rather simple example:

1. First, create a new file and name it `chapter3_15.py`.

2. Suppose you have a user model with the following structure:

```
from pydantic import BaseModel, EmailStr, ValidationError, model_
validator
from typing import Any, Self

class UserModelV(BaseModel):
    id: int
    username: str
    email: EmailStr
    password1: str
    password2: str
```

The model is simple like the previous ones, and it contains two password fields that are required to match to enable the registration of a new user. Additionally, you want to impose another validation—the data that comes into the model via deserialization must not contain private data (such as a social security number or card number). Model validators allow you to perform flexible validations such as this.

3. Continuing the previous model, you can write the following model validators under the class definition:

```python
@model_validator(mode='after')
def check_passwords_match(self) -> Self:
    pw1 = self.password1
    pw2 = self.password2
    if pw1 is not None and pw2 is not None and pw1 != pw2:
        raise ValueError('passwords do not match')
    return self


@model_validator(mode='before')
@classmethod
def check_private_data(cls, data: Any) -> Any:
    if isinstance(data, dict):
        assert (
            'private_data' not in data
        ), 'Private data should not be included'
    return data
```

4. Now, try to validate of the following data:

```python
usr_data = {
    "id": 1,
    "username": "freethrow",
    "email": "email@gmail.com",
    "password1": "password123",
    "password2": "password456",
    "private_data": "some private data",
}

try:
    user = UserModelV.model_validate(usr_data)
    print(user)
except ValidationError as e:
    print(e)
```

You will be informed of just one error—the one related to the `before` mode, stating that private data should not be included.

5. If you comment out or delete the line that sets the `private_data` field and re-run the example, the error becomes the following:

```
Value error, passwords do not match [type=value_error, input_
value={'id': 1, 'username': 'fr...ssword2': 'password456'}, input_
type=dict]
```

There are a couple of new concepts involved in the previous example; you are using the `Self` Python type, introduced for denoting instances of the wrapping class, so you practically expect the output to be an instance of the `UserModelV` class.

Another new concept is present in the `check_private_data` function as it checks whether the data passed to the class is an instance of a dictionary, and then proceeds to verify whether the undesired `private_data` field is present in the dictionary—this is just Pydantic's way of checking for the data passed as it is stored inside a dictionary.

The next section will detail how to compose nested models with Pydantic to validate models of increasing complexity.

## Nested models

The treatment of nested models in Pydantic through composition is very straightforward and intuitive if you are coming from a basic MongoDB background. To understand how to implement nested models, the easiest way is to start from an existing data structure that needs to be validated and run through Pydantic:

1.  Begin with the structure of a JSON document that returns car brands and makes (or models). Create a new file named `chapter3_16.py` and add the following lines of code:

    ```
    car_data = {
        "brand": "Ford",
        "models": [
            {"model": "Mustang", "year": 1964},
            {"model": "Focus", "year": 1975},
            {"model": "Explorer", "year": 1999},
        ],
        "country": "USA",
    }
    ```

    You can start from the inside of the data structure and begin identifying the smallest units or the most deeply nested structures—in this case, the smallest unit is the car model (a Ford Mustang from 1964).

2.  This can be the first Pydantic model:

    ```
    class CarModel(BaseModel):
        model: str
        year: int
    ```

3.  Once this first abstraction is made, it is easy to create a model for the brand:

    ```
    class CarBrand(BaseModel):
        brand: str
        models: List[CarModel]
        country: str
    ```

The car brand model has distinct names and countries of origin and contains a list of models.

Model fields can be other models (or lists or sets or other sequences thereof) and this feature makes mapping Pydantic data structures to data, and especially MongoDB documents, a very pleasant and intuitive process.

While MongoDB can support up to 100 levels of nesting, you will probably not hit that limit in your data modeling process. However, it's worth noting that Pydantic will support you as you delve deeper and deeper into your data structures. Embedding data also becomes much more manageable from the Python side, as you can rest assured that data coming into your collections is stored as intended.

The next and final section will detail another useful tool that Pydantic offers—a little help with managing environment variables and settings, a problem that you face in every web-related project.

## Pydantic Settings

Pydantic Settings is an external package that needs to be installed separately. It provides Pydantic features for loading a settings or config class from environment variables or secret files.

That is basically the definition from the Pydantic website (`https://docs.pydantic.dev/latest/concepts/pydantic_settings/`), and the whole concept revolves around the `BaseSettings` class.

A model that inherits from this class attempts to read the values of any fields passed as keyword arguments by scanning the environment.

This simple functionality allows you to define clear and straightforward configuration classes from environment variables. Pydantic settings can also automatically pick up environment modifications and, when needed, manually override settings for testing, development, or production.

In the following exercise, you will create a simple `pydantic_settings` setup that will allow you to read environment variables and easily override them in case the necessity arises:

1.  Install Pydantic settings with `pip`:

    ```
    pip install pydantic-settings
    ```

2.  Create a `.env` file at the same level as your project files:

    ```
    API_URL=https://api.com/v2
    SECRET_KEY=s3cretstr1n6
    ```

3.  Now you can set up a simple `Settings` configuration (the `chapter3_17.py` file):

    ```python
    from pydantic import Field
    from pydantic_settings import BaseSettings


    class Settings(BaseSettings):
        api_url: str = Field(default="")
        secret_key: str = Field(default="")

        class Config:
            env_file = ".env"
    print(Settings().model_dump())
    ```

4.  If you run this code, both the Python and the `.env` file are on the same path, so you will see that Pydantic was able to read the environment variables from the `.env` file:

    ```
    {'api_url': 'https://api.com/v2', 'secret_key': 's3cretstr1n6'}
    ```

    However, if you set an environment variable, it will take precedence over the `.env` file.

5.  You can test it by adding this line before the `Settings()` call and observing the output of the program:

    ```python
    os.environ["API_URL"] = 'http://localhost:8000'
    ```

Pydantic Settings makes managing configurations such as your Atlas and MongoDB URLs, secrets for hashing passwords, and other configurations much more structured and organized.

# Summary

This chapter detailed aspects of Python that are either new and still evolving, or often simply overlooked, such as type hinting, and the implications that their use can have on your projects.

FastAPI is based on Pydantic and type hinting. Working with these solid principles and conventions will make your code more robust, maintainable, and future-proof even when working with other frameworks. You have a solid Python types foundation and have learned the basic functionalities provided by Pydantic—validation, serialization, and deserialization.

You have learned how to deserialize, serialize, and validate data through Pydantic, and even add some transformations during the process, creating structures of increased complexity.

This chapter has equipped you to learn more web-specific aspects of FastAPI and to blend data seamlessly between MongoDB, Python data structures, and JSON.

The next chapter will explore FastAPI and its Pythonic foundations.

# 4

# Getting Started with FastAPI

The **application programming interface** (**API**) is the cornerstone of your FARM stack, functioning as the brain of the system. It implements business logic that dictates how the data flows in and out of the system, but more importantly, how it relates to the business requirements inside your system.

Frameworks such as FastAPI are much easier to showcase through examples. In this chapter, you'll explore some simple endpoints that make up for a minimal, self-contained REST API. These examples will help you understand how FastAPI handles requests and responses.

This chapter focuses on introducing the framework, along with the standard REST API practices and how they are implemented in FastAPI. You'll learn how to send requests and modify them according to your needs, and how to retrieve all the data from HTTP requests, including parameters and request bodies. You'll also understand how to handle responses and how you can use FastAPI to easily set cookies, headers, and other standard web-related topics.

This chapter will cover the following topics:

- An overview of the FastAPI framework

- Setup and requirements for a simple FastAPI app

- Python features in FastAPI, such as type hinting, annotations, and `async/await` syntax

- How FastAPI handles typical REST API tasks

- Working with form data

- Anatomy of a FastAPI project and routers

# Technical requirements

For this chapter, you will need the following:

- Python setup
- Virtual environments
- Code editor and plugins
- REST client

The following sections cover these requirements in more detail.

## Python setup

If you do not have Python installed, visit the Python download site (`https://www.python.org/downloads/`) to get the installer for your OS. In this book, you will be using **version 3.11.7** or later.

FastAPI relies heavily on Python hints and annotations, and Python versions after 3.6 treat type hints in a similar, modern way; so, while theoretically any version later than 3.6 should work, the code in this book uses Python version 3.11.7, for compatibility reasons.

Ensure that your Python installation is upgraded to one of the latest Python versions—as stated, at least version 3.11.7—and is reachable and the default version. You can check this by:

- Typing `python` in your terminal of choice.
- Using **pyenv**, a handy tool that manages multiple Python versions on the same machine.

## Virtual environments

If you have ever worked with a Python project before, chances are you needed to include some, if not dozens, Python third-party packages. After all, one of Python's main strengths lies in its vast ecosystem, which is one of the primary reasons it's chosen for the FARM stack.

Without getting into the detailed specifics of how Python manages third-party package installations, let's just go over the main problems that can arise should you decide to use only one Python installation for all of your projects, or even worse, should that installation be the default operating system Python installation.

Following are a few challenges:

- Operating systems often lag in terms of Python versions, so the latest couple of versions likely won't be available.
- Packages will get installed into the same namespace or in the same packages folder, creating havoc in any application or package that depends on that package.
- Python packages depend on other packages and those packages also have versions. Let's suppose that you are using package A, which depends on packages B and C, and for some reason, you

need to keep package B to a specific version (i.e., 1.2.3). You might need package B for a totally different project and that project might require a different version.

- Reduced or impossible reproducibility: without a separate Python virtual environment, it would prove very difficult to quickly replicate the desired functionality with all the required packages.

Python virtual environments are the solution to the aforementioned problems as they allow you to work in a pristine Python development with only the packages and package versions that you need. In our case, the virtual environment will certainly include the core packages: FastAPI and Uvicorn. FastAPI, on the other hand, depends on Starlette, Pydantic, and so on, so it is really important to have the package versions under control.

The best practice for Python development states that each project, no matter how big or small, should have its own virtual environment. While there are several ways of creating a virtual environment, which is a separated and isolated Python environment, you will use `virtualenv`.

The basic syntax for creating new virtual environments with `virtualenv` is given in the following command. Once you are in the project folder, name your folder `FARM` or `chapter4`, open a terminal, and enter the following command:

```
python - m venv venv
```

This command will create a new virtual environment for your project, a copy of the Python interpreter (or if you are using macOS, a brand new Python interpreter) and the necessary folder structure, a couple of commands necessary for activating and deactivating the environment, as well as a copy of the `pip` installer (pip installs packages).

In order to activate your new virtual environment, you will choose one of the following commands, depending on your operating system. For Windows systems, type the following in the shell:

```
venv/Scripts/activate
```

On Linux or macOS systems, use the following command:

```
source venv/bin/activate
```

In both cases, your shell should now be prepended with the name that you have given to your environment. In the command to create a new virtual environment, the final parameter is the name of the environment, so it was `venv` in this case.

Some considerations when working with virtual environments are as follows:

- There are different schools of thought when it comes to virtual environment placement. For now, it will suffice if you keep them inside your project folder like you did.

- Similar to the `activate` command, there is also a `deactivate` command to exit your virtual environment.

- Saving the exact package versions in a `requirements.txt` file and pinning the dependencies is not only useful but also often mandatory when deploying.

There are many alternatives to `virtualenv` in the Python community, as well as many complementary packages. Poetry is a tool that manages virtual environments and dependencies simultaneously, `virtualenvwrapper` is a set of utilities that further simplify the process of environment management. `pyenv` is a bit more complex—it manages Python versions and allows you to have different virtual environments based on different Python versions.

## Code editors

While there are many great code editors and **integrated development environments** (**IDEs**) for Python, a common choice is **Visual Studio Code** (**VS Code**) from Microsoft. Released in 2015, it's cross-platform, providing a lot of integrated tools, such as an integrated terminal for running your development server. It's lightweight and offers hundreds of plugins for virtually any programming task you may have. Since you'll be working with JavaScript, Python, React, and CSS for styling, along with running command-line processes, using VS Code is the easiest option.

There's also an excellent MongoDB plugin named **MongoDB for VS Code**, that allows you to connect to a MongoDB or Atlas cluster, navigate through databases and collections, get a quick overview of the schema and indexes, and view documents in collections. This proves very handy in a full stack scenario when you find yourself dealing with backend code in Python, frontend code in JavaScript and React or Next.js, running shells, and needing to quickly view the state of the MongoDB database. The extension is available here: `https://marketplace.visualstudio.com/items?itemName=mongodb.mongodb-vscode`. You can install it from the **Extensions** tab in Visual Studio Code as well, just by searching for MongoDB.

## Terminal

Besides Python and Git, you'll need a shell program. Linux and Mac users usually have one pre-installed. For Windows, you can use Windows PowerShell or a console emulator such as **Cmder** (`https://cmder.app`), which offers additional features.

## REST clients

To effectively test your REST API, you'll need a REST client. While **Postman** (`https://www.postman.com/`) is robust and customizable, there are other viable alternatives. **Insomnia** (`https://insomnia.rest/`) and the REST GUI offer a simpler interface, while **HTTPie** (`https://httpie.io/`), a command-line REST API client, allows quick testing without leaving the shell. It offers features such as an expressive syntax, handling of forms and uploads, and sessions.

HTTPie is probably the easiest REST client to install, as it can be done using `pip` or some other package manager, such as Chocolatey, apt (for Linux), or Homebrew.

The easiest way to install HTTPie is to activate your virtual environment and use `pip`, as shown in the following command:

```
pip install httpie
```

Once it's been installed, you can test HTTPie with the following command:

```
(venv) http GET "http://jsonplaceholder.typicode.com/todos/1"
```

The output should begin with an `HTTP/1.1 200 OK` response.

`venv` signifies that the virtual environment is active. HTTPie simplifies issuing HTTP requests by simply adding `POST` for `POST` requests, payloads, form values, and so on.

## Installing the necessary packages

After setting up the virtual environment, you should activate it and install the Python libraries required for your first simple application: FastAPI and Uvicorn.

For FastAPI to run, it needs a server. In this case, a server is a software designed to serve web applications (or REST APIs). FastAPI relies on the **asynchronous server gateway interface** (**ASGI**), which enables async non-blocking applications, which is something you can completely use with your FastAPI capabilities. You can read more about ASGI in the following documentation: `https://asgi.readthedocs.io/`.

At present, the FastAPI documentation lists three compatible Python ASGI-compatible servers: **Uvicorn**, **Hypercorn**, and **Daphne**. This book will focus on Uvicorn, the most widely used and recommended option for working with FastAPI. Uvicorn offers high performance, and if you get stuck, there's extensive documentation available online.

To install the first two dependencies, ensure you're in your working directory with the desired virtual environment activated, then execute the following:

```
pip install fastapi uvicorn
```

Now, you have a Python coding environment that contains a shell, one or two REST clients, a great editor, and a great REST framework. If you've previously developed a **Django** or **Flask** application, this should all be familiar ground.

Finally, choose a folder or clone this book's GitHub repository and activate a virtual environment. It is customary to create the environment in a folder named `venv` within the working directory, but feel free to structure your directories and code as you prefer.

Later, this chapter will briefly discuss some options for structuring your FastAPI code. For now, ensure you're in a folder with your newly created virtual environment activated.

# FastAPI in a nutshell

In *Chapter 1*, *Web Development and the FARM Stack*, it was mentioned why FastAPI is the preferred REST framework in the FARM stack. What sets FastAPI apart is its coding speed and the resulting clean code, with which you can spot bugs quickly and early. The author of the framework himself, *Sebastian Ramirez*, often modestly emphasizes that FastAPI is just a mix of Starlette and Pydantic, while heavily relying on modern Python features, especially type hinting.

Before diving into an example and building a FastAPI app, it is useful to quickly go over the frameworks that FastAPI is based on.

## Starlette

Starlette is an ASGI framework known for its top performance and numerous features, which are also available in FastAPI. These include WebSocket support, events on startup and shutdown, session and cookie support, background tasks, middleware implementations, and templates. While you will not be coding directly in Starlette, it is important to know how FastAPI works under the hood and what its origins are.

If you're interested in knowing its functionalities, visit Starlette's excellent documentation (`https://www.starlette.io/`).

## Asynchronous programming

You will likely have learned about the asynchronous programming paradigm when developing apps with Node.js. It involves running slow operations, such as network calls and file reading, allowing the system to respond to other requests without blocking. This is achieved by using an event loop, an asynchronous task manager that enables it to move requests to the next one, even though the previous one hasn't finished and yielded a response.

Python added support for asynchronous I/O programming in version 3.4 and the `async`/`await` keywords in version 3.6. ASGI emerged shortly afterward in the Python world, outlining how applications should be structured and called, and defining the events that can be sent and received. FastAPI relies on ASGI and returns an ASGI-compatible app.

In this book, all the endpoint functions are prefixed with the `async` keyword, even before they become necessary, since you will be using the asynchronous Motor Python MongoDB driver.

> **Note**
> If you are developing a simple application not expecting high stress, you can use simple synchronous code and the official PyMongo driver.

Functions with the `async` keyword are coroutines; they run on the event loop. While simple examples in this chapter may work without `async`, the real power of asynchronous programming in

FastAPI will be visible when you connect to your MongoDB server through an `async` driver, such as **Motor** (`https://motor.readthedocs.io/en/stable/`).

## Standard REST API operations

This section will discuss some common terminologies in API development. Usually, communication occurs via the HTTP protocol, through HTTP requests and responses. You'll explore how FastAPI handles these aspects and leverages additional libraries such as Pydantic and type hints to improve efficiency. In the examples, you'll be using Uvicorn as the server.

The basis of any REST API communication is a system of URLs and paths. The URL for your local web development server will be `http://localhost:8000` since `8000` is the default port that Uvicorn uses. The path part (optional) of an endpoint could be `/cars`, while `http` is the scheme. You will see how FastAPI handles paths, query strings, and the request and response bodies, the significance of defining endpoint functions in a certain order, and how to extract variables from dynamic path segments effectively.

In every path or address, the URL and the path combined, there's a set of approved actions that can be performed on it—HTTP verbs. For example, a page or URL might list all the cars on sale, but you cannot issue a `POST` request since this is not allowed.

In FastAPI, these verbs are implemented as Python **decorators**. To put it better, they are exposed as decorators, and they are implemented only if you, the developer, implement them.

FastAPI encourages the proper and semantic use of HTTP verbs for data resource operations. For example, you should always use `POST` (or the `@post` decorator) when creating new resources, `GET` for reading data (individual or lists of items), `PATCH` for updating, and so on.

HTTP messages consist of a request/status line, headers, and, optionally, body data. FastAPI offers tools to easily create and modify headers, set response codes, and manipulate request and response bodies in a clean and intuitive way.

This section describes the programming concepts and specific Python features that underpin FastAPI's performance and enable maintainable code. In the next section, you'll learn about standard REST API operations and see how they're achieved with FastAPI.

## How does FastAPI speak REST?

Observing even a minimal FastAPI application, the classic **Hello World** example, you can start examining how FastAPI structures endpoints. In this context, an endpoint specifies the following details:

- A unique combination of a URL: This will be the same in your development server—`localhost:8000`.

- A path: The part after the slash.

- An HTTP method.

In a new folder named `Chapter4`, for example, create a new Python file named `chapter4_01.py` by using Visual Studio Code:

```python
from fastapi import FastAPI


app = FastAPI()


@app.get("/")
async def root():
    return {"message": "Hello FastAPI"}
```

With this code, you can accomplish several things. Here's a breakdown of what each part does:

- In the first line of `chapter4_01.py`, you imported the FastAPI class from the `fastapi` package.
- Next, you instantiated an application object. This is just a Python class with all the API functionalities that exposes an ASGI-compatible application, which must be passed to Uvicorn.

Now, the application is ready and instantiated. But without endpoints, it can't do or say much. It has one endpoint, the root, which you can view at `http://127.0.0.1:8000/`. FastAPI exposes decorators for HTTP methods to tell the application how and whether to respond. However, you must implement them.

After that, you used the `@get` decorator, which corresponds to the `GET` method, and passed a URL—in this case, the root path, `/`, is used.

The decorated function, named `root`, is responsible for responding to requests. It accepts any arguments (in this case, there aren't any). The value returned by the function, typically a Python dictionary, will be transformed into a **JavaScript Object Notation (JSON)** response by the ASGI server and returned as an HTTP response. This may seem obvious, but it is useful to break things down to understand the fundamentals.

The preceding code defines a fully functional application with a single endpoint. To test it, you need a Uvicorn server. Now, you must run the live server with Uvicorn in your command line:

```
uvicorn chapter4_01:app --reload
```

You will use this code snippet quite often when developing with FastAPI, so the following note will break it down.

> **Note**
>
> Uvicorn is your ASGI-compatible web server. You can call it directly by passing it the combination of the executable Python file (without the extension) and the instantiated app (the FastAPI instance), separated by a colon (`:`). The `--reload` flag instructs Uvicorn to reload the server each time you save your code, similar to *Nodemon* in Node.js. Unless specified otherwise, you can run all the examples in this book containing FastAPI apps using this syntax.

Here's the output when testing your only endpoint with HTTPie. Remember, when you omit the keyword for the method, it defaults to a GET request:

```
(venv) http http://localhost:8000/
HTTP/1.1 200 OK
content-length: 27
content-type: application/json date: Fri, 01 Apr 2022 17:35:48 GMT
server: uvicorn
{
    "message": "Hello FastAPI"
}
```

HTTPie informs you that your simple endpoint is running. You will get a 200 OK status code, the content-type is correctly set to application/json, and the response is a JSON object containing the desired message.

Every REST API guide begins with similar *hello world* examples, but with FastAPI, this is particularly useful. With a couple of lines of code, you can see the anatomy of a simple endpoint. This endpoint only covers the GET method directed toward the root URL (/). So, if you try to test this app with a POST request, you should get a 405 Method Not Allowed error (or any method other than GET).

If you want to create an endpoint that responds with the same message but for POST requests, you will just have to change the decorator. Add the following code to the end of your file (chapter4_01.py):

```
@app.post("/")
async def post_root():
    return {"message": "Post request success!"}
```

HTTPie will respond accordingly in the terminal:

```
(venv) http POST http://localhost:8000 HTTP/1.1 200 OK
content-length: 35
content-type: application/json date: Sat, 26 Mar 2022 12:49:25 GMT
server: uvicorn
{
    "message": "Post request success!"
}
```

Now that you've created a couple of endpoints, head over to http://localhost:8000/docs and see what FastAPI has generated for you.

## Automatic documentation

When developing REST APIs, you will find yourself needing to constantly perform API calls—GET and POST requests—analyze the responses, set payloads and headers, and so on. Choosing a viable REST client is largely a matter of preference and is something that should be carefully considered. While there are numerous clients on the market— ranging from full-blown API IDEs such as Postman (https://www.postman.com/) to the slightly more lightweight Insomnia (https://insomnia.rest/) or Visual Studio Code's REST Client (https://marketplace.visualstudio.com/items?itemName=humao.rest-client)—this book mostly uses the very simple command-line based HTTPie client, which exposes a minimalistic command-line interface.

This, however, is the right moment to introduce another of FastAPI's most beloved features—interactive documentation—a tool that facilitates the development process of REST APIs in FastAPI.

With each endpoint or router that you develop, FastAPI creates automatically generated documentation. It is interactive, allowing you to test your API as you develop it. FastAPI lists all the endpoints you define and provides information about expected inputs and responses. The documentation is based on the OpenAPI specification and relies heavily on Python hints and the Pydantic library. It allows setting the JSON or form data to be sent to the endpoints, displays responses or errors, is tightly coupled with Pydantic, and is able to handle simple authorization procedures such as the bearer token flow that will be implemented in *Chapter 6, Authentication and Authorization*. Rather than having to use a REST client, you can just open the documentation, select the desired endpoint to be tested, input the test data conveniently into a standard web page, and hit the **Submit** button!

In this section, you created a minimal, yet fully functional API with a single endpoint, giving you insights into the syntax and structure of an app. In the next section, you will learn about the basic elements of a REST API request-response cycle and how you can control every single aspect of the process. Standard REST clients provide a more transferable experience and enable you to compare different APIs, even those that aren't Python-based.

# Building a showcase API

REST APIs revolve around HTTP requests and responses, which power the web and are implemented in every web framework using the HTTP protocol. To showcase the capabilities of FastAPI, you will now create simple endpoints that focus on specific parts of code that achieve the desired functionalities. Rather than the usual CRUD operations, the next sections will focus on the process of retrieving and setting request and response elements.

## Retrieving path and query parameters

The first endpoint will be for retrieving a fictional car by its unique ID.

1.  Create a file called chapter4_02.py and insert the following code:

```
from fastapi import FastAPI
```

```
app = FastAPI()
@app.get("/car/{id}")
async def root(id):
    return {"car_id": id}
```

The third line of the code snippet defines a dynamic path defined with `car/:id`, while `{id}` is a standard Python string-formatted dynamic parameter in the sense that it can be anything—a string or a number since you haven't used any hinting.

2. Try it out and test the endpoint with an ID equal to 1:

```
(venv) http "http://localhost:8000/car/1"
HTTP/1.1 200 OK
content-length: 14
content-type: application/json date: Mon, 28 Mar 2022 20:31:58 GMT
server: uvicorn
{
    "car_id": "1"
}
```

3. You got your JSON response back, but here, 1 in the response is a string (hint: quotes). You can try this same route with an ID equal to a string:

```
(venv) http http://localhost:8000/car/billy HTTP/1.1 200 OK
{
    "car_id": "billy"
}
```

FastAPI returns your string, which was provided as part of the dynamic parameter. However, Python's newer features, such as type hinting, come into play.

4. Returning to your FastAPI route (or endpoint) to make the car ID become an integer, it is enough to hint at the type of the variable parameter. The endpoint will look like this:

```
@app.get("/carh/{id}")
async def hinted_car_id(id: int):
    return {"car_id": id}
```

You have given it a new path: `/carh/{id}` (the h after `car` means hint). Apart from the function's name (`hinted_car_id`), the only difference is in the argument: the semicolon followed by `int` means that you can expect an integer, but FastAPI takes this very seriously and you can already see how the framework puts the hinting system to good use.

If you take a look at the interactive documentation at `http://localhost:8000/docs` and try to insert a string in the `id` field for the `/carh/` endpoint, you will get an error.

Now, try it out in your REST client and test the /carh/ route by passing it a string. First, FastAPI sets the status code for you correctly—that is, 422 Unprocessable Entity—and in the body of the response, it pointed out what the problem was—the value is not a valid integer. It also informs you of the exact location where the error occurred: in the id path.

This is a trivial example but imagine that you are sending a complex request with a complicated path, several query strings, and maybe additional information in the header. Using type hinting quickly solves these problems.

If you try to access the endpoint without specifying any ID, you will get yet another error:

```
(venv) http http://localhost:8000/carh/ HTTP/1.1 404 Not Found
{
    "detail": "Not Found"
}
```

FastAPI has, again, correctly set the status code, giving you a 404 Not Found error, and repeated this message in the body. The endpoint you hit does not exist; you must specify a value after the slash.

Situations may arise where you have similar paths: both dynamic and static. A typical case is an application that has numerous users. Directing the API at the URL defined by /users/id would give you some information about the user with the selected ID, while /users/me would typically be an endpoint that displays your information and allows you to modify it, in some way.

In these situations, it is important to remember that, like in other web frameworks, order matters. Because of said order of path handler declarations, the following piece of code will not yield the desired results as the application will try to match the /me route with the first endpoint that it encounters—the one that requires an ID—and since the /me part is not a valid ID, you will get an error.

Create a new file called chapter4_03.py and paste the following code:

```
from fastapi import FastAPI


app = FastAPI()
@app.get("/user/{id}")
async def user(id: int):
    return {"User_id": id}


@app.get("/user/me")
async def me_user():
    return {"User_id": "This is me!"}
```

When you run the application and test the /user/me endpoint, you will get a 422 Unprocessable Entity error, like previously. This is quite logical once you remember that order matters—FastAPI finds the first matching URL, checks the types, and throws an error. If the first match is the one with the fixed path, everything works as intended. Just change the order of the two routes and everything will work as expected.

Another powerful feature of the path treatment of FastAPI is how it limits the path to a specific set of values and a path function, imported from FastAPI, which enables you to perform additional validation on the path.

Suppose you want to have a URL path that accepts two values and allows the following:

- `account_type`: This can be `free` or `pro`.
- `months`: This must be an integer between 3 and 12.

FastAPI solves this by letting you create a class based on `Enum` for the account type. This class defines all the possible values for the account variable. In this case, there are just two—`free` and `pro`. Create a new file and name it `chapter4_04.py` and edit it:

```
from enum import Enum
from fastapi import FastAPI, Path


app = FastAPI()


class AccountType(str, Enum):
    FREE = "free"
    PRO = "pro"
```

Finally, in the actual endpoint, you can combine this class with the utilities from the `Path` function (do not forget to import it along with FastAPI from `fastapi`). Paste the following code at the end of the file:

```
@app.get("/account/{acc_type}/{months}")
async def account(acc_type: AccountType, months: int = Path(..., ge=3,
le=12)):
    return {"message": "Account created", "account_type": acc_type,
"months": months}
```

In the preceding code, FastAPI sets the type of the `acc_type` part of the path to your previously defined class and ensures that only the `free` or `pro` value can be passed. The `months` variable, however, is handled by the `Path` utility function. When you try to hit this endpoint, `account_type` will show that there are only two values available, while the actual value of the enumeration can be accessed through the `.value` syntax.

FastAPI allows you to declare path parameters using standard Python types. If no type is declared, FastAPI will assume that you're working with strings.

For more details on these topics, you can visit the excellent documentation site and see what other options are available (`https://fastapi.tiangolo.com/tutorial/path-params/`). In this case, the `Path` function received three parameters. The three dots mean that the value is required and that no default value has been provided, `ge=3` means that the value can be greater than or equal to 3, while `le=12` means that it can be smaller than or equal to 12. This syntax allows you to define validation right inside the path functions quickly.

## Query parameters

Now that you've learned how to validate, restrict, and properly order your path parameters and endpoints, it's time to look at **query parameters**. These parameters are a simple mechanism of passing data to a server through the URL and they are represented as key-value pairs, separated by an equals sign (=). You can have multiple pairs of keys and values separated by an ampersand (&).

Query parameters are added at the end of the URL by using the question mark/equals notation: `?min_ price=2000&max_price=4000`.

The question mark, ?, is a separator that tells you where the query string begins, while the ampersand, &, allows you to add more than one (the equals sign, =) assignment.

Query parameters are usually used to apply filters, sort, order, or limit query sets, paginate a long list of results, and similar tasks. FastAPI treats them very similarly to path parameters as it automatically picks them up and makes them available for processing in your endpoint functions.

1.  Create a simple endpoint that accepts two query parameters for the minimum and maximum prices of the car, and name it `chapter4_05.py`:

    ```
    from fastapi import FastAPI


    app = FastAPI()


    @app.get("/cars/price")
    async def cars_by_price(min_price: int = 0, max_price: int = 100000):
        return {"Message": f"Listing cars with prices between {min_price}
    and {max_price}"}
    ```

2.  Test this endpoint with HTTPie:

    ```
    (venv) http "http://localhost:8000/cars/price?min_price=2000&max_
    price=4000"
    HTTP/1.1 200 OK
    content-length: 60
    content-type: application/json date: Mon, 28 Mar 2022 21:20:24 GMT
    server: uvicorn
    {
    "Message": "Listing cars with prices between 2000 and 4000"
    }
    ```

In this solution, you can't ensure the basic condition that the minimum price should be lower than the maximum price. This is handled by the object-level validation of Pydantic.

FastAPI picks your query parameters and performs the same parsing and validation checks it did previously. It provides the Query function, like the Path function. You can use the *greater than*, *less than*, or *equal* conditions, as well as set default values. They can also be set to default to None. Query parameters will be converted into Boolean values as needed. You can write rather complex combinations of path and query parameters, as FastAPI can distinguish between them and handle them inside the function.

With that, you've seen how FastAPI enables working with data that is passed through the path and query parameters, as well as the tools it uses under the hood to perform parsing and validation as soon as possible. Now, you will examine the main data vehicle of REST APIs: the **request body**.

## The request body—the bulk of the data

REST APIs enable two-way communication between a client—a web browser or a mobile application and an API server. The bulk of this data is carried over in the request and response body. A request body has data sent from the client to your API, while the response body is data sent from the API server to the client(s).

This data can be encoded in various ways, but many users prefer to encode data with JSON since it is exceptionally nice with our database solution of choice, MongoDB—which operates with BSON, a close relative to JSON.

When modifying data on the server, you should always use:

- POST requests: To create new resources
- PUT and PATCH: To update resources
- DELETE: To delete resources

Since the body of a request will contain raw data—in this case, MongoDB documents or arrays of documents—you can use Pydantic models. But first, see how the mechanism works, without any validation or modeling. In HTTP terminology, the GET method should be *idempotent*, meaning it should always return the same value for the same set of parameters.

In the following code for a hypothetical endpoint used to insert new cars in your future database, you can pass the generic request body as the data. It can be a dictionary without entering into the specifics of how that dictionary should be shaped. Create a new file called chapter4_06.py and paste the following code:

```
from typing import Dict
from fastapi import FastAPI, Body

app = FastAPI()
@app.post("/cars")
async def new_car(data: Dict = Body(...)):
    print(data)
    return {"message": data}
```

Intuitively, the Body function is similar to the previously introduced Path and Query functions. Yet the difference is, when working with the request body, this function is mandatory.

The three dots indicate that the body is required (you must send something), but this is the only requirement. Try to insert a car (a Fiat 500, made in 2015):

```
(venv) http POST "http://localhost:8000/cars" brand="FIAT" model="500"
year=2015
HTTP/1.1 200 OK
content-length: 56
content-type: application/json date: Mon, 28 Mar 2022 21:27:31 GMT
server: uvicorn
{
  "message": {
  "brand": "FIAT",
  "model": "500",
  "year": "2015"
}
```

FastAPI does the heavy lifting. You can retrieve all the data passed to the request body and make it available to your function for further processing – database insertion, optional preprocessing, and so on.

On the other hand, you could have passed any key-value pairs to the body. Of course, this is just an illustration of the general mechanism—in reality, Pydantic will be your data guardian, ensuring you only let the right data in.

While all went well, FastAPI sends you a 200 response status again, even though a 201 Resource Created error is more appropriate and exact. You could, for instance, have some document inserted into MongoDB at the end of the function and a 201 CREATED status message would be appropriate. You will see how easy it is to modify the response body as well, but for now, you will be able to see why Pydantic shines when it comes to request bodies.

To create new car entries, you would only need the brand, model, and production year fields.

So, create a simple Pydantic model with the desired types in the chapter4_07.py file:

```python
from fastapi import FastAPI, Body
from pydantic import BaseModel

class InsertCar(BaseModel):
    brand: str
    model: str
    year: int

app = FastAPI()

@app.post("/cars")
async def new_car(data: InsertCar):

    print(data)
    return {"message": data}
```

By now, you know that the first two parameters are expected to be strings, while the year must be an integer; all of them are required.

Now, if you try to post the same data that you did previously but with additional fields, you will only get these three fields back. Also, these fields will go through Pydantic parsing and validation and throw meaningful error messages if something does not conform to the data specification.

This combination of Pydantic model validation and the Body function provides all the necessary flexibility when working with request data. This is because you can combine them and pass different bits of information using the same request bus ride.

If you want to pass a promo code attached to a user, along with the new car data, you could try defining a Pydantic model for the user and extracting the promo code with the Body function. First, define a minimal user model in a new file and name it chapter4_08.py:

```
class UserModel(BaseModel):
    username: str
    name: str
```

Now, create a more complex function that will process two Pydantic models and an optional user promo code – set the default value to None:

```
@app.post("/car/user")
async def new_car_model(car: InsertCar, user: UserModel, code: int =
Body(None)):
    return {"car": car, "user": user, "code": code}
```

For this request, which contains a full-fledged JSON object with two nested objects and some code, you might opt to use Insomnia or a similar GUI client since it's easier than typing JSON in the command prompt or resorting to piping. While it is largely a matter of preference, when developing and testing REST APIs, it is useful to have a GUI tool such as Insomnia or Postman and a command-line client (such as cURL or HTTPie).

The Body class constructor's parameters are very similar to the Path and Query constructors, and since they will often be much more complex, it is useful to try and tame them with Pydantic. Parsing, validation, and meaningful error messages – Pydantic provides us with the whole package before allowing the request body data to make it to the real data processing functionality. The POST requests are almost exclusively fed an appropriate Pydantic model as a parameter.

After playing around with the combination of request bodies and Pydantic models, you have seen that you can control the inflow of the data and be confident that the data that's available to your API endpoint will be what you want and expect it to be. Sometimes, however, you may want to go to the bare metal, and work with the raw request object. FastAPI covers that case too, as is discussed in the next section.

## The request object

FastAPI is built on the Starlette web framework. The raw request object in FastAPI is Starlette's request object and it can be accessed in your functions once it's been imported from FastAPI directly. By using the request object directly, you are missing out on FastAPI's most important features: Pydantic's parsing and validation and self-documentation! However, there might be situations in which you need to have the raw request.

Look at the following example in the `chapter4_09.py` file:

```python
from fastapi import FastAPI, Request


app = FastAPI()


@app.get("/cars")
async def raw_request(request: Request):
    return {"message": request.base_url, "all": dir(request)}
```

In the preceding code, you created a minimal FastAPI app, imported the `Request` class, and used it in the endpoint. If you test this endpoint with your REST client, you will only get the base URL as the message, while the `all` part lists all the methods and properties of the `Request` object so that you have an idea of what is available.

All of these methods and properties are available for you to use in your application.

With that, you've seen how FastAPI facilitates your work with the main HTTP transport mechanisms—request bodies, query strings, and paths. Next, you'll explore equally important aspects of any web framework solution—cookies, headers, form data, and files.

## Cookies and headers, form data, and files

Speaking of the ways the web framework ingests data, topics such as handling form data, handling files, and manipulating cookies and headers must be included. This section will provide simple examples of how FastAPI handles these tasks.

## Headers

Header parameters are handled in a similar way to query and path parameters and, as you'll see later, cookies. You can collect them, so to speak, using the `Header` function. Headers are essential in topics such as authentication and authorization as they often carry **JSON Web Tokens (JWTs)**, which are used for identifying users and their permissions.

Try to read the user agent by using the `Header` function in a new file called `chapter4_10.py`:

```python
from typing import Annotated
from fastapi import FastAPI, Header


app = FastAPI()
```

```
@app.get("/headers")
async def read_headers(user_agent: Annotated[str | None, Header()] = None):
    return {"User-Agent": user_agent}
```

Depending on the software you use to execute the test for the endpoint, you'll get different results. Here's an example of using HTTPie:

```
(venv) http GET "http://localhost:8000/headers"
HTTP/1.1 200 OK
content-length: 29
content-type: application/json date: Sun, 27 Mar 2022 09:26:49 GMT
server: uvicorn
{
"User-Agent": "HTTPie/3.2.2"
}
```

You can extract all the headers in this way and FastAPI will provide further assistance—it will convert names into lowercase, convert the keys into snake case, and so on.

## Cookies

Cookies work similarly, although they can be extracted manually from the Cookies header. The framework offers a utility function, conveniently named Cookie, that does all the work in a way similar to Query, Path, and Header.

## Forms (and files)

So far, you've only dealt with JSON data. It is the ubiquitous language of the web and your main vehicle for moving data back and forth. There are cases, however, that require a different data encoding – forms might be processed directly by your API, with data encoded as multipart/form-data or form-urlencoded. Since the arrival of modern React Server Actions, form data has become more popular in frontend development too.

> **Note**
>
> Although you can have multiple Form parameters in a path operation, you cannot declare the Body fields expected in JSON. The HTTP request will have the body encoded using only application/x-www-form-urlencoded instead of application/json. This limitation is part of the HTTP protocol and is not specific to FastAPI.

The simplest way to cover both form cases—with and without including files for upload—is to start by installing python-multipart, a streaming multipart parser for Python. For this, you must stop your server and use pip to install it:

```
pip install python-multipart==0.0.9
```

The Form function works similarly to the previously examined utility functions, but with the difference that it looks for form-encoded parameters. For simple fields, data is usually encoded using the media type (application/x-www-form-urlencoded), while if files are included, the encoding corresponds to mutlipart/form-data.

Look at a simple example in which you wish to upload an image and a couple of form fields, such as the brand and the model.

You will use a photo that can be found on Pexels (https://www.pexels.com/photo/white-vintage-car-parked-on-green-grass-8746027/), renamed to car.jpeg and saved in the current directory.

Create a file named chapter4_11.py and paste the following code:

```python
from fastapi import FastAPI, Form, File, UploadFile


app = FastAPI()
@app.post("/upload")
async def upload(
    file: UploadFile = File(...), brand: str = Form(...), model: str =
Form(...)
):
    return {"brand": brand, "model": model, "file_name": file.filename}
```

The preceding code handles the form parameters via the Form function and the uploaded file by using the UploadFile utility class.

The photo, however, isn't saved on the disk—its presence is merely acknowledged, and the filename is returned. Testing this endpoint, that has a file upload, in HTTPie looks like this:

```
http -f POST localhost:8000/upload  brand='Ferrari'
model='Testarossa'  file@car.jpeg
```

The preceding HTTPie call returns the following output:

```
HTTP/1.1 200 OK
content-length: 63
content-type: application/json
date: Fri, 22 Mar 2024 11:01:38 GMT
server: uvicorn

{
    "brand": "Ferrari",
    "file_name": "car.jpeg",
    "model": "Testarossa"
}
```

To save the image to a disk, you must copy the buffer to an actual file on the disk. The following code achieves this (chapter4_12.py):

```
import shutil
from fastapi import FastAPI, Form, File, UploadFile


app = FastAPI()


@app.post("/upload")
async def upload(
    picture: UploadFile = File(...),
    brand: str = Form(...),
    model: str = Form(...)
):
    with open("saved_file.png", "wb") as buffer:
        shutil.copyfileobj(picture.file, buffer)
    return {"brand": brand, "model": model, "file_name": picture.filename}
```

The open block opens a file on the disk using a specified filename and copies the FastAPI file that's sent through the form. You will have hardcoded the filename, so any new upload will simply overwrite the existing file, but you could use some randomly generated filename while using the **universally unique identifier (UUID)** library, for example.

File uploading is an operation that can be achieved in different ways—file uploads can be also handled by the Python async file library known as aiofiles or as a background task, which is another feature of FastAPI, as will be shown later in *Chapter 5, Setting Up a React Workflow*.

## FastAPI response customization

The previous sections discussed numerous examples of FastAPI requests how you can reach every corner of the request—the path, the query string, the request body, headers, and cookies—and how to work with form-encoded requests.

Now, let's take a closer look at FastAPI's response objects. In all previous cases, you returned a Python dictionary that was serialized into JSON by FastAPI. The framework enables customizations to the response.

The first thing you might want to change in an HTTP response is the status code, for instance to provide some meaningful errors when things do not go as planned. FastAPI conveniently raises classic Python exceptions when HTTP errors are present. It also uses standard-compliant meaningful response codes that minimize the need to create custom payload messages. For instance, you don't want to send a 200 OK status code for everything and then notify users of errors by using the payload—FastAPI encourages good practices.

## Setting status codes

HTTP status codes indicate whether an operation was successful or there was an error. These codes also provide information about the type of operation, and they can be divided into several groups: informational, successful, client errors, server errors, and so on. It isn't necessary to memorize the status codes, although you probably know what a 404 or 500 code is.

FastAPI makes it incredibly easy to set a status code—it is enough to just pass the desired status_code variable to the decorator. Here, you are using the 208 status code for a simple endpoint (chapter4_13.py):

```python
from fastapi import FastAPI, status

app = FastAPI()

@app.get("/", status_code=status.HTTP_208_ALREADY_REPORTED)
async def raw_fa_response():
    return {"message": "fastapi response"}
```

Testing the root route in HTTPie yields the following output:

```
(venv) http GET "http://localhost:8000"
HTTP/1.1 208 Already Reported content-length: 30
content-type: application/json date: Sun, 27 Mar 2022 20:14:25 GMT
server: uvicorn
{
    "message": "fastapi response"
}
```

Similarly, you can set status codes for the delete, update, and create operations.

FastAPI sets the 200 status code by default if it doesn't encounter exceptions, so it is up to you to set the correct codes for the various API operations, such as 204 No Content for deleting and 201 for creating. This is a good practice that is particularly encouraged.

Pydantic can be used for response modeling. You can limit or modify the fields that should appear in the response and perform similar checks that it does for the request body by using the response_model argument.

FastAPI does not enable customizing the response, but modifying and setting headers and cookies is as simple as reading them from the HTTP request and the framework has you covered.

Although beyond the scope of this book, it is worth noting that JSON is by no means the only response that FastAPI can provide: you can output an HTMLResponse and use classic Flask-like Jinja templates, StreamingResponse, FileResponse, RedirectResponse, and so on.

## HTTP errors

Errors are bound to happen. For example, users somehow find a way to send the wrong parameters to a query, the frontend sends the wrong request body, or the database goes offline (although this is unlikely with MongoDB)—anything can happen. It is crucial to detect these errors as soon as possible (this is a leitmotiv in FastAPI) and send clear and complete messages to the frontend, as well as the user by raising exceptions.

FastAPI relies on web standards and enforces good practices in every facet of the development process, so it puts a lot of emphasis on using HTTP status codes. These codes provide a clear indication of the type of problem that has arisen, while the payload can be used to further clarify the cause of the problem.

FastAPI uses a Python exception, aptly called `HTTPException`, to raise HTTP errors. This class allows you to set a status code and set an error message.

Returning to the example of inserting new cars into the database, you could set a custom exception like the following (`chapter4_14.py`):

```python
from pydantic import BaseModel
from fastapi import Fastapi, HTTPException, status


app = FastAPI()


class InsertCar(BaseModel):
    brand: str
    model: str
    year: int


@app.post("/carsmodel")
async def new_car_model(car: InsertCar):
    if car.year > 2022:
        raise HTTPException(
            status.HTTP_406_NOT_ACCEPTABLE, detail="The car doesn't exist
yet!"
        )
    return {"message": car}
```

When trying to insert a car that hasn't been built yet, the response is as follows:

```
(venv) λ http POST http://localhost:8000/carsmodel brand="fiat" mode3
l="500L" year=2023
HTTP/1.1 406 Not Acceptable content-length: 39
content-type: application/json date: Tue, 29 Mar 2022 18:37:42 GMT
server: uvicorn
{
    "detail": "The car doesn't exist yet!"
}
```

This is a pretty contrived example of making custom exceptions for a possible problem that might arise. However, this gives a good idea of what is possible and the flexibility that FastAPI gives you.

## Dependency injection

To make a brief but self-contained introduction to FastAPI, the system of dependency injection must be mentioned. In broad terms, **dependency injection** (**DI**) is a way of providing necessary functionalities (classes, functions, database connections, authorization statuses and so on) to a path operation function at the right time. FastAPI's DI system is very useful for sharing logic across endpoints, sharing database connections, for instance, as you will see when you connect to your MongoDB Atlas instance—performing security and authentication checks, and so on.

Dependencies aren't special; they are just normal functions that can take the same arguments as path operations. In fact, the official documentation compares them to path operations without the decorator. Dependencies are used a bit differently, though. They are given a single parameter (typically a callable) and they are not called directly; they are just passed as a parameter to Depends().

An example inspired by the official FastAPI documentation is the following; you can use a pagination dependency and use it in different resources (chapter4_15.py):

```
from typing import Annotated
from fastapi import Depends, FastAPI


app = FastAPI()


async def pagination(q: str | None = None, skip: int = 0, limit: int =
100):
    return {"q": q, "skip": skip, "limit": limit}



@app.get("/cars/")
async def read_items(commons: Annotated[dict, Depends(pagination)]):
    return commons



@app.get("/users/")
async def read_users(commons: Annotated[dict, Depends(pagination)]):
    return commons
```

One of the most common cases of DI used in a full stack FastAPI project is authentication; you can use the same authentication logic, that is, some class or function that checks the header for an authorization token and applies it to all the routes or routers that need to require authentication, as you will see in *Chapter 6, Authentication and Authorization.*

## Structuring FastAPI applications with routers

Although putting all of our request/response logic in one big file is possible, as you start building even a moderately sized project, you will quickly see that this is not feasible, maintainable, or pleasant to work with. FastAPI, like Express.js in the Node.js world, or Flask with its blueprints, provides **APIRouter**—a module designed to handle a group of path operations relating to a single type of object or resource. With this approach, you can assign a separate APIRouter to handle, for instance, cars, at the /cars path, another to handle the creation and management of users at /users, and so on. FastAPI proposes a type of project structure that is simple and intuitive enough, yet able to accommodate the most common cases.

### API Routers

FastAPI provides a class named APIRouter that is used for grouping routes, usually related to the same type of resource (users, shopping items, and so on). This concept, known in Flask as **Blueprints** and present in every modern web framework, allows the code to be more modular and distributed in smaller units, with each router managing only a certain type of resource. These APIRouters are finally included in the main FastAPI instance and provide very similar functionality.

Instead of applying the path decorators (@get, @post and so on) directly on the main application instance (usually called app), they are applied to the APIRouter instance. Below is a simple example of an application broken into two APIRouters:

1. First, create a chapter4_16.py file that will host the main FastAPI instance:

```python
from fastapi import FastAPI
from routers.cars import router as cars_router
from routers.user import router as users_router


app = FastAPI()


app.include_router(cars_router, prefix="/cars", tags=["cars"])
app.include_router(users_router, prefix="/users", tags=["users"])
```

2. Now, create a new folder named /routers, and in this folder, create an APIRouter in a file named users.py:

```python
from fastapi import APIRouter
router = APIRouter()


@router.get("/")
async def get_users():
    return {"message": "All users here"}
```

3.  Create another file, in the same /routers directory, named cars.py:

    ```
    from fastapi import APIRouter


    router = APIRouter()


    @router.get("/")
    async def get_cars():
        return {"message": "All cars here"}
    ```

When connecting the routers to the main application, in the chapter4_17.py file, you are able to provide different optional arguments to the APIRouter—tags and a set of dependencies, such as an authentication requirement. The prefix, however, is mandatory, as the application needs to know at which URL to mount the APIRouter.

If you test this application with Uvicorn with the following command:

```
uvicorn chapter4_17:app
```

And then, head over to the automatically generated documentation, you will see that the two APIRouters are mounted just as if you defined two separate endpoints. They are, however, grouped under the respective tags, for easier navigation and testing.

If you now navigate to the documentation, you should indeed find just one route defined at /cars and responding only to GET requests. It is intuitive that this procedure can have you build parallel or same-level routers in no time, but one of the biggest benefits of using APIRouters is that they support nesting, which enables managing quite complex hierarchies of endpoints effortlessly!

Routers are subsystems of an application and are not meant to be used autonomously, although you are free to mount entire separate FastAPI applications under specific paths, but that is beyond the scope of this book.

## Middleware

FastAPI implements the concept of **middleware**—something that you might have encountered in Django or Express.js, and more recently Next.js—popular frameworks that make extensive use of the concept. Middleware is simply a set of functions that run on every request and tap into the request/response cycle, intercepting the request, manipulating it in some desired way, then taking the response before it is sent to the browser or client, performing additional manipulation if needed, and finally, returning the final response.

Middleware is based on the ASGI specification, and it is implemented in Starlette, so FastAPI enables using it in all your routes and optionally tying it to a part of an application (via APIRouter) or the entire app.

Similarly to the mentioned frameworks, the FastAPI middleware is just a function that receives the request and a `call_next` function. Create a new file named `chapter4_17.py`:

```
from fastapi import FastAPI, Request
from random import randint

app = FastAPI()

@app.middleware("http")
async def add_random_header(request: Request, call_next):
    number = randint(1,10)
    response = await call_next(request)
    response.headers["X-Random-Integer "] = str(number)
    return response

@app.get("/")
async def root():
    return {"message": "Hello World"}
```

If you now start this small application, and test the only route, the route at `http://127.0.0.1:8000/`, you will notice that the returned headers contain an integer between 1 and 10, and on every request this integer will be different.

Middleware plays a large role in authentication with **cross-origin resource sharing** (**CORS**), something you're bound to face when developing full stack applications, but also for redirecting, managing proxies, and so on. It is a very powerful concept that can greatly simplify and enhance your application efficiency.

## Summary

This chapter covered very simple examples of how FastAPI achieves the most common REST API tasks and the way it can help you by leveraging modern Python features and libraries such as Pydantic.

This chapter also detailed how FastAPI enables you to perform requests and responses through HTTP and how you can tap into it, at any point, and customize and access the elements of the request, as well as the response. Finally, it also detailed how to split your API into routers and how to organize your app into logical resource-based units.

The next chapter will give you a quick introduction to React—the user interface library of choice in the FARM stack.

# 5

# Setting Up a React Workflow

This chapter focuses on the React library and discusses the important topics and features that you should be aware of so that you can create a very simple React app, really just a frontend. In this chapter, you will learn about the main features and the most salient concepts of React.

You will begin with the prerequisites and tools, such as Node.js, some Visual Studio Code extensions, and more. You will also learn how to use the new standard and recommended build tool called **Vite**. Compared to **Create React App**, Vite is more efficient and allows for fast **hot module replacement** (**HMR**) and on-demand file serving, without the need for bundling. Bundling is the process of combining and joining multiple JavaScript files into a single file, reducing the number of HTTP requests needed to load the page. HMR, on the other hand, allows for the updating of single modules while the application is running, in real time.

You will design a simple application with a few components and see how decoupling helps you write modular and maintainable code. This chapter covers two of the most important React Hooks and how they solve some common web development problems. However, the main objective of this chapter is to discuss the tools needed to be able to explore React and its various functionalities.

By the end of this chapter, you will have a simple but fully functional React web app. The concepts in this chapter will prepare you to be a frontend developer who values relatively simple tools to be able to achieve complex functionalities, without being confined within a strict framework.

This chapter will cover the following topics:

- Introduction to React and how to use Vite to create React apps
- Styling techniques with Tailwind CSS
- The functional components and JSX, the language of React

- How to use the `useState` and `useEffect` Hooks for state management and API communication
- Features of React Router and other packages within the React ecosystem

# Technical requirements

Creating a React-based application involves several steps, including setting up a build system and a transpiler, creating a directory structure, and more. You must install the following tools before you start developing your application:

- **Vite**: Vite requires Node.js versions 18+ or 20+ in order to run, but you can always check the documentation at `https://vitejs.dev` for updates.
- **Node.js**: You can download Node.js for your operating system from `https://nodejs.org/en/download/`. When installing, check all the boxes – you want **npm** (**Node.js' package manager**) and optional additional command-line tools if you are on a Windows machine.
- **Visual Studio Code**: Install a React extension called **ES7+ React/Redux/React-Native snippets** to help speed up the creation of components of a React app.
- **React Developer Tools** : Install the React Developer Tools browser extension (`https://react.dev/learn/react-developer-tools`). This enables debugging your React apps quicker and spotting potential problems easily.

# Creating a React app using Vite

React is a JavaScript library for building **user interfaces** (**UIs**), particularly for **single-page applications** (**SPAs**) but also for traditional server-side-rendered applications. It offers reusable UI components that are able to manage their own state, allowing for the creation of complex and dynamic web applications with simplicity and high scalability.

React is based on the virtual **document object model** (**DOM**). It minimizes manipulations of the actual DOM, improving performance. As stated in the introduction, React's robust ecosystem includes libraries, tools, and frameworks such as **Next.js**, **Remix.js**, mobile-centric **React Native**, and numerous Hooks. These features enable developers to build versatile and high-performance applications.

Vite is a modern build tool designed to simplify and speed up the development of web applications with React, but also with Vue.js, Svelte, and other frameworks and libraries. It offers a fast development server that supports features such as hot module replacement, ensuring quick updates without losing the application's current state. Unlike traditional setups, Vite separates app modules into dependencies and source code, employing `esbuild` for fast dependency bundling and serving source code using native **ECMAScript Modules** (**ESMs**). This approach results in faster server start and update times, enhancing productivity during development.

> **Note**
> Vite supports the scaffolding of numerous types of projects, such as Svelte, Preact, Solid.js, and more.

Let's start by creating a simple app that you will be building upon in this introduction:

1. Pick a folder of your choice, for example, `chapter5`. Set it to the working directory with `cd`, and from your terminal of choice, run the following command to create a React template:

```
npm create vite@latest frontend -- --template react
```

2. Unlike the Create React App tool, Vite requires manual installation of all the Node.js dependencies. Change the working directory into your `/frontend` directory:

```
cd frontend
```

3. Next, you can install the dependencies by running the following command:

```
npm install
```

   Once this process is complete, you will have a properly initiated React project ready to be developed.

4. Although you can start your project with a simple command (`npm run dev`), this is the opportunity to install your CSS framework, **Tailwind CSS**, as it is easier to begin with the Tailwind CSS setup and not have to deal with the few bundled Vite-specific CSS styles. Run the following commands to install the CSS framework in order to install the Tailwind framework and initialize its configuration file:

```
npm install -D tailwindcss postcss autoprefixer
npx tailwindcss init -p
```

   While the first command installs Tailwind itself and a couple of needed packages as development dependencies, the second creates a `tailwind.config.js` file, the file that you will be using for fine-tuning and configuring your instance of Tailwind.

5. It is useful to set up a simple project to showcase basic React concepts. Configure your newly created `tailwind.config.js` file by replacing the contents of the file with the following code. The configuration of Tailwind for React is the following:

```
/** @type {import('tailwindcss').Config} */
export default {
  content: [
    "./index.html",
    "./src/**/*.{js,ts,jsx,tsx}",
  ],
  theme: {
    extend: {},
  },
  plugins: [],
}
```

6.  Finally, edit the `src/index.css` file that Vite created and populated with some default styles. Delete everything, and insert the `tailwind` directives instead:

```
@tailwind base;
@tailwind components;
@tailwind utilities;
```

Now, you have a basic React application with a Tailwind setup.

The latest documentation of this process is usually available on the excellent Tailwind CSS website (`https://tailwindcss.com/docs/guides/vite`) along with similar documents for Next.js, Remix.js, and other frameworks.

Delete the `App.css` file since you will not be using it, and then perform the following steps to populate the landing page of your application.

7.  Replace the contents of `App.jsx` by pasting the following code:

```
export default function App() {
  return (
      <div className="bg-purple-800 text-white min-h-screen p--4 flex
  flex-col justify-center  items-center">
          <h1 className="text-3xl font-thin">
            Hello FARM stack!
          </h1>
      </div>
    )
}
```

8.  Back in the terminal, start your React project with the following command:

```
npm run dev
```

If you open a browser tab on port `5173` (`http://localhost:5173/`), which is the default for Vite, you will be greeted by a purple screen and the title *Hello FARM stack!* in  the middle of the page. However, behind this page, there is some code and many packages, and you can examine this generated code by looking inside the frontend folder that the Vite build tool built for you.

> **Note**
>
> In your project, there is a `node_modules` directory that contains all the project dependencies. You don't need to touch this folder except for extreme debugging operations.

In the `public` folder, there are a couple of generic files that you will not use in this project, such as the png logos and the `favicon.ico` file. This folder will contain static assets that Vite will not process, such as images, fonts and so on. You can leave it as is or use it later for files that will be served to users without any Vite modification.

In the /src directory there is an important HTML file called index.html. This bare-bones file contains a div element with the id parameter of the root. This div element is the place where React will load your entire application.

You will be creating most of the application in the /src directory. The App.jsx file that represents your entire application will be living inside this file, which, in turn, will be rendered in your single div element with the id parameter of the root in the index.html file. This complexity is necessary for the declarative approach that React will be able to provide us with while developing, in just a few more steps. At this point, different approaches are possible depending on your use case, so you might want to create additional folders for components or pages or group functionalities by features.

React enables you to style applications in a myriad of ways. You can use classic CSS style sheets or **syntactically awesome style sheets** (**SASS**), you can opt for JavaScript-style objects, or you can choose a modern but efficient solution such as **styled-components**. Additionally, all the major UI/CSS frameworks have a React version, for example, Material UI, Bootstrap, and Semantic UI.

Throughout this book, you will be using Tailwind CSS, which has an atypical approach that busy developers tend to like, as it doesn't get in the way. It is excellent for defining basic, simple styles that make the page look simple and clean, but it is also good for achieving pixel-perfect designs from Figma or Adobe XD files if needed.

## Tailwind CSS and installation

Tailwind CSS is a utility-first framework that translates CSS into classes that can be used directly in the markup and enables you to achieve complex designs. Just by adding classes to your HTML elements, you will be able to create completely styled documents. Check out the Tailwind documentation at https://tailwindcss.com/, as you will be using it for all your React styling needs.

Your App.jsx file has a div element with the following list of classes:

- bg-purple-800: To make the background purple
- text-white: To make the text white
- min-h-screen: To make the height full-screen
- p-4: To add padding
- flex: To display a flex container
- flex-col: To set the flex direction to a vertical one
- justify-center: To justify the item's center
- items-center: To center the items across the secondary axis

className is from **JavaScript Syntax Extension** (**JSX**), React's language for creating HTML. Visual Studio Code does some autocompletion as soon as you type in the first quote.

This is a basic **React + Tailwind** setup. If you want to practice Tailwind CSS a bit, try creating a full-height page with some dashed borders and some titles.

The next section will tackle the most fundamental parts of React by using JSX.

# Components and building blocks of JSX

According to the latest Stack Overflow Developer Survey from 2023[1], React is the developers' top choice, and still the most popular frontend JavaScript library by a large margin. Like FastAPI, React boasts an incredibly well-written and structured documentation website (`https://react.dev/`), so starting from there and making your way up is one of the best things you can do when starting your React journey and even when you have become a seasoned developer.

To put it simply, React enables you to craft UIs using a much simpler and more efficient way compared to plain JavaScript or first-generation JavaScript libraries such as jQuery, as it takes care of operations that would prove to be very tedious and error-prone if performed with plain JavaScript. React achieves this with the help of JSX, which is an enhanced JavaScript and HTML mix that React compiles into JavaScript.

To be more precise, JSX is a JavaScript extension used in React to build interactive functionalities and UIs in a visually intuitive way. It allows you to write HTML-like code within JavaScript, making the code easier to understand and maintain.

React performs two essential functions, which are visible in the `main.jsx` file of your newly created Vite project. If you open and inspect the file, you will see two packages imported. React is responsible for using features such as JSX, while ReactDOM performs operations on the DOM.

The keyword in every React description is **declarative,** so you, as a developer, can describe (declare) the UI and the associated data flow and actions. Then, React will figure out how to achieve the desired functionality through its mechanisms and optimizations.

JSX is the glue that holds the whole React concept together. The smallest building blocks of a React page or app are **React elements**. A simple element might be as follows:

```
const title = <h1>The Car Sales App</h1>
```

This code looks like an `h1` `HTML` element, but it also looks like JavaScript. Both observations are valid, because JSX enables you to create React elements that can be inserted into React's virtual DOM tree, which is different from the actual HTML. React takes care of the tedious job of updating the DOM to match the virtual DOM through a process called **diffing**, and then compiles the JSX elements (through a tool called Babel) into actual HTML elements.

React elements are immutable, which means that once you create them, you cannot change them, and as the React website states, they are like single frames in a movie. However, they can be replaced with new elements or frames.

It is important to note that every React component, including your `App.jsx` file, which is currently the only component that you have, must return only one element—a `div` element or a fragment (essentially, an empty tag, `<>`) and all the React elements enclosed in it. The following examples will show you how to craft some components:

---

1    `https://survey.stackoverflow.co/2023/#most-popular-technologies-web-frame`

Create some simple elements in your `App.jsx` file by pasting the following code:

```jsx
export default function App() {

    const data = [{
            id: 1,
            name: "Fiat"
        },
        {
            id: 2,
            name: "Peugeot"
        },
        {
            id: 3,
            name: "Ford"
        },
        {
            id: 4,
            name: "Renault"
        },
        {
            id: 5,
            name: "Citroen"
        }
    ]


    return (
        <div className="bg-purple-800 text-white min-h-screen p-4 flex
flex-col items-center">

            <div className="mb-4 space-y-5">
                <h2>Your budget is {budget}</h2>
                <label htmlFor="budget">Budget : </label>
                <input type="number" className="text-black" step={1000}
id="budget" value={budget} onChange={(e) => setBudget(e.target.value)} />
            </div>

            <div className="grid grid-cols-3 gap-4">
                {data.filter((el) => el.price <= budget).map((el) => {
                    return (
                        <Card car={el} key={el.id} />
                    )
                }
                )}
```

```
            </div>

        </div >
    );
}
```

When you run your web app, you should see the following page rendered:

Figure 4.1: A simple page generated by using React

## Recap

Let us review what you created in your React app:

1.  First, you declared some data, a simple list of car brands in an array. For now, the data is hard-coded, but this data might be loaded from an external API.

2.  Then, in the `return` statement, you map over this array by using the JavaScript `map` function, iterating by referencing each element of the array as `el`.

Finally, you return these elements. In this case, they are strings, and you wrap them in **template literals** (another ES6 feature) and transform them to uppercase by using another JavaScript function. The whole function returns exactly one `div` element. Since **class** is a reserved name in JavaScript, React uses the `className` keyword, and you can see how it was used quite a bit since Tailwind is very verbose. Finally, there's a little addition to the `App.jsx` file, so React doesn't complain in the console—a key property so React can handle our list even when it changes. You can read about the purpose and need for this key in the documentation here: https://react.dev/learn/rendering-lists#keeping-list-items-in-order-with-key.

The key is a unique identifier that React needs anytime it creates arrays of DOM elements, so it knows which one to replace, keep, or remove. This is a rather simplistic example, but it shows the basics of the power of JSX. An important thing to remember is that you must return *exactly one element*, such as a `div` element, a title, or a React fragment. Functional components are, after all, functions (and you will only be working with functional components).

React does not have a dedicated templating language with a special syntax for looping over arrays of objects or `if-else` constructs. Instead, you can rely on the full power of JavaScript and use the standard language features such as `map` for iterating through arrays, `filter` for filtering data, ternary operators for `if-else` constructs, template literals for string interpolations, and more.

The next section will discuss React components.

## Components

Components are reusable pieces of the UI. They are the functions returning pieces or units of UI written in JSX. They are the building blocks of UI in React, allowing you to create modular, reusable pieces of code that can be composed to form the desired output of the user interface.

*Figure 4.2* shows an application user interface that is visually broken into separate components. Each rectangle represents an independent component that is imported into the main app component. Some might be repeated several times, while others, such as the header and the footer, might be present with only one instance:

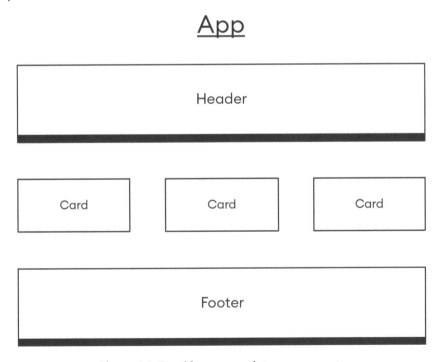

Figure 4.2: Breaking an app into components

One of the first stages of planning the development of a React site is the identification of areas, or pieces, that could be abstracted into components and reused in some way or at least abstracted into separate units.

Next, we will create a minimal component for displaying the header on a page. The component should have an easy task: to display the header, in your case, the title of the page.

Functional components in React.js are defined as files with .jsx or .js extensions, and like your App.jsx file (the root component), they must return a single JSX element. The filenames should be capitalized. This is a great moment in which to use your previously installed React extension for Visual Studio Code as it provides useful snippets for creating standard components. Follow these steps:

1.  Create a folder and name it components in your /src folder along with a new file called Header.jsx in it.

2.  Now, open the newly created file and type in rafce. The editor should suggest creating a component shell called reactArrowFunctionExportComponent.

3.  Select this entry from the suggestion list and you will see your file filled with a typical ES6 arrow function component exported:

    ```
    const Header = () => {
        return (
            <div>Header</div>
        )
    }
    export default Header
    ```

    This file defines a single JSX topmost element—called Header—and exports it at the bottom.

4.  Make some edits to this file, making use of our Tailwind CSS framework classes to make a div element. At this point, don't worry about responsiveness or fancy coloring. Replace the Header element with the following code:

    ```
    const Header = () => {
      return <div className="text-3xl border-yellow-500 border-4
    p-4">Header</div>;
    };
    export default Header;
    ```

5.  After these edits, which are purely Tailwind-related, import the first component to our App.jsx file. Imports are handled in terms of the relative path—remember that the dot denotes the current directory of the file (/src, in your case), while /components is the folder in which you are keeping your components. The App.jsx file should also include an instance of the Header component. Replace the contents of the App.jsx file with the following code:

```
import Header from "./components/Header";
export default function App() {
  const data = [
    { id: 1, name: "Fiat" },
    { id: 2, name: "Peugeot" },
    { id: 3, name: "Ford" },
    { id: 4, name: "Renault" },
    { id: 5, name: "Citroen" },
  ];
  return (
    <div className="bg-purple-800 text-white min-h-screen p-4 flex
flex-col justify-between items-center">
      <Header/>
      <h1 className="text-3xl font-thin border-b-white border-b m-3">
        Hello FARM stack!
      </h1>
      <div>
        {data.map((el) => {
          return (
            <div key={el.id}>
              Cars listed as{" "}
              <span className="font-bold">{el.name.toUpperCase()}</
span>
            </div>
          );
        })}
      </div>
    </div>
  );
```

6.   Vite should automatically reload the app for you if you haven't stopped the npm run dev process.

You will see that your simple web page now has a simple header component. It is an H1 element and has some basic formatting, as it is purple, centered, and has a yellow border. You imported the component as a self-closing tag. It is worth noting that components can be self-closing or (like an H1 tag, for instance) enclose the data provided via children.

You just made your first, very simple, React functional component. In this way, you can break down the functionality of your entire website. You can add a footer, some navigation, and more. The process of breaking an app down into components and deciding what should constitute a single component is so important that the React documentation has an excellent page dedicated to the process: https://reactjs.org/docs/thinking-in-react.html.

## Creating dynamic components

Crafting components like this is nice and quick, but it can become tedious if the output is fixed. Fortunately, React components are functions, and functions can take arguments then do something useful with those arguments. Suppose you want to create a component that will replace your plain list of car brands and display the information in a more pleasing and informative way. You can pass the data for each car in your data array (an object) and have it formatted in a specified way.

To redo your procedure for displaying the list, follow these steps:

1.  Create a new file in the `components` folder, name it `Card.jsx`, and type `rafce` in order to get the correct component template. Replace the `Card` component with the following code:

```
const Card = ({ car: { name, year, model, price } }) => {
    return (
        <div className="bg-white rounded m-4 p-4 shadow-lg">
            <h1 className="text-2xl text-gray-600">{name}</h1>
            <p className="text-sm text-gray-600">{year} - {model}</p>
            <p className="text-lg text-right text-gray-600 align-
text-bottom">${price}</p>
        </div>
    )
}
export default Card
```

This component, unlike the `Header` component that you made earlier, accepts props, or properties that define the component behavior. The `Card` component is a simple reusable abstraction that is repeated across the page wherever needed. You also made use of ES7 object *destructuring* to make the component a bit easier on the eyes and not have to repeat `props.name`, `props.model`, and so on.

2.  Update the `App.jsx` main file to make proper use of `Card`. Replace the contents of `App.jsx` with the following code:

```
import { useState } from "react";
import Card from "./components/Card";
export default function App() {

    const data = [
        { id: 1, name: "Fiat", year: 2023, model: "Panda", price:
12000 },
        { id: 2, name: "Peugeot", year: 2018, model: "308", price:
16000 },
```

```
        { id: 3, name: "Ford", year: 2022, model: "Mustang", price:
25000 },
        { id: 4, name: "Renault", year: 2019, model: "Clio", price:
18000 },
        { id: 5, name: "Citroen", year: 2021, model: "C3 Aircross",
price: 22000 },
        { id: 6, name: "Toyota", year: 2020, model: "Yaris", price:
15000 },
        { id: 7, name: "Volkswagen", year: 2021, model: "Golf", price:
28000 },
        { id: 8, name: "BMW", year: 2022, model: "M3", price: 45000 },
        { id: 9, name: "Mercedes", year: 2021, model: "A-Class",
price: 35000 },
        { id: 10, name: "Audi", year: 2022, model: "A6", price: 40000
}
    ]
    const [budget, setBudget] = useState(20000)

    return (
        <div className="bg-purple-800 text-white min-h-screen p-4 flex
flex-col items-center">

            <div className="mb-4 space-y-5">
                <h2>Your budget is {budget}</h2>
                <label htmlFor="budget">Budget : </label>
                <input type="number" className="text-black"
step={1000} id="budget" value={budget} onChange={(e) => setBudget(e.
target.value)} />
            </div>
            <div className="grid grid-cols-3 gap-4">
                {data.map((el) => {
                    return (
                        <Card car={el} key={el.id} />
                    )
                }
                )}
            </div>
        </div>
    );
}
```

3.  Next, the goal is to use the newly created `Card` component and pass it all the needed data. Update `Card.jsx` with the following code:

```
const Card = ({ car: { name, year, model, price } }) => {
    return (
        <div className="bg-white rounded m-4 p-4 shadow-lg">
            <h1 className="text-2xl text-gray-600">{name}</h1>
            <p className="text-sm text-gray-600">{year} - {model}</p>
            <p className="text-lg text-right text-gray-600 align-
text-bottom">${price}</p>
        </div>
    )
}
export default Card;
```

Now, instead of returning the `div` elements when mapping through your data, you are returning your `Card` component and passing it the key—that is, the ID of the `car` object. Note that the ID has to be unique or React will throw warnings in the console indicating that we haven't specified it. Additionally, you're passing something that you can refer to as `el` and set to the element—the `car` object from your data array.

Your `Card` component is now able to display data related to the cars—each card holds the data of a single car. You passed data through props (short for properties) to each card. You just have to accept it in the component.

It is easy to pass props to components, but since props provide one-way communication, in most apps, you will have to deal with the **state** as well, which is discussed in the next section

## Events and state

React exposes and wraps all the standard DOM events—button and link clicks, form submissions, mouse hovers, keyups and keydowns, and more. Handling these events in React is relatively intuitive. A click event will be handled by a synthetic event called `onClick`; events are named by using the **camelCase naming convention**. In React, **event handlers** are functions that are triggered when an interaction occurs. These functions accept function handlers, which are other functions, as props. The simplest possible case would be clicking a button (although it could be any DOM element).

Create a simple component in a file called `Button.jsx` in the `/components` directory that contains a button that, when clicked, displays a message in the console:

1.  Paste the following code into your `Button.jsx` file after performing the `racfe` action:

```
const Button = () => {
    const handleClick = () => {
        console.log("click")
    }
```

```
        return ( <
            button className = "bg-white text-purple-800 hover:bg-gray-300
    p-3 rounded-md"
            onClick = {
                handleClick
            } > Button < /button>
        )
    }
    export default Button
```

This is a simple example and it showcases the underlying mechanism; onClick is React's way of knowing what event it should listen to and the handleClick function executes your (rather simple) business logic. If you import the button into the App.jsx file and click the button, you should see the messages in the console.

2.  The implementation is very simple; update the App.jsx component with the following:

```
    import { useState } from "react";
    import Card from "./components/Card";
    import Button from "./components/Card";
    export default function App() {
      const data = [
        { id: 1, name: "Fiat", year: 2023, model: "Panda", price: 12000 },
        // continued
      ];
      const [budget, setBudget] = useState(20000);

      return (
        <div className="bg-purple-800 text-white min-h-screen p-4 flex
    flex-col items-center">
            <div className="mb-4 space-y-5">
              <h2>Your budget is {budget}</h2>
              <Button />
              <label htmlFor="budget">Budget : </label>
              <input
                type="number"
                className="text-black"
                step={1000}
                id="budget"
                value={budget}
                onChange={(e) => setBudget(e.target.value)}
              />
            </div>
            <div className="grid grid-cols-3 gap-4">
              {data.map((el) => {
```

```
            return <Card car={el} key={el.id} />;
        })}
      </div>
    </div>
  );
```

## React Hooks with events and state

The components of React are essentially functions that convert a state to a user interface. A React component isa function that takes props as arguments. It can be thought of as an updatable data structure responsible for the component behavior. The output of the function, the component, is a JSX element. Essentially, React Hooks are functional constructs that enable you to tap into the life cycle of a component and change its state.

While there are many standard React Hooks and numerous external ones, you will work with only two, which are the most fundamental for React comprehension: useState and useEffect. These two Hooks will remain in the forthcoming React version 19, while others, such as useMemo, useCallback, and some others, will be gradually deprecated. It is also true that while mastering React takes some time, much of standard UI functionality can be achieved through clever combinations of these two Hooks.

### Creating stateful variables with useState

The useState Hook allows you to maintain a certain state throughout your component. For example, you might want to maintain some kind of state in your SPA, so the website doesn't show you any cars that are too expensive based on your specified budget. You can make a simple textbox, set it to display just numeric values, and hook it up with a state variable that you can name budget.

Replace the contents of the App.jsx file with the following code:

```
import { useState } from "react";
import Card from "./components/Card";
export default function App() {

  const data = [
    { id: 1, name: "Fiat", year: 2023, model: "Panda", price: 12000 },
    { id: 2, name: "Peugeot", year: 2018, model: "308", price: 16000 },
    { id: 3, name: "Ford", year: 2022, model: "Mustang", price: 25000 },
    { id: 4, name: "Renault", year: 2019, model: "Clio", price: 18000 },
    { id: 5, name: "Citroen", year: 2021, model: "C3 Aircross", price:
22000 },
    { id: 6, name: "Toyota", year: 2020, model: "Yaris", price: 15000 },
    { id: 7, name: "Volkswagen", year: 2021, model: "Golf", price: 28000 },
    { id: 8, name: "BMW", year: 2022, model: "M3", price: 45000 },
    { id: 9, name: "Mercedes", year: 2021, model: "A-Class", price: 35000
  },
```

```
      { id: 10, name: "Audi", year: 2022, model: "A6", price: 40000 }
  ]
  const [budget, setBudget] = useState(20000)


  return (
    <div className="bg-purple-800 text-white min-h-screen p-4 flex flex-col
items-center">

      <div className="mb-4 space-y-5">
        <h2>Your budget is {budget}</h2>
        <label htmlFor="budget">Budget : </label>
        <input type="number" className="text-black" step={1000} id="budget"
value={budget} onChange={(e) => setBudget(e.target.value)} />
      </div>

      <div className="grid grid-cols-3 gap-4">
        {data.filter((el) => el.price <= budget).map((el) => {
          return (
            <Card car={el} key={el.id} />
          )
        }
        )}
      </div>

    </div >
  );
}
```

In the preceding example, you first import the useState Hook from React. The useState Hook returns two values:

- A variable, which can be anything you want—an array or an object, a simple number, or a string

- A function that sets the value for this state variable

Although you can use any legal JavaScript name, it is a good convention to use the name of the variable—in your case, budget—and the same name prepended with set: setBudget. With this simple line of code, you have told React to set up a state unit called budget and to set up a setter. The argument of the useState() call is the initial value. In the following case, you have set it to 20,000 dollars.

The following image shows the updated web app with the updateable budget box:

Your budget is 20000

Budget : 20000

**Fiat**
2023 - Panda
$12000

**Peugeot**
2018 - 308
$16000

**Renault**
2019 - Clio
$18000

**Toyota**
2020 - Yaris
$15000

Figure 4.3: Listing cars

Now, you are free to use this state variable across the page. Here, you placed the useState call inside the App functional component—if you try to place it elsewhere, it will not work: Hooks tap into the lifecycle of components from the inside of the bodies of the functions defining the components themselves!

Moving down to the bottom of the component, you added a simple textbox. You can set it to display only numeric values with HTML and a step of 1000 and add an onChange handler.

This is a good moment to emphasize yet again that React uses the so-called **synthetic event**, a wrapper around the browser's native events that enables React to achieve cross-browser compatibility. Once you have remembered a couple of differences (that the events are using camelCase rather than lowercase, and you must pass them a function in JSX), you will be writing event handlers in no time.

In your app, you added an onChange event to the textbox and set it to handle the state, then you set the new value of the budget. Every time you change the value, the setBudget function fires, and, as a consequence, the budget updates and different Card instances are displayed that match your budget constraints.

This onChange event takes the current value of the textbox (target.value, just like the original DOM events, as it's just a wrapper) and sets your budget state to this value using our useState call defined just above the function.

Finally, you've added a div element component that uses this budget value and displays it. You have added a state variable to your app's root component. You can set it, get it, and display it on the page.

Now, you have accomplished another task typical for developing React apps. You have allowed the user to enter their budget and you are displaying it on the page. If you want to differentiate between cars that fit said budget and those that do not, you will make use of some simple JavaScript and component state. To get this to work, set your small data sample that is currently hardcoded to be a state variable itself, so the user can just filter it and display only those cars within the price range.

The procedure is simple and involves pure JavaScript to accomplish the task of displaying an array of cars satisfying the condition that their price is less than or equal to your budget. Hint: Use JavaScript filtering arrays as shown in bold in the following code sample:

```
{data.filter((el) => el.price <= budget).map((el) => {
    return (
        <Card car={el} key={el.id} />
        )
    }
)}
```

At this point, you can dive into the excellent React.js documentation and learn more about the useState Hook and its sibling, the useReducer Hook (https://react.dev/reference/react/useState). This is a Hook that might be thought of as a generalization of the useState Hook. It is best suited when you have to deal with numerous pieces of state that are interconnected, so managing them with many simple useState Hooks could end up being tedious and difficult to maintain.

In this section, you have seen how the useState Hook enables you to add a stateful variable in a very simple and straightforward way and how to manipulate the state through regular events.

Next, you will learn how you can get your data from your efficient FastAPI backend into your React.js frontend. You will get to know another Hook called useEffect.

# Communicating with APIs and the outside world using useEffect

Here, you can use a free mock REST API. However, you do need to address the problem of accessing external data and the management of external events. External to what, you might wonder?

You have seen that React and its mighty Hooks are centered around the task of synchronizing the UI to the state and the data. Components can contain other components, and together, they form what is known as a **component tree**, which is then constantly compared to the current state. React does all of this coordination work, to determine what should be rendered, updated, and more.

Events that are outside of the React data flow process are called **side effects**. Notable examples of React side effects are as follows:

- Performing API calls—sending or receiving data from an external server
- Subscribing to external data sources via websockets or streams
- Setting or getting data values to and from the local storage or session storage
- Event listeners and their cleanup functions

Remember that React works in a continuous data flow, with an underlying system constantly scanning for updates and ready to re-render components that it deems in need of an update. The following example will illustrate this.

Consider that you are working on your *Car Sales* application and you need to list all the users that have registered an account. The task at hand is a simple and common one. You have a dedicated page—it will live in a URL called /users or something similar, and it should be populated with the data (think of a JavaScript array of objects) from an external API. This API will be powered by FastAPI, but for now, you will use a readymade mock solution called Jsonplaceholder.

The GET call you need to make should be directed toward the URL https://jsonplaceholder. typicode.com/users/.

You already understand how to make components, provide them with props, and set their state, so that shouldn't be a problem. When it comes to loading data from an external API, you might just use something such as Fetch or Axios, as if you were using a normal plain JavaScript app. Fetch and Axios are the two most popular JavaScript libraries used for making HTTP requests to servers.

Trying to fetch the data in a React component and then setting the state to the resulting JSON would start an **infinite loop**. Bear in mind that React came before the server component with async code existed.

Whenever the state of a component changes and the component is re-rendered, the new render again triggers a fetch call to the API, the state changes again to be set to the list of users, and so on.

In this component's data flow, the fetching of the data is considered external—not part of the main component life cycle. It is executed after the component has been executed.

To deal with this problem, React has a very elegant solution—the useEffect Hook. You can create a new application by editing the App.jsx main component, and then display a list of users from your API endpoint.

You can implement a possible solution using the useEffect Hook. Paste the following code into your App.jsx file (refer App3.jsx):

```
import { useState, useEffect } from "react";

export default function App() {
    const [users, setUsers] = useState([]);
    useEffect(() => {
        fetchUsers();
    }, []);

    const fetchUsers = () => {
        fetch("https://jsonplaceholder.typicode.com/users")
            .then((res) => res.json())
            .then((data) => setUsers(data));
    };
```

```
    return (
        <div className="bg-purple-800 text-white min-h-screen p-4 flex
flex-col items-center">
            <h2 className="mb-4">List of users</h2>
            <div className="grid grid-cols-3 gap-4">
                <ol>
                    {users.map((user) => (
                        <li key={user.id}>{user.name}</li>
                    ))}
                </ol>
            </div>
        </div>
    );
}
```

At the top of the `App.jsx` file, import `useState` and `useEffect` and then you can begin creating your sole state variable—the `users` array—initializing it to an empty array.

The `fetchUsers` function is simple—it makes a call to the API and returns data in JSON format, using promises. It could also have been an `async/await` function.

The `useEffect` Hook, as with all Hooks, is executed inside the component function. It does not return a value, however, and it accepts two arguments: the function to be executed (in this case, `fetchUsers`), and a dependency array, an array of values whose change in value will trigger a new execution of the effect. If the function should trigger only once, the array should be empty. If you want to fetch other users from the next API URL, you must add the URL to the array.

As with `useState`, there are many more subtleties involved. For example, you can provide a cleanup function at the bottom of the `useEffect` body to make sure that any long-lasting effects are removed, but this should give you a basic idea of how to handle actions that reach out to an external API.

Additionally, `useContext` allows React to cover an entire area of components and pass values directly without having to pass them through several components that might not actually need it, a procedure called prop drilling. You can even create your own Hooks and abstract functionality that can be reused in several places of the app, ensuring better maintainability and less repetition.

With the introduction of Hooks, the whole ecosystem becomes much clearer and cleaner, and the mapping of business logic to UIs is much more streamlined and logical.

You now have the knowledge that is necessary to set and get states in your components or apps and to communicate with external API services in a predictable and controllable way, while crafting clean and simple code. Just using React and its Hooks can give you web developer proficiency, but there is a whole ecosystem of packages and modules built around React that can be just as important and useful as the core libraries.

## Exploring React Router and other useful packages

So far, you have only created a couple of single-page apps, but you haven't touched some advanced functionalities. However, single-page apps are not limited to a single URL. For example, if you navigate to your Gmail account, you will see that the URL changes with every action that you might take.

While there are several solutions that enable you to achieve routing in SPAs, React Router is the standard solution, and it is a well-tested, mature package.

The underlying idea of a frontend page router is that it should enable rendering different components on the same page depending on the route that is loaded. For instance, the `/about` route would cause the app to load a component called `About.jsx` in the main `App` component, removing other previously loaded components. The package provides a basic structure, within the `BrowserRouter` class, which can be used to wrap an entire root `App` component.

React is such a popular framework that there is a diverse ecosystem of tools and integrations that you can learn about. As you've already seen earlier, besides Tailwind, you can use virtually any UI or CSS framework either directly or through some optimized React version, such as Bootstrap, or more tightly coupled with React, such as Ant Design. You can enhance your user experience with subtle animations through Framer Motion, and you can speed up the development of forms with some excellent form libraries such as React Hook Form. For complex state problems, Redux is the most popular and widely adopted industry standard, but there are many smaller or specialized libraries for local and global state management, such as **Recoil**, **Zustand**, or **React Query**.

## Summary

This chapter provided a short introduction to the world's most popular user interface library—React.js.

This chapter also detailed what JSX is and why it's so convenient for developers. It explored the basic building blocks of React, functional components, and the basic rules that must be followed when designing them. It also introduced two fundamental React Hooks that, when combined, allow you to begin building basic user interfaces, maintain and change the state of the components, and interact with external APIs.

Finally, the chapter covered the implementation of some of the React libraries that will make your life easier when developing custom applications. These libraries all have excellent documentation and are updated frequently.

The next chapter will use some of this basic knowledge and React to create a simple but fully functional and dynamic application.

# 6

# Authentication and Authorization

The concepts of authentication—proving that the user is who they claim to be—and authorization—making sure that the authenticated user should or should not be able to perform certain operations on your API—are very complex. In this chapter, you will explore the topics of authentication and authorization from a very practical standpoint and from the FARM stack perspective.

The chapter will detail a simple yet robust and extensible setup for your FastAPI backend, based on **JSON Web Token** (**JWT**)—arguably the most popular and practical authentication method that has emerged in the last years. Then, you will see how to integrate your JWT-based authentication methods into React, leveraging some of React's powerful features—namely, Hooks, Context, and React Router.

By the end of this chapter, you should have a solid grasp of authentication methods that both FastAPI on the backend and React on the frontend have to offer, and you will be able to authenticate users and control what they can and cannot do within your application with granularity and precision.

The chapter will cover the following topics:

- The user model and how it relates to other resources
- JWT authentication mechanism—the big picture
- Authentication and authorization tools in FastAPI
- How to protect the routes, routers, or the entire app
- Various solutions for authenticating with React

# Technical requirements

To run the sample application in this chapter, you should have the following:

- Node.js version 18 or later
- Python 3.11.7 or later

The requirements are identical to those in the previous chapters, and the new packages that you will install will be described as they are used.

# Understanding JSON Web Token

HTTP is a stateless protocol, and that fact alone implies several important consequences. One of them is that if you want to persist some kind of state between requests, you must resort to a mechanism that will be able to remember a set of data, such as who the logged-in user was, what the selected items during a previous browser session were, or what the site preferences were. In order to achieve such functionality, and identify the current user, you as a developer have numerous options at your disposal. Some of the most popular and modern solutions are the following:

- **Credential-based authentication:** It requires the user to enter personal credentials, such as a username or email, along with a password
- **Passwordless login:** Users receive a secure, time-limited token via email or another communication channel for authentication instead of using a traditional password after creating an account. The secure token is used for session authentication, eliminating the need to type or remember passwords.
- **Biometric passwords:** It utilizes a bio-feature of the user, such as a fingerprint, for authentication.
- **Social authentication:** Users leverage their existing social media accounts (e.g., Google, Facebook, or LinkedIn) for authentication. This associates the user's social media account with their account on the platform.
- **Classic personal credentials method:** Users provide an email and choose a password during registration. Optionally, users can also select a username.

This chapter will consider the classic personal credentials method. When users register, they provide an email and choose a password and, optionally, a username.

## What is JWT?

While there are different ways of maintaining the identity of a user across different parts of an app, JWT is arguably the most common and popular method of connecting frontend applications (React, Vue.js, and Angular) or mobile apps with an API (in our case, a REST API). JWT is nothing but a standard, a way of structuring a big string composed of seemingly random characters and numbers that encapsulate user data in a secure way.

JWTs contain three parts—the **header**, the **payload**, and the **signature**. The header hosts metadata about the token itself—the algorithm used for signing the token and the type of the token.

The payload is the most interesting part. It contains the following information necessary for authentication:

- Data (claims): The ID of the user (or the username)

- The **issued at field** (**iat**): The date and time of issuing the token

- The time at which the token ceases to be valid: Tied to the duration of the token

- Optionally, other fields: For example, the username, roles etc.

The payload is decodable and readable by everyone. You can read more about tokens and understand how they look in the JWT documentation: `https://jwt.io`.

Finally, the most important part of the token is the signature. The signature guarantees the claims made by the token. The signature is reproduced (calculated) and compared with the original—thus preventing the modification of the claims.

For example, consider a JWT stating that the username is `John`. Now, if someone were to attempt to change this to `Rita`, they would also need to modify the signature to match. However, altering the signature would render the token invalid. This mechanism ensures that the token's content remains unchanged and authentic.

The token is hence able to completely replace the authentication data—user or email and password combinations that do not need to be transmitted more than once.

In the upcoming sections, you will learn how to implement a JWT-based authentication flow in your app.

# FastAPI backend with users and dependencies

Web applications (or mobile apps, for that matter) are not very useful if they are not secure. You must have heard about tiny errors in the authentication implementations that result in hundreds of thousands or even millions of compromised accounts, potentially exposing sensitive and valuable information.

FastAPI is based on OpenAPI—previously known as **Swagger**—an open specification for crafting APIs. OpenAPI enables you to define various security schemes, compatible with the various protocols (`apiKey`, `http`, `OAuth 2.0`, `openIdConnect`, and so on). While the FastAPI documentation website (`https://fastapi.tiangolo.com/tutorial/security/`) provides an excellent and detailed tutorial on creating an authentication flow, it is based on the `OAuth 2.0` protocol, which uses form data to send the credentials (username and password).

In the following sections, you will devise a simple user model that will enable an authentication flow. You will then learn how to encode the user data into a JWT and how to use the token for accessing protected routes.

## User model for authentication

The basis of every authentication flow is the user model, which has to be able to store a minimum set of data needed for unequivocally identifying the users. The most common unique fields are an email address, a username, and, of course, a primary key—an `ObjectId` instance in the case of MongoDB.

Modeling data with MongoDB is inherently different from modeling relational databases as discussed in *Chapter 2, Setting Up the Database with MongoDB*. The driving idea is to think of queries upfront and model your relationships taking into account the queries that your app is going to be making most frequently.

## Authentication and authorization with FastAPI: a walk-through

Authentication and authorization with FastAPI are much easier to understand through an example. In the next few sub-sections, you will develop a simple yet fully functional authentication system that will contain all the mandatory steps. To highlight the important parts, while keeping the example as concise as possible, you will not use a real MongoDB connection. Instead, you will make your own JSON file-based **database** that will store users as they register into the app and effectively mock a MongoDB collection. The first and foremost step is to review your authentication system.

## Reviewing all the parts of your authentication system

The following list provides a quick recapitulation of the tools and packages needed for implementing a FastAPI authentication workflow:

- To implement a FastAPI authentication workflow, you must use FastAPI's security tools. In FastAPI, when you need to declare dependencies with **OAuth2** scopes, you will use the `Security()` class. The other FastAPI import that will be needed is the type of dependable—in this case, you will use **bearer** tokens for authorization. You can refer to the FastAPI documentation: `https://fastapi.tiangolo.com/reference/security/#fastapi.security.HTTPBearer`.

- You also need password hashing and comparing functionality, which `passlib` can provide. The `passlib.context` module contains one main class: `passlib.context.CryptContext`, designed to take care of many of the more frequent coding tasks associated with hashing and comparing strings through various algorithms. Your authentication system requires two main functionalities: hashing passwords during user registration and comparing hashed passwords during login with those stored in your database.

- Finally, **PyJWT** will provide the functionality to encode and decode JWT.

## Creating the model

The next steps involve creating the basic FastAPI application in a new virtual environment, activating the environment, installing the necessary packages, and creating a suitable model of the users with the required fields:

1. Create a new directory, set it as the working directory with the `cd` (change directory) command, create a new Python environment in `/venv`, and activate it:

```
mkdir chapter6
cd chapter6
python -m venv venv
source ./venv/bin/activate
```

2. Once the new Python environment is active, install the needed packages for the authentication system and the application overall:

```
pip install fastapi uvicorn bcrypt==4.0.1 passlib pyjwt
```

> **Note**
>
> If you want to be able to reproduce exactly the code in the book, you are strongly encouraged to use the `/backend/requirements.txt` file from the accompanying repository and install the packages with the `pip install -r requirements.txt` command.

The following are the last three packages needed for your authentication system:

- `Passlib` is a password hashing library for Python, and it supports a wide range of hashing algorithms, including `bcrypt`. It is very useful as it provides a unified interface for hashing and verifying passwords.

- The `bcrypt` package is a Python module that provides the password hashing method based on the Blowfish password hashing algorithm that you will be using. Please stick to the provided version of the package as there are some unresolved issues with later versions.

- `PyJWT` is the Python library for encoding and decoding JWT.

3.  Next, create the models for the application. As this app will only deal with users, the `models.py` file is rather simple:

```python
from pydantic import BaseModel, Field
from typing import List

class UserBase(BaseModel):
    id: str = Field(...)
    username: str = Field(
        ...,
        min_length=3,
        max_length=15)
    password: str = Field(...)

class UserIn(BaseModel):
    username: str = Field(
        ...,
        min_length=3,
        max_length=15)
    password: str = Field(...)

class UserOut(BaseModel):
    id: str = Field(...)
    username: str = Field(
        ...,
        min_length=3,
        max_length=15)

class UsersList(BaseModel):
    users: List[UserOut]
```

The models are self-explanatory, and they are left to be as explicit as possible. `UserBase` corresponds to the user representation that will be stored in your dummy database, or in a MongoDB collection (pay special attention to `Object_id`). In the given solution, the `id` field will be a UUID, so you set it to a string type.

> **Note**
>
> A Python **UUID** (which stands for **universally unique identifier**) is a 128-bit string that uniquely identifies an object, entity, or resource in both space and time. In our case, it will mimic MongoDB's `ObjectId()` class for the purpose of this demonstration.

The `models.py` file contains two additional auxiliary Pydantic models: `UserIn`, which accepts the user data for registration or login (typically username and password, but can easily be extended to include email or other data), and `UserOut`, which is responsible for representing users within the application, excluding the hashed password but including the ID and the username.

`UsersList` finally just outputs the list of all users, and you will use this model as an example for your protected route. Now, build your `app.py` file and create the actual application.

### Creating the application file

After defining the models, you can now proceed and create the main FastAPI application and the authentication class:

1. Open a new Python file and name it `app.py`. Inside this file, create a minimal FastAPI application:

   ```
   from fastapi import FastAPI
   app = FastAPI()
   ```

   We will return to this file shortly, but for now, let's keep it as short as possible. Now it is time to build out the heart of your authentication system.

2. In the same folder, create the `authentication.py` file and start building it. Having all this at hand, open the newly created `authentication.py` file and begin crafting the authentication class. For this, you must first scaffold the `AuthHandler` class and add the required imports:

   ```
   import datetime
   import jwt
   from fastapi import HTTPException, Security
   from fastapi.security import HTTPAuthorizationCredentials, HTTPBearer
   from passlib.context import CryptContext

   class AuthHandler:
       security = HTTPBearer()
       pwd_context = CryptContext(schemes=["bcrypt"], deprecated="auto")
       secret = "FARMSTACKsecretString"
   ```

Now that you have learned about all these imports, you can craft a class named `AuthHandler`, that uses FastAPI's `HTTPBearer` as the security dependency and defines a password-processing context from `passlib`.

### Adding security dependency and password-processing context

This procedure consists of multiple steps. You'll need to add a secret string that would ideally be generated randomly and kept safe in an environment variable, far from any `git commit`. The secret string is necessary for hashing the passwords. Here, you will hardcode it in this file for simplicity.

So, continue with the same file and code the desired functionality step by step, as follows:

1. **Hashing the passwords**

   First, you will need a function for generating the hashed password. Add the following code into your `authentication.py` file under the `AuthHandler` class:

   ```
   def get_password_hash(self, password: str) -> str:
           return self.pwd_context.hash(password)
   ```

   This function simply creates a hash of the given password, and this result is what you will be storing in your database. It is making good use of your previously defined `passlib` context.

2. **Verifying the hashed passwords**

   In the next step, you need a way of verifying that the hash of the provided plain password matches the stored hashed version. Add the following code into your `authentication.py` file:

   ```
   def verify_password(
       self,
       plain_password: str,
       hashed_password: str) -> bool:
       return self.pwd_context.verify(
          plain_password,
           hashed_password)
   ```

   Similar to the previous function, `verify_password` simply verifies that the hash of `plain_password` is indeed equal to the (already) hashed password and it returns `True` or `False`.

3. **Token encoding**

   Now you can take care of the token encoding. Add the following code at the end of your `authentication.py` file:

   ```
   def encode_token(self, user_id: int, username: str) -> str:

   payload = {
               "exp": datetime.datetime.now(datetime.timezone.utc)
               + datetime.timedelta(minutes=30),
               "iat": datetime.datetime.now(datetime.timezone.utc),
               "sub": {"user_id": user_id, "username": username},
           }
           return jwt.encode(payload, self.secret, algorithm="HS256")
   ```

The encode_token method of your class leverages the PyJWT package's encode method to create the JWT itself, and it is very explicit; the payload contains the expiration time (very important—you do not want the JWTs to last for too long) and the *issued-at time* (the iat part). Also, it references the dictionary named sub, which contains all the data that you wish to encode—in this case, the user ID and the username, although you could also add a role (regular user, administrator, and so on) or other data. To recap, the JWT encodes three pieces of data:

- The expiration duration, in this example, 30 minutes.

- The time of issuing the token, in this example, it is set to now().

- The sub part is the data (in the form of a dictionary) that you want to include in the token. In this example, it is the user ID and the username.

4. **Decoding the token**

   Continue building out the class, as now the reverse functionality is required—a way of decoding the token:

   ```
   def decode_token(self, token: str):
       try:
           payload = jwt.decode(
               token,
               self.secret,
               algorithms=["HS256"])
           return payload["sub"]
       except jwt.ExpiredSignatureError:
           raise HTTPException(
               status_code=401,
               detail="Signature has expired")
       except jwt.InvalidTokenError:
           raise HTTPException(
               status_code=401,
               detail="Invalid token")
   ```

   The previous snippet is also pretty straightforward. Here, you try to decode the JWT and in case of expiry or an invalid token, you raise a nice exception with the status code and a descriptive message.

5. **Defining the dependency**

   Finalize your class with the dependency to be injected in the routes that will need protection:

   ```
   def auth_wrapper(
       self,
       auth: HTTPAuthorizationCredentials = Security(security)) -> dict:
       return self.decode_token(auth.credentials)
   ```

You will use this `auth_wrapper` as the dependency—it will check for the presence of a valid JWT passed as a bearer token in the request headers for all the routes or entire routers that need authorization.

The `authorization.py` file is a minimal implementation of an authentication/authorization flow.

In the previous steps you wrapped most of the authentication and authorization functionality into a simple and compact class. The creation of the token, its encoding and decoding, as well as the password hashing and verification. Finally, you have created a simple dependency that will be used for verifying the user and enabling or disabling access to protected routes.

Building the FastAPI router for the application will be very similar to the ones that you have already built in *Chapter 2, Setting Up the Database with MongoDB*. You will have two basic endpoints for registering and logging in, and they will rely heavily on the `AuthHandler` class.

### Creating the APIRouter for the users

In this section, you will create the APIRouter for the users and implement the login and register functionalities with the help of the authentication class and a mock database service implemented with dictionaries and UUID. To achieve this functionality, perform the following steps:

1.  Create a folder `routers` in the root of your application and a file named `users.py` inside of it. Add the following code to the `users.py` file:

    ```
    import json
    import uuid
    from fastapi import APIRouter, Body, Depends, HTTPException, Request
    from fastapi.encoders import jsonable_encoder
    from fastapi.responses import JSONResponse


    from authentication import AuthHandler
    from models import UserBase, UserIn, UserOut, UsersList
    ```

2.  After adding the imports at the start of the file, create the APIRouter and the registration endpoint. The registration function uses the fake JSON database to store the username and the hashed password, by using the `authentication.py` file that you created before.

    ```
    router = APIRouter()
    auth_handler = AuthHandler()


    @router.post("/register", response_description="Register user")
    async def register(request: Request, newUser: UserIn = Body(...)) ->
    UserBase:
        users = json.loads(open("users.json").read())["users"]
        newUser.password = auth_handler.get_password_hash(newUser.
    password)
    ```

```
        if any(user["username"] == newUser.username for user in users):
            raise HTTPException(status_code=409, detail="Username already
    taken")
        newUser = jsonable_encoder(newUser)
        newUser["id"] = str(uuid. uuid4())
        users.append(newUser)
        with open("users.json", "w") as f:
            json.dump({"users": users}, f, indent=4)


        return newUser
```

In order to demonstrate a basic JWT-based authentication and authorization system, a fake data storage solution is used. Instead of connecting through a driver to a MongoDB cluster, you use a simple JSON file for storing users along with their hashed passwords—a solution similar to the popular JSON Server Node package, used for testing and scaffolding purposes. However, all the functionality and logic presented will apply to real database scenarios, and it is easily adaptable for MongoDB drivers or ODMs, such as PyMongo, Motor, or Beanie.

After the imports, which include a couple of packages that you will likely not need when working with a real MongoDB database, such as **JSON** and uuid, you have instantiated APIRouter and the custom-made AuthHandler class.

The /register endpoint accepts the new user's data in the body and molds it through the UserIn Pydantic class defined in the models.py file, while the output is set to be of class UserBase. This is something that you would likely avoid as it will send the hashed password back to the newly registered user.

Instead of a real MongoDB database, you are reading the contents of a JSON file called users.json—this file will host a very simple data structure that will mimic your users' MongoDB collection: a simple array of dictionaries containing user data – the ID, the username, and the hashed password.

Now that you have this "database," or array of users, it is easy to just loop over them and verify whether it contains a user with the same username as the user trying to register—if so, you just dismiss it with a gentle HTTP 409 response code and a Username already taken message.

If the username is not taken, proceed to start using your auth_handler instance and set the plain-text raw password to its hashed counterpart, safe to be stored inside the database.

In order to be able to store the user as a Python dictionary, use jsonable_encoder and add a new key to it: the uuid string that will be used as the ID of the new user.

Finally, append the user (represented as a dictionary with an ID, username, and hashed password) to your list of users, write the modified list to the JSON file, and return the user.

3.  Now, continuing with the `users.py` router, you can create the `login` endpoint as well by adding the following code at the end of the file:

```
@router.post("/login", response_description="Login user")
async def login(request: Request, loginUser: UserIn = Body(...)) ->
str:
    users = json.loads(open("users.json").read())["users"]
    user = next(
        (user for user in users if user["username"] == loginUser.
username), None
    )

    if (user is None) or (
        not auth_handler.verify_password(loginUser.password,
user["password"])
    ):
        raise HTTPException(status_code=401, detail="Invalid username
and/or password")

    token = auth_handler.encode_token(str(user["id"]),
user["username"])

    response = JSONResponse(content={"token": token})
    return response
```

This code follows a similar logic: it loads the user data and attempts to find the login user by their username (similar to a find query). If the user is not found or the password verification fails, the endpoint raises an exception. It's considered a good security practice to inform the user that the entire combination of username and password is invalid, without specifying which part exactly failed. If both checks pass, you encode the token and return it to the user.

4.  Time to hook up the router. Edit the previously created `app.py` file by replacing the contents of the file with the following code:

```
from fastapi import FastAPI
from fastapi.middleware.cors import CORSMiddleware

from routers.users import router as users_router

origins = ["*"]

app = FastAPI()

app.add_middleware(
    CORSMiddleware,
    allow_origins=origins,
    allow_credentials=True,
    allow_methods=["*"],
```

```
          allow_headers=["*"],
    )
    app.include_router(users_router, prefix="/users", tags=["users"])
```

Here, you added the **CORS middleware** in order to facilitate the connection with your future React frontend, and you added the `users` router.

5.  Now, create a file called `users.json` in the root of your project and populate it with an empty `users` array:

```
    {
        users:[]
    }
```

6.  Save the file and start the FastAPI application from the shell:

```
    uvicorn app:app --reload
```

7.  You should be able to perform a user registration and a user login. Try it with the HTTPie client:

```
    http 127.0.0.1:8000/users/register username="marko" password="marko123"
```

8.  The server should send the following response, but bear in mind that your hash and UUID will be different:

```
    HTTP/1.1 200 OK
    content-length: 138
    content-type: application/json
    date: Sun, 07 Apr 2024 18:38:41 GMT
    server: uvicorn

    {
        "id": "45cd212b-71eb-42b4-9d06-a74f2609764b",
        "password": "$2b$12$owWXcY5KgI9s6Rdfjcpx7eXaZOMWf8NaxN.SoLJ4h8O.
    xzFpRqEee",
        "username": "marko"
    }
```

If you peek in the `users.json` file, you should see something like this:

```
    {
        "users": [
            {
                "username": "marko",
                "password": "$2b$12$owWXcY5KgI9s6Rdfjcpx7eXaZOMWf8NaxN.
    SoLJ4h8O.xzFpRqEee",
                "id": "45cd212b-71eb-42b4-9d06-a74f2609764b"
            }
        ]
```

> **Note**
>
> In a real-world system, you would not want to send the hashed password even to the logged-in user, but this whole system is for demonstration purposes and created to be as illustrative as possible.

You have created a full authentication flow (for demonstration purposes—you will not use a JSON file with dictionaries and UUIDs in production) and you have crafted all the mandatory functionalities: creating users (registration), checking for the validity of the submitted data, and user login. Finally, you tested the registration functionality by creating a test user.

### Testing the login functionality with HTTPie

Now, test the login functionality with the correct user/password combination and then a wrong one.

1.  First, log in. In the terminal, issue the following HTTPie command:

    ```
    http POST 127.0.0.1:8000/users/login username="marko"
    password="marko123"
    ```

    The response should be just a big string—your JWT—the value of this token (here, it starts with the string *eyJhbGciOiJ...*) should be copied and saved for testing the authenticated route later:

    ```
    HTTP/1.1 200 OK
    content-length: 241
    content-type: application/json
    date: Sun, 07 Apr 2024 18:43:07 GMT
    server: uvicorn
    {
        "token":
    "eyJhbGciOiJIUzI1NiIsInR5cCI6IkpXVCJ9.
    eyJleHAiOjE3MTI1MTcxODgsImlhdCI6MTcxMjUxNTM4OCwic3ViIjp7InVzZXJfaWQ
    iOiI0NWNkMjEyYi03MWViLTQyYjQtOWQwNi1hNzRmMjYwOTc2NGIiLCJlc2VybmFtZS
    I6Im1hcmtvIn19.tFcJoKhTdDBDIBhCX-dCUEkCD3Fc8E-smQd2M_h5h2k"
    }
    ```

2.  Try something like the following (notice the password is wrong):

    ```
    http POST 127.0.0.1:8000/users/login username="marko"
    password="marko111"
    ```

    The response will be similar to the following:

    ```
    HTTP/1.1 401 Unauthorized
    content-length: 45
    content-type: application/json
    date: Sun, 07 Apr 2024 18:44:34 GMT
    server: uvicorn
    ```

```
{
    "detail": "Invalid username and/or password"
}
```

You have just implemented your own authentication system with FastAPI from scratch. Now it would be great to put it to use in a route.

## Creating a protected route

Say that now you want a new endpoint that lists all the users in your system, and you want to make it visible only to logged-in users. This method would allow you to protect any route in different routers, just by leveraging the powerful FastAPI dependency injection system:

1. Open the users.py file and add the following route at the end:

```
@router.get("/list", response_description="List all users")
async def list_users(request: Request, user_data=Depends(auth_handler.
auth_wrapper)):

    users = json.loads(open("users.json").read())["users"]
    return UsersList(users=users)
```

The key to this route is the user_data part—if the dependency is not met, the route will respond with an exception and the messages defined in authentication.py.

2. Try to log in, grab the JWT that you got from the login endpoint and have copied (if it hasn't expired!), and then pass it as the bearer token:

```
http GET 127.0.0.1:8000/users/list 'Authorization:Bearer <your Bearer
Token>'
```

The result should contain all the users that you have created so far:

```
HTTP/1.1 200 OK
content-length: 76
content-type: application/json
date: Sun, 07 Apr 2024 19:07:45 GMT
server: uvicorn
{
    "users": [
        {
            "id": "45cd212b-71eb-42b4-9d06-a74f2609764b",
            "username": "marko"
        }
    ]
}
```

3.  If you try to modify the token, or if you let it expire, the result will be the following:

```
HTTP/1.1 401 Unauthorized
content-length: 26
content-type: application/json
date: Sun, 07 Apr 2024 19:10:12 GMT
server: uvicorn
{
    "detail": "Invalid token"
}
```

In this section, you saw how to create a simple but efficient authentication system on your FastAPI backend, create a JWT generator, verify the tokens, protect some routes, and provide the routes needed for creating (registering) new users and logging in. The next section will show how things work on the front end.

# Authenticating the users in React

In this section, you will go through a basic mechanism that will enable you to have a simple authentication flow on the client side. Everything will revolve around the JWT and the way you decide to handle it.

React.js is an unopinionated UI library. It provides numerous ways of implementing user authentication and authorization. Since your FastAPI backend implements JWT-based authentication, you have to decide how to deal with the JWT in React.

In this chapter, you are going to store it in memory, then in `localStorage` (an HTML5 simple web storage object in JavaScript that allows applications to store key-value pairs in a user's web browser with no expiration date). This chapter will not cover cookie-based solutions, which tend to be the most robust and secure, as one such solution will be covered in the next chapter.

Each of these methods has its benefits and drawbacks, and it is very useful to get acquainted with them. Authentication should always be taken very seriously and, depending on your application scope and requirements, it should always be a topic that requires thorough analysis.

There is an ongoing debate on what the optimal solution for storing authentication data is—in this case, the JWT. As always, there are pros and cons to each solution.

Cookies have been around for a very long time—they can store data in key-value pairs in the browser and are readable from both the browser and the server. Their popularity coincided with the classic server-side-rendered websites. However, they can store a very limited amount of data and the structure of said data has to be very simple.

`localstorage` and `sessionStorage` were introduced with HTML5 as a way to address the need for storing complex data structures in **single-page applications** (**SPAs**), among other things. Their capacity is around 10 MB, depending on the browser's implementation, compared to 4 KB of cookie capacity. Session storage data persists through a session, while local storage remains in the browser even after it is closed and reopened until manually deleted, making SPAs the most pleasant but also the most vulnerable solution. Both can host complex JSON data structures.

Storing JWTs in `localstorage` is easy and it provides a great user and developer experience.

The majority of authorities on the subject suggest storing JWTs in HTTP-only cookies, as they cannot be accessed through JavaScript and require the frontend and the backend to run on the same domain.

This can be accomplished in different ways, through routing requests or using a proxy. Another popular strategy is the use of so-called refresh tokens. In this method, the application issues one token upon login, and then this token is used to generate other (refresh) tokens automatically, allowing you to strike the right balance between security and user experience.

### The Context API

In *Chapter 3*, *Python Type Hints and Pydantic*, you learned how to manage simple pieces of the state of a component through the `useState` hook.

Imagine that you have a top-level component—maybe even the root `App.js` component—and you need to pass some piece of state to a deeply nested component inside the React component tree. You would need to pass that piece of data to a component that is inside the `App.js` stateful component and then pass it further down the tree until it reaches the subcomponent that actually needs said data.

This pattern is known as **prop drilling**—passing a state value through props and having multiple components that do not use this state value; they just pass it on. Prop drilling has several implications, most of which are best avoided:

- Refactoring and changing code is more difficult because you must keep the state value channels of communication intact at all times

- Code is less reusable as components need to always provide the state value

- More code needs to be written, as components need to accept and forward props

React introduced the **Context API** as a way of providing values across components without the need for prop drilling.

### Creating a simple SPA

In the following section, you will create a very simple SPA that will allow users to register (if they are not registered yet), log in with a username and password, and, if authenticated, see the list of all registered users. The UI will tightly mimic your backend.

> **Note**
>
> In order for the frontend to be functional and testable, it is mandatory to provide the backend from the previous section, so be sure to run the FastAPI backend with:
>
> ```
> uvicorn app:app --reload
> ```

The frontend will connect to the running FastAPI backend through the API. While FastAPI is serving the application on the address `http://127.0.0.1:8000`, the React frontend will use this same URL to connect, perform GET and POST requests, authenticate users and list resources.

You will go through the main concepts of the Context API storing the JWT in the application. Begin with the following steps:

1.  Create a new Vite React project, install Tailwind, and add Tailwind CSS as it simplifies the styling of the application. Please refer to *Chapter 5, Setting up a React Workflow*, in order to do so. Also, delete files and folder that will not be needed (assets such as `App.css`).

2.  Create in the `/src` folder a new file and name it `AuthContext.jsx`. The `.jsx` extension is a reminder that the context is indeed a React component that will wrap all the other components that need access to the context variables, functions, objects, or arrays:

```
import {
    createContext
} from 'react';
const AuthContext = createContext();
export const AuthProvider = ({
    children
}) => {
    const [user, setUser] = useState(null);
    const [jwt, setJwt] = useState(null);
    const [message, setMessage] = useState(null);
    return (<AuthContext.Provider value={
        {
            user,
            jwt,
            register,
            login,
            logout,
            message,
            setMessage
        }
    } > {
            children
        } </AuthContext.Provider>)
}
```

The preceding code shows the structure of the context creation – you imported `createContext` from React and created your first context (`AuthContext`). After defining a couple of state variables and setters (for the user, the `jwt` token and the message), you returned the `AuthContext` component and the values that will be available in the context. The syntax is a bit different from the one used for the hooks examined in *Chapter 4, Getting Started with FastAPI*, but this is a straightforward template that you will reuse many times, should you opt for the Context API.

3.  While simple, creating a context involves several steps:

    I.   First, you will need to create the actual context that will be shared across the application.

    II.  After that, the context should be provided to all the components needing access to its values.

    III. The components that need to access the context values need to subscribe to the context in order to be able to read, but also write to it.

    So, the first step when creating a context should be defining exactly what type of information you need to pass to components. If you think about it, you would definitely want the JWT since that is the whole point of this exercise. In order to showcase context functionality, you will also include the logged-in user and a message that will display the state of the application.

    But since the context can also contain and pass functions—and that's indeed one of its most useful features—you will also add to the context the `register`, `login`, and `logout` functions. That may not be something you would do in a production system, but it will showcase the capabilities of Context API.

4.  Now, the only thing left to do is add the functions to the context. To do that, edit the existing `AuthContext.jsx` file and, after declaring the state variables, define the function for registering new users:

```
const register = async (username, password) => {
  try {
    const response = await fetch('http://127.0.0.1:8000/users/
register', {
      method: 'POST',
      headers: {
        'Content-Type': 'application/json',
      },
      body: JSON.stringify({
        username,
        password
      }),
    });
    if (response.ok) {
      const data = await response.json();
      setMessage(`Registration successful: user ${data.username}
created`);
    } else {
      const data = await response.json();
      setMessage(`Registration failed: ${JSON.stringify(data)}`);
    }
  } catch (error) {
    setMessage(`Registration failed: ${JSON.stringify(error)}`);
  }
};
```

This simple JavaScript function is part of the context, and the only thing that interacts with your context is the setting of the status message—if a user is successfully created, the message confirms it. In case of an error, the message is set to the error. You will want to provide a more complex validation logic and a nicer UI, but this is quite illustrative of the context functioning.

5.  Now add the other function related to authentication—the `login()` function:

```javascript
const login = async (username, password) => {
  setJwt(null)
  const response = await    fetch('http://127.0.0.1:8000/users/
login', {
    method: 'POST',
    headers: {
      'Content-Type': 'application/json',
    },
    body: JSON.stringify({
      username,
      password
    }),
  });
  if (response.ok) {
    const data = await response.json();
    setJwt(data.token);
    setUser({
      username
    });
    setMessage(`Login successful: token ${data.token.slice(0, 10)}...,
user ${username}`);
  } else {
    const data = await response.json();
    setMessage('Login failed: ' + data.detail);

    setUser({
      username: null
    });
  }

};
```

The preceding code is similar to the `register` function—it sends a POST request to the FastAPI `/login` endpoint with the user-provided username and password, and it clears any pre-existing JWT in the process. If the request is successful, the retrieved token is set to its state variable and the username accordingly.

6.  The final piece of the puzzle is logging the user out. Since you are dealing only with the Context API and not some persistent storage solutions, the code is very short; it just needs to clear the context variables and set the appropriate message:

```
const logout = () => {

    setUser(null);
    setJwt(null);
    setMessage('Logout successful');
};
```

7.  Your AuthContext is nearly complete—the only thing left is to inform the context that it needs to provide the previously defined functions. So, modify the return statement to include everything:

```
return ( <
    AuthContext.Provider value = {
        {
            user,
            jwt,
            register,
            login,
            logout,
            message,
            setMessage
        }
    } > {
        children
    } <
    /AuthContext.Provider>
);
```

8.  As a final touch, add a useContext React hook that facilitates working with contexts:

```
export const useAuth = () => useContext(AuthContext);
```

This simple one-line hook allows you to now use AuthContext in any component that has access to the context—so any component wrapped inside AuthContext—with some simple ES6 destructuring. With your AuthContext now in place, you can put it directly in the App.jsx component and wrap it around all the other components.

9.  Open the `App.jsx` file and edit it:

```
import { AuthProvider } from "./AuthContext";
const App = () => {
  return (
    <div className="bg-blue-200 flex flex-col justify-center items-
center min-h-screen">
      <AuthProvider>
        <h1 className="text-2xl text-blue-800"> Simple Auth App </h1>
      </AuthProvider>{" "}
    </div>
  );
};
```

```
export default App
```

This root component doesn't contain anything that you haven't seen already—apart from importing `AuthProvider`—the component of your custom authentication context responsible for wrapping the area of components and a bit of Tailwind styles.

10. Now comes the part where you will define the components that will be wrapped inside the context – as those components will be able to consume the context, have access to the context data, and modify it. For a bit more complex application, you would likely resort to the React Router package, but since this will be a very simple application, you will cram all the components into one page. There aren't many of them:

- **Login**: A simple login component form that will accept a username and password and then call the `login()` function from the context.

- **Register**: Similar to the login component, but for registering new users.

- **Message**: The simplest component, used only to display the status of the app.

- **Users**: The component whose state depends on the authentication status: if the user is logged in, they can see the list of users, meaning the JWT is present and valid; otherwise, the user is prompted to make a login.

11. The `Register` component will be used for user registration. It needs to display a form. Create the `Register.jsx` file in the `/src` folder and create a simple form with two fields:

```
import { useState } from 'react';
import { useAuth } from './AuthContext';

const Register = () => {
    const [username, setUsername] = useState('');
    const [password, setPassword] = useState('');
    const { register } = useAuth();
```

```
        const handleSubmit = (e) => {
            e.preventDefault();
            register(username, password)
            setUsername('')
            setPassword('')
        };


        return (
            <div className="m-5 p-5  border-2">
                <form onSubmit={handleSubmit} className='grid grid-rows-3
    gap-2'>
                    <input
                        type="text"
                        placeholder="Username"
                        className='p-2'
                        value={username}
                        onChange={(e) => setUsername(e.target.value)}
                    />
                    <input
                        type="password"
                        placeholder="Password"
                        className='p-2'
                        value={password}
                        onChange={(e) => setPassword(e.target.value)}
                    />
                    <button type="submit" className='bg-blue-500 text-
    white rounded'>Register</button>
                </form>
            </div>
        );
    };
    export default Register
```

You have just created a React-specific form with the help of two local state variables that take care of keeping track and sending the username and password to your FastAPI instance. The register function is imported from AuthContext through the useAuth() hook. That line really shows how easy it is to work with the context from within the wrapped components.

Finally, handleSubmit performs the call to the register function, clears the fields, and prevents the default HTML form behavior.

12. Create the `Login.jsx` file, which is nearly identical (and here you could practice your React skills and perform some refactoring). The component has a login form that will be used for logging in:

```
import { useState } from 'react';
import { useAuth } from './AuthContext';

const Login = () => {
    const [username, setUsername] = useState('');
    const [password, setPassword] = useState('');
    const { login } = useAuth();

    const handleSubmit = (e) => {
        e.preventDefault();
        login(username, password);
        setUsername('');
        setPassword('');
    };

    return (
        <div className="m-5 p-5  border-2">
            <form onSubmit={handleSubmit} className='grid grid-rows-3
gap-2'>
                <input
                    type="text"
                    placeholder="Username"
                    className='p-2'
                    value={username}
                    onChange={(e) => setUsername(e.target.value)}
                />
                <input
                    type="password"
                    placeholder="Password"
                    className='p-2'
                    value={password}
                    onChange={(e) => setPassword(e.target.value)}
                />
                <button type="submit" className='bg-blue-500 text-
white rounded'>Login</button>
            </form>
        </div>
    );
};
export default Login
```

13. There are two components left to be inserted in your simple auth application powered by FastAPI and React. First, create the `src/Message.jsx` component, which will be used to display the status message:

```jsx
import { useAuth } from "./AuthContext"
const Message = () => {
    const { message } = useAuth()
    return (
        <div className="p-2 my-2">
            <p>{message}</p>
        </div>
    )
}
export default Message
```

The `Messages` component reads the message state variable from the context and displays it to the users.

14. Now, you can finally create the `src/Users.jsx` component and edit it:

```jsx
import { useEffect, useState } from 'react';
import { useAuth } from './AuthContext';

const Users = () => {
    const { jwt, logout } = useAuth();
    const [users, setUsers] = useState(null);

    useEffect(() => {
        const fetchUsers = async () => {
            const response = await fetch('http://127.0.0.1:8000/users/
list', {
                headers: {
                    Authorization: `Bearer ${jwt}`,
                },
            });
            const data = await response.json();
            setUsers(data.users);
        };

        if (jwt) {
            fetchUsers();
        }
    }, [jwt]);

    if (!jwt) return <div>Please log in to see all the users</div>;
```

```
        return (
            <div>
                {users ? (
                    <div className='flex flex-col'>
                        <h1>The list of users</h1>
                        <ol>
                            {users.map((user) => (
                                <li key={user.id}>{user.username}</li>
                            ))}
                        </ol>
                        <button onClick={logout} className='bg-blue-500
text-white rounded'>Logout</button>
                    </div>
                ) : (
                    <p>Loading...</p>
                )}
            </div>
        );
    };
```

```
export default Users;
```

This component does a bit of heavy lifting compared to the others. It imports jwt (along with the logout function) from the context. This is important since the output of the Users.jsx component depends entirely on the existence and validity of the JWT.

After declaring a local state variable—users—the component uses the useEffect React hook to perform a call to the REST API, and since the /users/list endpoint is protected, the JWT token needs to be present and valid.

If the call to the /users/list endpoint is successful, the retrieved users data is sent to the users variable and displayed. Finally, if there is no jwt in the context, the user is asked to perform a login and the **Logout** button you added simply calls the logout function from the context.

15. Finally, to tie everything together, replace the App.jsx file with the following code to import the components, and finalize the root component:

```
import { useState } from 'react';
import { AuthProvider } from './AuthContext';
import Register from './Register';
import Login from './Login';
import Users from './Users';
import Message from './Message';
```

```
const App = () => {

  const [showLogin, setShowLogin] = useState(true)
  return (
    <div className='bg-blue-200 flex flex-col justify-center items-
center min-h-screen'>
      <AuthProvider>
        <h1 className='text-2xl text-blue-800'>Simple Auth App</h1>
        <Message />
        {showLogin ? <Login /> : <Register />}
        <button onClick={() => setShowLogin(!showLogin)}>{showLogin ?
'Register' : 'Login'}</button>
        <hr />
        <Users />
      </AuthProvider>
    </div>
  );
};
export default App;
```

Now, you'll be able to test the application—try registering, logging in, entering invalid data, and so on. You have created a very simple but complete full stack authentication solution. In the next section, you will learn about some methods of persisting the login data.

## Persisting authentication data with localStorage

As mentioned before, the most developer-friendly option for persisting authentication is the use of `localStorage` or `sessionStorage`. `localStorage` becomes very useful when it comes to storing temporary, local data. It is widely used for tasks such as remembering shopping cart data or user login on any website where security is not paramount. `localStorage` has a higher storage limit than cookies (5 MB versus 4 KB) and does not get sent with every HTTP request. This makes it a better choice for client-side storage.

To use `localStorage`, you can set and get JSON items using the `setItem()` and `getItem()` methods, respectively. One important thing to remember is that `localStorage` only stores strings, so you will need to use `JSON.stringify()` and `JSON.parse()` to convert between JavaScript objects and strings.

Armed with this knowledge, try to summarize what the app requirements are – you want the user to be able to refresh or close and reopen the application window/tab and remain logged in if they were logged in, in the first place. Translated into React language, you need a `useEffect` hook that will run and verify whether there is a token stored in `localStorage`. If it is present, you want to check this token through the FastAPI /me endpoint and set the username accordingly:

1.  Open the existing `AuthContext.jsx` file, and after the `useState` hook, define the `useEffect` call:

```
export const AuthProvider = ({ children }) => {
const [user, setUser] = useState(null);
const [jwt, setJwt] = useState(null);
const [message, setMessage] = useState(null);
useEffect(() => {

    const storedJwt = localStorage.getItem('jwt');
    if (storedJwt) {
        setJwt(storedJwt);
        fetch('http://127.0.0.1:8000/users/me', {
            headers: {
                Authorization: `Bearer ${storedJwt}`,
            },
        })
            .then(res => res.json())
            .then(data => {

                if (data.username) {
                    setUser({ username: data.username });
                    setMessage(`Welcome back, ${data.username}!`);
                }
            })
            .catch(() => {
                localStorage.removeItem('jwt');
            });
    }
}, []);
```

The bulk of your persistence logic is located in the `useEffect` call. First, you can try to get the `jwt` token from `localStorage` and then use that token to get the user data from the `/me` route. If the username is found, it is set in the context and the user is (already) logged in. If not, you clear `localStorage` or send a message that the token has expired (in the `Users.jsx` component).

2.  The `login()` function also has to be modified in order to take account of `localStorage`. In the same `AuthContext.jsx`, modify the `login()` function:

```
const login = async (username,
  password) => {

    setJwt(null)
    const response = await fetch(
      'http://127.0.0.1:8000/users/login', {
        method: 'POST',
        headers: {
          'Content-Type': 'application/json',
        },
        body: JSON.stringify({
          username,
          password
        }),
      });
    if (response.ok) {
      const data = await response
        .json();
      setJwt(data.token);
      localStorage.setItem('jwt', data.token);
      setUser({
        username
      });
      setMessage(
        `Login successful: token ${data.token.slice(0, 10)}..., user
${username}`
      );
    } else {
      const data = await response
        .json();
      setMessage('Login failed: ' +
        data.detail);
      setUser({
        username: null
      });
    }

  };
```

The only modification involves setting the new JWT to the `localStorage` jwt variable. Hence, the `logout()` function will also need to clear `localStorage`.

3. In the same AuthContext.jsx file, modify the logout function:

```
const logout = () => {
    setUser(null);
    setJwt('');
    localStorage .removeItem('jwt');
    setMessage('Logout successful');
};
```

4. Finally, in order to make your application even more explicit and informative, open the Users.jsx component and replace it with the following code:

```
import { useEffect, useState } from 'react';
import { useAuth } from './AuthContext';

const Users = () => {
    const { jwt, logout } = useAuth();
    const [users, setUsers] = useState(null);
    const [error, setError] = useState(null);

    useEffect(() => {
        const fetchUsers = async () => {
            const response = await fetch('http://127.0.0.1:8000/users/
list', {
                headers: {
                    Authorization: `Bearer ${jwt}`,
                },
            });
            const data = await response.json();
            if (!response.ok) {
                setError(data.detail);
            }
            setUsers(data.users);
        };

        if (jwt) {
            fetchUsers();
        }
    }, [jwt]);

    if (!jwt) return <div>Please log in to see all the users</div>;

    return (
        <div>
            {users ? (
```

```
                <div className='flex flex-col'>
                    <h1>The list of users</h1>
                    <ol>
                        {users.map((user) => (
                            <li className='' key={user.id}>{user.
    username}</li>
                        ))}
                    </ol>
                    <button onClick={logout} className='bg-blue-500
    text-white rounded'>Logout</button>
                </div>
            ) : (
                <p>{error}</p>
            )}
        </div>
    );
};


export default Users;
```

The app is now able to persist the logged-in user, retrieve the stored JWT, and restore the previous authentication state. Before trying to log in, make sure that the FastAPI backend is working properly on port 8000.

Try logging in, refreshing the browser, closing the tab, and reopening it.

You can also try this with the token inside the **Application** tab in the developer toolbar of Chrome or Firefox and see what happens if you tamper with it or delete it.

## Other authentication solutions

It is important to emphasize again that the **FARM** stack can be a great prototyping tool. So, knowing your way around it when creating an authentication flow, even if it is not ideal or bulletproof, might be just good enough to get you over that **MVP** hump in the race for the next great data-driven product. You could easily implement a similar solution with cookies instead of localStorage for instance, but keeping in mind the specificities of both solutions.

Finally, it is important to get acquainted with the various third-party authentication options. **Firebase** and **Supabase** are popular database and authentication services that can be used solely for managing users and authenticating them. **Clerk** and **Kinde** are newer players in the field and are particularly geared toward the React/Next.js/Remix.js ecosystem, while **Auth0** and **Cognito** are industry-standard solutions. Almost all third-party authentication systems offer a generous free or almost-free tier, but once your application grows, you are bound to hit a paid tier, and the costs vary and replacing these services, should the need arise, is not easy.

# Summary

In this chapter, you've seen a very basic, but quite representative, implementation of two versions of an authentication mechanism. You learned how FastAPI enables the use of standard-compliant authentication methods and implemented one of the simplest possible yet effective solutions – without persisting the authentication data and storing the **JWT** in `localStorage`.

You have learned how elegant and flexible FastAPI is when it comes to defining granular roles and permissions, especially with MongoDB, with the aid of **Pydantic** as the middleman. This chapter was focused exclusively on **JWTs** as the means of communication because it is the primary and most popular tool in SPAs nowadays, and it enables great connectivity between services or microservices. **JWT** mechanisms shine when you need to develop different applications with the same FastAPI and MongoDB-powered backend—for instance, a React web application and a React Native or Flutter-based mobile app.

Furthermore, carefully considering your authentication and authorization strategy is crucial, especially when extracting user data from third-party systems may not be feasible or practical. This highlights the importance of devising robust authentication and authorization methods.

In the next chapter, you will create a more complex FastAPI backend, with image uploading through a third-party service and use a MongoDB database for persistance.

# 7

# Building a Backend with FastAPI

In the previous chapters, you learned the basic mechanics of authentication and authorization, and now you are ready to implement it and secure a web API, built with FastAPI. In this chapter, you will put this knowledge to good use and create a simple, yet fully functional REST API showcasing used cars and their pictures.

In this chapter, you will learn about the following actions, which can be thought of as a loosely coupled blueprint when creating a REST API with FastAPI.

This chapter will cover the following topics:

- Connecting the FastAPI instance to MongoDB Atlas by using the Python Motor driver
- Defining the Pydantic models according to the specification and initial creation of the FastAPI application
- Creating the API router and implementing CRUD operations
- Securing the API with a JWT
- Deployment to Render

# Technical requirements

The requirements for this chapter are similar to those defined earlier. You will work with:

- Python 3.11.7 or higher
- Visual Studio Code
- An account on MongoDB Atlas

Later on, you will need to create an account on the image-hosting service **Cloudinary** (free) and the **Render** platform for hosting the API (also a free tier account). Again, you will use HTTPie for manually testing the API endpoints that you are going to implement.

Let's start by understanding the application to be developed and what the backend will require.

# Introducing the application

It is much easier to start working with a framework while having a specific problem that needs solving, even if the requirements are somewhat vague. The task at hand is rather simple: you need to create a REST API backend for storing and retrieving data about used cars for a fictional car sales company.

The data structure that describes a vehicle is rather simple but can become more complicated as soon as you delve into the details such as engine models, interior colors, types of suspension, and so on.

In your first simple **create**, **read**, **update**, **delete** (**CRUD**) application, you will keep the resource data limited. A car will be described by the following fields:

- `Brand`: The brand of the car (Ford, Renault, etc.), represented by a *string*
- Make or model: For example, Fiesta or Clio, represented by a *string*
- `Year`: The year of production, an *integer* limited to a reasonable range (1970–2024)
- `Cm3`: The displacement of the engine, proportional to the power of the engine, a ranged *integer*
- `kW`: Power of the engine in kW, an *integer*
- `Km`: How many kilometers the car has travelled, an *integer* in the hundreds of thousands range
- `Price`: The price in euros
- An image URL: This is optional

An essential feature of every car sales website is the presence of images, so you will implement an image-uploading pipeline with one of the leading services for image hosting and processing—**Cloudinary**. Later, you will aid the employees even more by generating compelling copy text for each car model, which will make the API richer while showcasing FastAPI's simplicity.

# Creating an Atlas instance and a collection

Log in to your Atlas account, and create a new database called `carBackend` inside a collection named `cars`. You can refer to *Chapter 2*, *Setting Up the Database with MongoDB*. After creating the database and the collection, take note of the MongoDB connection string and save it in a text file for later, when you will be creating your secret environment keys.

## Setting up the Python environment

After creating the MongoDB database on Atlas and connecting it, it is time for you to set up a brand new Python virtual environment and install the requirements:

1.  First, create a plain text file called `requirements.txt` and insert the following lines in it:

    ```
    fastapi==0.111.0
    motor==3.4.0
    uvicorn==0.29.0
    pydantic-settings==2.2.1
    ```

2.  The package versioning is important if you want to be able to reproduce exactly the code used in this book and you can always refer to the `requirements.txt` file in the book's repository. Run the `pip` installation command that reads the previously defined requirements file:

    ```
    pip install -r requirements.txt
    ```

Your environment is ready. Now, armed with the knowledge of Python type hints and Pydantic from *Chapter 3*, *Python Type Hints and Pydantic*, you will model this relatively simple car data structure.

## Defining the Pydantic models

Let's begin with the first Pydantic model, for a single car. Here, one of the main problems that need to be solved upfront is how to serialize and define the MongoDB `ObjectID` key in Pydantic. While there are different ways of representing the `ObjectID`, the simplest and the one currently recommended by MongoDB is to cast the `ObjectID` to a string. You can refer to the following documentation for further details: `https://www.mongodb.com/developer/languages/python/python-quickstart-fastapi/`.

MongoDB uses the field name `_id` for the identifier. In Python, since attributes that start with an underscore have a special meaning, you cannot use the original field name for model population.

Pydantic aliases provide a simple and elegant solution; you can name the field `id` but also give it an alias of `_id` and set the `populate_by_name` flag to `True`, as shown in *Chapter 3*, *Python Type Hints and Pydantic*.

Finally, you will need to cast the `ObjectID` as a string. To do so, you will use a simple Python annotation, and the Pydantic `BeforeValidator` module.

1. Create a folder named `Chapter7` and a `models.py` file inside of it, and start with the imports and the `ObjectID` type:

```
#models.py
from typing import Optional, Annotated, List
from pydantic import BaseModel, ConfigDict, Field, BeforeValidator,
field_validator


PyObjectId = Annotated[str, BeforeValidator(str)]
```

2. After the imports, and creating a new type, `PyObjectId`, which will be used to represent MongoDB's original **BSON** `ObjectID` as a string, continue populating the model:

```
class CarModel(BaseModel):

    id: Optional[PyObjectId] = Field(
        alias="_id", default=None)
    brand: str = Field(...)
    make: str = Field(...)
    year: int = Field(..., gt=1970, lt=2025)
    cm3: int = Field(..., gt=0, lt=5000)
    km: int = Field(..., gt=0, lt=500000)
    price: int = Field(..., gt=0, lt=100000)
```

These fields should be very familiar if you read the chapter on Pydantic; you are simply declaring the car fields, marking all of them as required, and setting some reasonable limits on the numerical quantities (`cm3`, `km`, `price`, and `year`).

Bear in mind that the number of car brands is limited, so it is possible and probably advisable to create an **enumerated** type for the brand name, but in this case, you will keep things simple.

3. Add two convenient field validators that act as modifiers. You want to return the title of every car brand and model:

```
@field_validator("brand")
@classmethod
def check_brand_case(cls, v: str) -> str:
    return v.title()


@field_validator("make")
@classmethod
def check_make_case(cls, v: str) -> str:
    return v.title()
```

4. To complete the model, finally, add a configuration dictionary that will allow it to be populated by name and allow arbitrary types:

```
model_config = ConfigDict(
    populate_by_name=True,
    arbitrary_types_allowed=True,
    json_schema_extra={
        "example": {
            "brand": "Ford",
            "make": "Fiesta",
            "year": 2019,
            "cm3": 1500,
            "km": 120000,
            "price": 10000,
        }
    },
)
```

5. You can now test the model by adding the following (temporary) lines at the end of the file, outside of the class definition, and running it:

```
test_car = CarModel(
    brand="ford", make="fiesta", year=2019, cm3=1500, km=120000,
price=10000
)
print(test_car.model_dump())
```

6. Run the `models.py` file:

```
python models.py
```

You will get the following output:

```
{'id': None, 'brand': 'Ford', 'make': 'Fiesta', 'year': 2019, 'cm3':
1500, 'km': 120000, 'price': 10000}.
```

Now, it's time to define other models for updating a single instance and getting a list of cars. The `update` model will need to allow only specific fields to be changed. In theory, only the `price` should be updatable since cars are pretty immutable objects in their own right, but this system will allow for some ambiguity and situations in which the inserted data is just wrong and needs to be manually corrected via the API.

7.  After deleting or commenting out the testing lines from `models.py`, proceed with creating the `UpdateCarModel` model:

```
class UpdateCarModel(BaseModel):

    brand: Optional[str] = Field(...)
    make: Optional[str] = Field(...)
    year: Optional[int] = Field(..., gt=1970, lt=2025)
    cm3: Optional[int] = Field(..., gt=0, lt=5000)
    km: Optional[int] = Field(..., gt=0, lt=500 * 1000)
    price: Optional[int] = Field(..., gt=0, lt=100 * 1000)
```

The remaining part of the class is identical to the `CarModel` class and will be omitted for brevity.

8.  Finally, the `ListCarsModel` class will be very simple, as it only needs to handle a list of `CarModel` classes:

```
class CarCollection(BaseModel):
    cars: List[CarModel]
```

With the models now in place, you are ready to make a simple test and see how `ListCarsModel` works.

9.  Create a new testing file called `test_models.py`, add the following lines in order to create two different car models and a list, and then print a model dump:

```
from models import CarCollection, CarModel
test_car_1 = CarModel(
    brand="ford", make="fiesta", year=2019, cm3=1500, km=120000,
price=10000
)
test_car_2 = CarModel(
    brand="fiat", make="stilo", year=2003, cm3=1600, km=320000,
price=3000
)
car_list = CarCollection(cars=[test_car_1, test_car_2])
print(car_list.model_dump())
```

If you run the `test_models.py` file with Python, the output should be the following:

```
{'cars': [{'id': None, 'brand': 'Ford', 'make': 'Fiesta', 'year':
2019, 'cm3': 1500, 'km': 120000, 'price': 10000}, {'id': None,
'brand': 'Fiat', 'make': 'Stilo', 'year': 2003, 'cm3': 1600, 'km':
320000, 'price': 3000}]}
```

The models, at least an initial iteration of them (and MongoDB is excellent for iterative data modeling), are complete, so you can start scaffolding your FastAPI application structure in the next section.

# Scaffolding a FastAPI application

**Scaffolding** is the term generally used to describe the process of creating the initial application with little or no functionality. In this section, you will build the FastAPI application and connect it to your MongoDB Atlas instance through the asynchronous MongoDB `Motor` driver. Initially, you will only create a generic and minimal FastAPI application, and gradually add functionality.

You will begin by storing the secret environment data—in your case, just the MongoDB Atlas database URL—into a `.env` file. These values should be always kept outside the reach of the repositories. You want to be able to connect to your MongoDB database and verify whether the connection is successful.

## Creating a .env file to keep the secrets

For managing values that should be kept secret and out of the version control system, you will use an environment file (`.env`). Perform the following steps to set up the environment variables and exclude them from the version control:

1.  First, create a `.env` file and, inside it, put your secret connection string in the following format, without quotes:

    ```
    DB_URL=mongodb+srv://<USERNAME>:<PASSWORD>@cluster0.fkm24.mongodb.
    net/?retryWrites=true&w=majority&appName=Cluster0
    DB_NAME=carBackend
    ```

    This `.env` file will later host other secret files for external services that you might need to use in your API development.

2.  Now, create a `.gitignore` file, and populate it with the basic entries: directories and files that are not to be tracked by Git. Open a file, name it `.gitignore`, and insert the following:

    ```
    __pycache__/
    .env
    venv/
    ```

    There are numerous examples of Python-related `.gitignore` files on the web, so feel free to look around, but this will be more than sufficient for our purposes.

3.  Now, you can put the working directory under version control with the following Git commands:

    ```
    git init
    git add .
    git commit -m "initial commit"
    ```

### Creating a Pydantic configuration with pydantic_settings

In the next steps, you will use the previously created environment variables and provide them to the pydantic_settings—the Pydantic class for managing application settings, covered in *Chapter 3, Python Type Hints and Pydantic*. This class will later be easily invoked wherever the environment variables will be necessary.

After this preparatory work, create a config.py file that will leverage the pydantic_settings package for managing your settings, as follows:

1.  Create a configuration file, aptly named config.py, which you will use for reading the settings of the application. You will be able to change them easily later when you introduce some automated testing or make different settings for production, a different database, and so on. Paste the following code into config.py:

    ```
    from typing import Optional
    from pydantic_settings import BaseSettings, SettingsConfigDict

    class BaseConfig(BaseSettings):
        DB_URL: Optional[str]
        DB_NAME: Optional[str]
        model_config = SettingsConfigDict(env_file=".env", extra="ignore")
    ```

    Now, you will use these configuration settings to get the environment data to connect to the MongoDB Atlas instance.

2.  Finally, you can start scaffolding the actual application file by creating a new Python file, named app.py. In this file, first, instantiate a FastAPI instance and create a root route with a simple message:

    ```
    from fastapi import FastAPI
    app = FastAPI()

    @app.get("/")
    async def get_root():
        return {"Message": "Root working"}
    ```

3.  You should be able to run this bare-bones application in the terminal with your server of choice:

    ```
    uvicorn app:app
    ```

The simple root message is available at 127.0.0.1:8000 and you have the application running.

## Connecting to Atlas

Now it is time to connect it to Atlas. To do so, you will use the **Lifespan Events** of FastAPI, which is the newer way of handling events that need to occur only once before the application starts up and begins receiving requests. Lifespan Events also allow you to handle events that should fire only after the application finishes handling requests.

> **Note**
>
> The FastAPI website has excellent documentation about the topic: `https://fastapi.tiangolo.com/advanced/events/`.

For the use case in this chapter, you will use an **asynchronous context manager** that will allow you to yield the application instance, and fire events before and after the application starts. Follow these steps:

1.  To showcase how this works, edit the `app.py` file:

    ```
    from contextlib import asynccontextmanager
    from fastapi import FastAPI


    @asynccontextmanager
    async def lifespan(app: FastAPI):
        print("Starting up!")
        yield
        print("Shutting down!")


    app = FastAPI(lifespan=lifespan)


    @app.get("/")
    async def get_root():
        return {"Message": "Root working!"}
    ```

    If you start the application with the same command as shown previously and then shut it down with *Ctrl+C*, you will see that the `print` statements display messages in the console.

    The `lifespan` event async context is the mechanism you will use to connect to your Atlas instance, through the use of the settings.

2.  Again, open up the `app.py` file, add the configuration settings, change the `lifespan` function, and bring in the `Motor` driver:

```
from fastapi import FastAPI
from motor import motor_asyncio
from config import BaseConfig

settings = BaseConfig()

async def lifespan(app: FastAPI):
    app.client = motor_asyncio.AsyncIOMotorClient(settings.DB_URL)
    app.db = app.client[settings.DB_NAME]
    try:
        app.client.admin.command("ping")
        print("Pinged your deployment. You have successfully connected
to MongoDB!")
        print("Mongo address:", settings.DB_URL)
    except Exception as e:
        print(e)
    yield
    app.client.close()

app = FastAPI(lifespan=lifespan)

@app.get("/")
async def get_root():
    return {"Message": "Root working!"}
```

3.  If you start the application now, you should receive a message similar to the following:

```
INFO:     Started server process [28228]
INFO:     Waiting for application startup.
Pinged your deployment. You have successfully connected to MongoDB!
Mongo address: <your connection string>
INFO:     Application startup complete.
INFO:     Uvicorn running on http://127.0.0.1:8000 (Press
```

You have implemented quite a lot in this setup:

- You have created the FastAPI instance, the backbone of your API.

- You have set the environment variables with `pydantic_settings` and they are, thus, manageable and maintainable.

- You have connected to the Atlas cluster that you have set up.

- You have also "attached" the MongoDB database to the application, so you will be able to access it conveniently from the API routers through the request.

Now, let's start implementing the routes for the **CRUD** operations, starting from a solid and expansible setup.

# CRUD operations

The four basic operations at the heart of almost every web application are often referred by the acronym **CRUD** (**create**, **read**, **update**, and **delete**). These operations enable users to interact with data by creating new resources, retrieving one or more instances of existing resources, and modifying and deleting resources. Here, a more formal definition of APIs is used, but resources, in this case, are simply cars.

FastAPI is strongly tied to web standards, so these operations map to specific HTTP request methods: POST is used for creating new instances, GET is for reading one or more cars, PUT is for updating, and DELETE is for deleting resources. In your case, the resources are represented by cars, which map to MongoDB documents.

## Set up the API router

After having the application ready and serving a basic root endpoint, the environment variables set up, and the connection to the Atlas MongoDB database in place, you are now ready to start implementing the endpoints.

In fact, in the following sections, we will add a router for users; this will be needed to enable you to associate individual cars with particular users/salespersons, and to allow for some basic authentication and authorization.

Like most modern web frameworks (Express.js, Flask, etc.), FastAPI allows you to structure and group endpoints into API routers. APIRouter is a module designed to handle a group of operations related to a single type of object or resource: in your case, cars, and later, users.

Perform the following steps to create the API router for managing cars:

1.  Create a dedicated folder inside your app directory and name it /routers. This directory will contain all the API routers . Inside it, create an empty __init__.py file to turn the folder into a Python package.

2.  Now, create a file named /routers/cars.py. This will be the first router in this app but, potentially, you could add more should the application grow. It is a convention to name the routers according to the resources they manage.

3.  Inside /routers/cars.py, begin scaffolding the router:

    ```
    from fastapi import APIRouter, Body, Request, status
    from models import CarModel

    router = APIRouter()
    ```

The APIRouter instantiation is very similar to the creation of the main FastAPI instance—it can be thought of as a small FastAPI application that becomes an integral part of the main app, as well as its automated documentation.

APIRouter by itself doesn't have any functionality—it needs to be plugged into the main application (app.py) in order to perform its tasks.

4.  Before proceeding, let's modify the app.py file and plug the newly created APIRouter in:

```python
from fastapi import FastAPI, status
from fastapi.middleware.cors import CORSMiddleware
from motor import motor_asyncio
from fastapi.exceptions import RequestValidationError
from fastapi.responses import JSONResponse

from fastapi.encoders import jsonable_encoder
from collections import defaultdict
from config import BaseConfig
from routers.cars import router as cars_router
from routers.users import router as users_router

settings = BaseConfig()

async def lifespan(app: FastAPI):
    app.client = motor_asyncio.AsyncIOMotorClient(settings.DB_URL)
    app.db = app.client[settings.DB_NAME]

    try:
        app.client.admin.command("ping")
        print("Pinged your deployment. You have successfully connected
to MongoDB!")
    except Exception as e:
        print(e)
    yield
    app. client.close()

app = FastAPI(lifespan=lifespan)
app.include_router(cars_router, prefix="/cars", tags=["cars"])

@app.get("/")
async def get_root():
    return {"Message": "Root working!"}
```

You have created your first APIRouter that will be handling operations regarding cars and you have connected it, through the app.py file, to the main FastAPI instance.

Now, you will add functionality to the APIRouter by implementing handlers for various operations.

## The POST handler

Now, with the APIRouter connected, you can return to the /routers/cars.py file and create the first endpoint, a POST request handler for creating new instances:

```
@router.post(
    "/",
    response_description="Add new car",
    response_model=CarModel,
    status_code=status.HTTP_201_CREATED,
    response_model_by_alias=False,
)
async def add_car(request: Request, car: CarModel = Body(...)):
    cars = request.app.db["cars"]
    document = car.model_dump(
        by_alias=True, exclude=["id"])
    inserted = await cars.insert_one(document)

    return await cars.find_one({"_id": inserted.inserted_id})
```

The code is rather simple and self-explanatory as it uses the previously defined Pydantic model (CarModel), which is flexible enough to be reused (through the alias) as the input and output model.

The line that creates the document to be inserted from the model uses a couple of Pydantic features, which are covered in *Chapter 3, Python Type Hints and Pydantic*, namely, the *alias* and the *excluded* fields.

Now, launch the application:

```
uvicorn app:app
```

In another terminal, still inside the working directory of your project and with the virtual environment activated, test the endpoint with **HTTPie**:

```
http POST http://127.0.0.1:8000/cars/ brand="KIA" make="Ceed" year=2015
price=2000 km=100000 cm3=1500
```

Your terminal should output the following response:

```
HTTP/1.1 201 Created
content-length: 109
content-type: application/json
date: Sun, 12 May 2024 15:29:45 GMT
server: uvicorn
{
    "brand": "Kia",
    "cm3": 1500,
    "id": "6640e06ad82a890d261a8a40",
    "km": 100000,
    "make": "Ceed",
    "price": 2000,
    "year": 2015
}
```

You have created the first endpoint—you can test it further with HTTPie, or with the interactive documentation at http://127.0.0.1:8000/docs, and try inserting some invalid data, such as a year greater than 2024 or something similar.

The endpoint should respond with informative JSON that will quickly direct you to the problem or provide feedback to the end user. Now, you will create the GET handlers for viewing the cars inside your database.

## Handling the GET requests

For viewing resources—cars—in your system, you will use the HTTP GET method. FastAPI makes very good use of HTTP verb semantics and closely follows web standards and good practices.

Follow these steps:

1.  First, return the whole collection of cars—if you have played around with the POST endpoint, you might already have a couple of them inserted. Continuing the /routers/cars.py file, let's add the GET handler:

    ```
    @router.get(
        "/",
        response_description="List all cars",
        response_model=CarCollection,
        response_model_by_alias=False,
    )
    async def list_cars(request: Request):
        cars = request.app.db["cars"]
        results = []
    ```

```
        cursor = cars.find()
        async for document in cursor:
            results.append(document)

        return CarCollection(cars=results)
```

2. Test this endpoint with HTTPie:

```
http http://127.0.0.1:8000/cars/
```

After running the preceding command, you should get all the cars inserted up to this point, in a nice JSON structure. The function signature and the decorator are similar to the POST endpoint.

3. Instead of using `async for`, which can be a bit counterintuitive at first if you are not used to it, you could also swap the population of the empty results list with the following:

```
return CarCollection(
    cars=await cars.find().to_list(1000)
    )
```

Then, you could use the `to_list()` method to get the results in a list. If you wish to dive deeper into the `Motor` documentation on handling cursors, their page is a bit dry but complete: `https://motor.readthedocs.io/en/stable/api-tornado/cursors.html`.

Later, you will learn how to manually add pagination, since the collection will hopefully grow to hundreds of cars, as you will not want to send the user hundreds of results immediately. Now, create the GET endpoint for finding a single car by its ID.

4. In the same `/routers/cars.py` file, add the following GET handler:

```
@router.get(
    "/{id}",
    response_description="Get a single car by ID",
    response_model=CarModel,
    response_model_by_alias=False,
)
async def show_car(id: str, request: Request):

    cars = request.app.db["cars"]

    try:
        id = ObjectId(id)
    except Exception:
        raise HTTPException(status_code=404, detail=f"Car {id} not
found")
```

```
            if (car := await cars.find_one({"_id": ObjectId(id)})) is not
None:

            return car


        raise HTTPException(status_code=404, detail=f"Car with {id} not
found")
```

The logic of the endpoint is contained in the line that checks whether the collection contains a car with the desired ID and the ID is supplied via a path parameter. The Python walrus operator ( : =), also known as the assignment expression, makes your code more concise: if the car is found (it is not None), it is returned and the operand of the truthiness check—the car instance itself—is passed on; otherwise, the code proceeds to finish with an HTTP exception.

Again, for the HTTPie command for testing, you will need to look up an ID and provide it as a path parameter (your ID value will be different from the following):

```
http http://127.0.0.1:8000/cars/6640e06ad82a890d261a8a40
```

You have implemented two of the most important result listing methods that map to a GET HTTP method: retrieving a list of all items and a specific single item. Other GET endpoints can retrieve queries based on MongoDB aggregations, simpler queries, and filtering, but these two cover the basics.

Now, let's complete the API with the UPDATE and DELETE methods.

## Updating and deleting records

Now you will tackle the most complex endpoint—the PUT method that will be used for updating the car instance. Again, in the same /routers/cars.py file, after the GET routes, continue editing:

```
async def update_car(
    id: str,
    request: Request,
    user=Depends(auth_handler.auth_wrapper),
    car: UpdateCarModel = Body(...),
):

    try:
        id = ObjectId(id)
    except Exception:
        raise HTTPException(status_code=404, detail=f"Car {id} not found")

    car = {
        k: v
        for k, v in car.model_dump(by_alias=True).items()
        if v is not None and k != "_id"
    }
```

The first part of the endpoint function analyzes the provided user data and checks which fields should be updated, by merely acknowledging their presence in the provided `UpdateCarModel` Pydantic model. If the field is present in the request body, its value is passed to the `update` dictionary.

Thus, you get a transformed `car` object that, if not empty, will then be fed to the `find_one_and_ update()` function of MongoDB:

```
if len(car) >= 1:
    cars = request.app.db["cars"]

    update_result = await cars.find_one_and_update(
        {"_id": ObjectId(id)},
        {"$set": car},
        return_document=ReturnDocument.AFTER,
    )
    if update_result is not None:
        return update_result
    else:
        raise HTTPException(status_code=404, detail=f"Car {id} not
found")
```

The update result simply performs the asynchronous update and returns the updated document by leveraging PyMongo's `ReturnDocument.AFTER` to return the document after the update has been performed.

Finally, you must also take into account the case in which none of the fields is set for updating, and simply return the original document if it is found:

```
if (existing_car := await cars.find_one({"_id": id})) is not None:
    return existing_car

raise HTTPException(status_code=404, detail=f"Car {id} not found")
```

The endpoint provides two possibilities of a `404` exception in case the document is not found: when there are fields to be updated and when there are not.

Now, finish the implementation of the basic CRUD functionality with the method for deleting cars:

```
@router.delete("/{id}", response_description="Delete a car")
async def delete_car(
    id: str, request: Request, user=Depends(auth_handler.auth_wrapper)
):

    try:
        id = ObjectId(id)
    except Exception:
        raise HTTPException(status_code=404, detail=f"Car {id} not found")
```

```
cars = request.app.db["cars"]

delete_result = await cars.delete_one({"_id": id})

if delete_result.deleted_count == 1:
    return Response(status_code=status.HTTP_204_NO_CONTENT)

raise HTTPException(status_code=404, detail=f"Car with {id} not found")
```

This is probably the simplest endpoint; if the car with the ID is found, it is deleted and the appropriate HTTP status is returned on an empty (No Content) response.

This concludes the basic CRUD functionality, but before going on, let's tackle another aspect that, while not part of the basic functionality, will incur in every real-life project: result pagination.

### Result pagination

Every application that works with data and users must have an appropriate way to enable and facilitate their communication. Slamming hundreds of results into the browser isn't exactly the best solution.

Results pagination with MongoDB, as well as other databases, is achieved with the help of the skip and limit parameters.

In this case, you will create a simple frontend-friendly pagination system with a custom Pydantic model that will provide two additional JSON properties: the current page and the has_more flag, to indicate whether there are more result pages.

This pattern matches the pagination UI with the arrows and page numbers that indicate the total number of results to the user.

Start by commenting out the existing GET route. Open the models.py file and add the following model:

```
class CarCollectionPagination(CarCollection):
    page: int = Field(ge=1, default=1)
    has_more: bool
```

This model inherits the CarCollection model and adds the two desired fields – this pattern is useful when dealing with large and complex models.

In the cars.py file, after instantiating APIRouter, add a hardcoded constant that will define the number of default results per page:

```
CARS_PER_PAGE = 10
```

Now you will update (or better, replace entirely) the `get all` method in the `routers/cars.py` file:

```
@router.get(
    "/",
    response_description="List all cars, paginated",
    response_model=CarCollectionPagination,
    response_model_by_alias=False,
)
async def list_cars(
    request: Request,
    page: int = 1,
    limit: int = CARS_PER_PAGE,
):
    cars = request.app.db["cars"]

    results = []
```

The first part of the function is very similar to the previous version, but we have two new parameters: `page` and `limit` (the number of results per page). Now, create the actual pagination:

```
cursor = cars.find().sort("companyName").limit(limit).skip((page - 1) *
limit)
    total_documents = await cars.count_documents({})
    has_more = total_documents > limit * page
    async for document in cursor:
        results.append(document)

    return CarCollectionPagination(cars=results, page=page, has_more=has_
more)
```

The bulk of the work is handled directly by MongoDB, with the `limit` and `skip` parameters. The endpoint needs the total number of cars in the collection in order to provide information on the remaining results and their existence.

This endpoint will work just like the previous one so, to properly test it, open MongoDB Compass and import some data. The accompanying GitHub repository contains a file named `cars.csv` with 1,249 cars.

After importing this data, you can perform a GET request like the following:

```
http http://127.0.0.1:8000/cars/?page=12
```

The output should contain a list of cars, as in the previous case, but also the indication of the page and whether there are more results:

```
{
    "has_more": false,
    "page": 12
}
```

Since you are already pulling the total document count from the database, you could extend this pagination model to include either the total number of cars in the database or the total number of pages given the current pagination. That would be a good exercise that showcases how easy it is to extend and modify the FastAPI setup.

You have successfully created a fully functional REST API with FastAPI. Now, let's further enhance the application by providing image-uploading functionality.

# Uploading images to Cloudinary

While FastAPI is perfectly capable of serving static files – through the `StaticFiles` module (`https://fastapi.tiangolo.com/tutorial/static-files/`) – you will rarely want to use your server space and bandwidth to store images or videos.

Many specialized services can take care of digital asset media management and, in this section, you will learn how to work with one of the premier players in the area—**Cloudinary**.

Cloudinary, as its name suggests, is a cloud-based service that provides various solutions for digital media assets and web and mobile applications. These services include uploading and storing images and videos, and these are precisely the functions that we are going to use now.

However, Cloudinary and other similar specialized services offer much more (image and video manipulations, filters, automatic cropping and formatting, and real-time transformations) and they might be an excellent fit for many media workflows, especially very heavy ones.

To be able to use the service, you will first need to create a free account by following the instructions at `https://cloudinary.com/users/register_free`.

After successfully signing up and logging in, you will automatically get assigned a product environment key, visible in the top-left corner. For your purposes, you will only interact through the Python API as you need to be able to upload images to your environment through FastAPI.

To get started with the Python API, or any other for that matter, in addition to this environment key, you will need two more pieces of information: the *API key* and the *API secret*. Both can be obtained from the **Settings** page (`console.cloudinary.com./settings`) and by selecting **API Keys** from the left menu.

Copy the API key and API secret, or create new ones and copy them into your existing .env file:

```
DB_URL=mongodb+srv://xxxxxx:xxxxxxxx@cluster0.fkm24.mongodb.
net/?retryWrites=true&w=majority&appName=Cluster0
DB_NAME=carBackend
CLOUDINARY_SECRET_KEY=xxxxxxxxxxxxxxxx
CLOUDINARY_API_KEY=xxxxxxxxxx
CLOUDINARY_CLOUD_NAME=xxxxxxxx
```

The environment name is mapped as CLOUDINARY_CLOUD_NAME, while the secret key and API key are prepended by CLOUDINARY.

You will also need to modify the config.py file to accommodate the new variables:

```
from typing import Optional
from pydantic_settings import BaseSettings, SettingsConfigDict
class BaseConfig(BaseSettings):
    DB_URL: Optional[str]
    DB_NAME: Optional[str]
    CLOUDINARY_SECRET_KEY: Optional[str]
    CLOUDINARY_API_KEY: Optional[str]
    CLOUDINARY_CLOUD_NAME: Optional[str]

    model_config = SettingsConfigDict(env_file=".env", extra="ignore")
```

The next step is to install the cloudinary Python package:

```
pip install cloudinary
```

Another thing you can do is add it to your requirements.txt file, which, at this point, should look like this:

```
fastapi==0.111.0
motor==3.4.0
uvicorn==0.29.0
httpie==3.2.2
cloudinary==1.40.0
pydantic-settings==2.2.1
```

The Cloudinary documentation is much richer when it comes to JavaScript, and there seem to be a couple of quirks when setting up the upload client, but the essence is simple.

## Updating the models

First, you will update the models.py file to accommodate the new field – a string that will store the URL of the uploaded image from Cloudinary:

1.  Open the models.py file and add just one line in the CarModel class, after the other fields and before the validators:

    ```
    # add the picture file
        picture_url: Optional[str] = Field(None)
    ```

2.  At this point, you should open **MongoDB Compass** and drop the existing cars collection, as you will create a new, empty one. Now, comment out the previous route for the POST handler in the cars.py file and create a new one taking into account the image uploading process.

3.  Cloudinary provides a simple utility module called uploader that needs to be imported, along with the cloudinary module itself. After the existing imports, add the following lines (cars.py):

    ```
    import cloudinary
    from cloudinary import uploader  # noqa: F401
    ```

    These lines import cloudinary and the uploader package, while the # noqa line prevents code linters from removing the line upon saving (as it is imported from a package that is already imported as a whole).

4.  The next step is configuring your Cloudinary instance, and you can do it in the /routers/cars.py file for convenience, although this could be made application-wide.

    To be able to read the environment variables, you will need to instantiate the Settings class again in the same file and pass the variables to the cloudinary configuration object.

5.  Open the cars router and modify it. The first part of the /routers/cars.py file should now look like this:

    ```
    from bson import ObjectId
    from fastapi import (
        APIRouter,
        Body,
        File,
        Form,
        HTTPException,
        Request,
        UploadFile,
        status,
    )
    from fastapi.responses import Response
    from pymongo import ReturnDocument
    ```

```
import cloudinary
from cloudinary import uploader  # noqa: F401
from config import BaseConfig
from models import CarCollectionPagination, CarModel, UpdateCarModel

settings = BaseConfig()
router = APIRouter()
CARS_PER_PAGE = 10

cloudinary.config(
    cloud_name=settings.CLOUDINARY_CLOUD_NAME,
    api_key=settings.CLOUDINARY_API_KEY,
    api_secret=settings.CLOUDINARY_SECRET_KEY,
)
```

Now, you must treat the POST handler differently, since it will accept a form and a file (your car picture) and not JSON anymore. You will need to accept the form data:

```
@router.post(
    "/",
    response_description="Add new car with picture",
    response_model=CarModel,
    status_code=status.HTTP_201_CREATED,
)
async def add_car_with_picture(
    request: Request,
    brand: str = Form("brand"),
    make: str = Form("make"),
    year: int = Form("year"),
    cm3: int = Form("cm3"),
    km: int = Form("km"),
    price: int = Form("price"),
    picture: UploadFile = File("picture"),
):
```

All the CarModel fields are now mapped to form fields with names, while the picture is defined as an UploadFile and expects a file.

Continue with the same function, and add the uploading functionality:

```
cloudinary_image = cloudinary.uploader.upload(
    picture.file, crop="fill", width=800
)
picture_url = cloudinary_image["url"]
```

The code that handles the actual upload is very simple: just a call to uploader with the received file and there are numerous options, transformations, and filters that you could use.

> **Note**
>
> The Cloudinary documentation covers in detail the available transformations: https://cloudinary.com/documentation/transformations_intro.

In your case, you are just cropping the image and setting a maximum width. Cloudinary will return a URL once the picture is uploaded, and that URL will be part of the model, along with the data we used previously.

Finally, you can construct a Pydantic model of the car and pass it to the MongoDB `cars` collection:

```
car = CarModel(
    brand=brand,
    make=make,
    year=year,
    cm3=cm3,
    km=km,
    price=price,
    picture_url=picture_url,
)
```

```
cars = request.app.db["cars"]
document = car.model_dump(by_alias=True, exclude=["id"])
inserted = await cars.insert_one(document)
return await cars.find_one({"_id": inserted.inserted_id})
```

You can test the endpoint through the interactive documentation that FastAPI serves on `127.0.0.1:8000/docs`; just select an image and pass it to the file field that is present in the POST handler for the root route, and don't forget to fill the remaining fields or there will be an error—just like dealing with JSON.

You can also test the route with HTTPie, but first provide an image and name it accordingly:

```
http --form POST 127.0.0.1:8000/cars brand="Ford" make="Focus" year=2000
cm3=1500 price=12000 km=23000 picture="ford.jpg"
```

After having the `Cars` API router ready, now you will create the second router for handling users.

## Adding the user model

You have successfully created a REST API powered by the Cloudinary image hosting and processing power and, following a similar procedure, you could easily integrate other third-party services into your API, making your application more complex and powerful.

Without authentication, however, it would be very risky to deploy even the simplest API online. For instance, a malicious user (or even a kid willing to pull some pranks) could easily "bomb" your API with images that you wouldn't want displayed and in quantities that would quickly fill your free quota. Therefore, before committing your API to GitHub and deploying it—in this case, to Render.com— you will add a user model and a JWT-based authentication scheme very similar to the one shown in *Chapter 6, Authentication and Authorization.*

In the following section, you will create a simple user model and allow users to log in to the application, in order to perform some operations otherwise unavailable – namely, creating, updating, and deleting resources (cars). You will begin by abstracting the authentication logic into a class.

## Creating the authentication functionality

In this section, you will implement an authentication class, similar to the one used in *Chapter 6, Authentication and Authorization,* that will abstract the functionalities needed for authentication and authorization—password encryption, JWT encoding and decoding, and the dependency that will be used for protecting routes. Follow these steps:

1.  First, create a file called authentication.py in the root folder of your project and import the modules needed for authentication:

    ```
    from datetime import datetime
    import jwt
    from fastapi import HTTPException, Security
    from fastapi.security import HTTPAuthorizationCredentials, HTTPBearer
    from passlib.context import CryptContext
    ```

2.  Next, implement an AuthHandler class that will provide all the needed functionality for hashing and verifying passwords and encoding and decoding tokens:

    ```
    class AuthHandler:
        security = HTTPBearer()
        pwd_context = CryptContext(
            schemes=["bcrypt"], deprecated="auto"
        )
        secret = "FARMSTACKsecretString"

        def get_password_hash(self, password):
            return self.pwd_context.hash(password)

        def verify_password(
            self, plain_password, hashed_password
        ):
            return self.pwd_context.verify(
                plain_password, hashed_password
            )
    ```

```
def encode_token(self, user_id, username):
    payload = {
        "exp": datetime.datetime.now(
            datetime.timezone.utc)
        + datetime.timedelta(minutes=30),
        "iat": datetime.datetime.now(datetime.timezone.utc),
        "sub": {
            "user_id": user_id,
            "username": username},
    }
    return jwt.encode(payload, self.secret, algorithm="HS256")

def decode_token(self, token):
try:
    payload = jwt.decode(
        token, self.secret, algorithms=["HS256"]
    )
    return payload["sub"]

except jwt.ExpiredSignatureError:
    raise HTTPException(
        status_code=401,
        detail="Signature has expired"
    )
except jwt.InvalidTokenError:
    raise HTTPException(
        status_code=401,
        detail="Invalid token"
    )
```

3.  Finally, you will end the file with the `auth_wrapper` function, which will be injected as a dependency into the FastAPI endpoints that require an authenticated user:

```
def auth_wrapper(
    self,
    auth: HTTPAuthorizationCredentials =
        Security(security)
):
    return self.decode_token(auth.credentials)
```

The authentication class is nearly identical to the one defined in *Chapter 6, Authentication and Authorization*—it provides methods for password hashing and verification, for JWT encoding and decoding, and a handy `auth_wrapper` method that is used as a dependency injection.

4.  With the `authentication.py` file ready, add the user model, very similar to the one defined in the previous chapter, bearing in mind that this model could be much more complex.

5.  In the `models.py` file, edit the `CarModel` class and add another field—`user_id`. That way, you will be able to associate an inserted car with a particular user and require a valid user for every creation operation:

```python
class CarModel(BaseModel):

    id: Optional[PyObjectId] = Field(alias="_id", default=None)
    brand: str = Field(...)
    make: str = Field(...)
    year: int = Field(..., gt=1970, lt=2025)
    cm3: int = Field(..., gt=0, lt=5000)
    km: int = Field(..., gt=0, lt=500 * 1000)
    price: int = Field(..., gt=0, lt=100000)
    user_id: str = Field(...)
    picture_url: Optional[str] = Field(None)
```

6.  The model for updating the car will not need the `user_id` field as you do not want to make that field editable. Now, after all the car models, let's add the user-related models in the same `models.py` file:

```python
class UserModel(BaseModel):
    id: Optional[PyObjectId] = Field(alias="_id", default=None)
    username: str = Field(..., min_length=3, max_length=15)
    password: str = Field(...)


class LoginModel(BaseModel):
    username: str = Field(...)
    password: str = Field(...)


class CurrentUserModel(BaseModel):
    id: PyObjectId = Field(alias="_id", default=None)
    username: str = Field(..., min_length=3, max_length=15)
```

The three models correspond to the three ways you will be accessing the user data: the full model with all the data, the login and registration model, and the current user that should return `_id` and the username.

## Creating the User router

After the Pydantic models are set up, create a new router for users and allow some basic operations such as registration, logging in, and verifying the user based on the JWT.

Open the file named `users.py` inside the `routers` folder and add the imports:

```
from bson import ObjectId
from fastapi import APIRouter, Body, Depends, HTTPException, Request,
Response
from fastapi.responses import JSONResponse

from authentication import AuthHandler
from models import CurrentUserModel, LoginModel, UserModel

router = APIRouter()
auth_handler = AuthHandler()
```

The `authhandler` class encapsulates all of your authentication logic and you will see this functionality in the endpoint functions.

Let's create the registration route:

```
@router.post("/register", response_description="Register user")
async def register(request: Request, newUser: LoginModel = Body(...)) ->
UserModel:
    users = request.app.db["users"]

    # hash the password before inserting it into MongoDB
    newUser.password = auth_handler.get_password_hash(newUser.password)
    newUser = newUser.model_dump()
    # check existing user or email 409 Conflict:
    if (
        existing_username := await users.find_one({"username":
newUser["username"]})
        is not None
    ):
        raise HTTPException(
            status_code=409,
            detail=f"User with username {newUser['username']} already
exists",
        )
    new_user = await users.insert_one(newUser)
    created_user = await users.find_one({"_id": new_user.inserted_id})
    return created_user
```

The endpoint performs the same functionality as shown in *Chapter 6, Authentication and Authorization*, except, this time, you are working with a real MongoDB collection. The login functionality is also very similar:

```
@router.post("/login", response_description="Login user")
async def login(request: Request, loginUser: LoginModel = Body(...)) ->
str:
    users = request.app.db["users"]

    user = await users.find_one({"username": loginUser.username})

    if (user is None) or (
        not auth_handler.verify_password(loginUser.password,
user["password"])
    ):
        raise HTTPException(status_code=401, detail="Invalid username and/
or password")

    token = auth_handler.encode_token(str(user["_id"]), user["username"])
    Wrong indentation. check and replace with:
response = JSONResponse(
    content={
        "token": token,
        "username": user["username"]
    }
)

    return response
```

If a user is not found by `username` or the password doesn't match, the endpoint responds with an HTTP 401 status and throws a generic message; otherwise, a username and a token are returned.

The final endpoint consists of a `/me` route—a route that will be used periodically by the frontend (React) to check the existing JWT and its validity:

```
@router.get(
    "/me",
    response_description="Logged in user data",
    response_ model=CurrentUserModel
)
async def me(
    request: Request,
    response: Response,
    user_data=Depends(auth_handler.auth_wrapper)
):
    users = request.app.db["users"]
    currentUser = await users.find_one(
        {"_id": ObjectId(user_data["user_id"])}
    )

    return currentUser
```

With the `users` router finished, let's plug it into the `app.py` file, just below the `cars` router:

```
app.include_router(
    cars_router, prefix="/cars", tags=["cars"]
    )
app.include_router(
    users_router, prefix="/users", tags=["users"]
    )
```

The `cars.py` file, which contains the `APIRouter` for managing the cars, will have to be updated to take into account the newly added user data. The creation endpoint will now look like the following:

```
@router.post(
    "/",
    response_description="Add new car with picture",
    response_model=CarModel,
    status_code=status.HTTP_201_CREATED,
)
async def add_car_with_picture(
    request: Request,
    brand: str = Form("brand"),
    make: str = Form("make"),
    year: int = Form("year"),
    cm3: int = Form("cm3"),
    km: int = Form("km"),
    price: int = Form("price"),
    picture: UploadFile = File("picture"),
    user: str =Depends(auth_handler.auth_wrapper),
):
```

The user data is provided through dependency injection and `auth_wrapper`. The rest of the function is largely unaltered—you just need the `user_id` value from the logged-in user:

```
cloudinary_image = cloudinary.uploader.upload(
    picture.file, folder="FARM2", crop="fill", width=800
)
picture_url = cloudinary_image["url"]
car = CarModel(
    brand=brand,
    make=make,
    year=year,
    cm3=cm3,
    km=km,
    price=price,
```

```
        picture_url=picture_url,
        user_id=user["user_id"],
    )


    cars = request.app.db["cars"]
    document = car.model_dump(by_alias=True, exclude=["id"])
    inserted = await cars.insert_one(document)
    return await cars.find_one({"_id": inserted.inserted_id})
```

The API is now quite complete; it handles data of varying complexity and can handle images using a top-quality cloud service. However, before deploying your API to an online cloud platform for the world to see, there is one more thing that needs to be done: setting up the **cross-origin resource sharing (CORS)** middleware.

# FastAPI middleware and CORS

The concept of middleware is common in almost every reputable web framework, and FastAPI is no exception. Middleware is just a function that accepts requests before they are handed over to the path operations for processing and also responds before they are returned.

This simple concept is quite powerful and has many uses—a middleware can check for specific headers that contain authentication data (such as a bearer token) and accept or deny requests accordingly, it can be used for rate limiting (often with the Redis key-value database), and so on.

Creating middleware in FastAPI is based on *Starlette's* middleware, like most web-related concepts in FastAPI, and the documentation provides some nice examples: `https://fastapi.tiangolo.com/tutorial/middleware/`.

In your application, you will use a ready-made middleware to enable the FastAPI-based backend—which will be running on one machine—to communicate with a frontend (in your case, React) running on a different origin.

CORS refers to the policy that is applied when you incur situations when the backend and frontend reside on different origins and, by default, it is very restrictive— allowing only sharing data (such as calling JavaScript fetch functions) between systems using the same origin: the combination of a protocol (HTTP, for instance), domain (such as `www.packt.com`) and a port (for example, `3000` or `80`).

By default, the policy blocks all communication, so if you were to deploy your backend as it is currently, you couldn't reach it from a React.js or Next.js application running even on the same machine but a different port.

FastAPI's solution for this task is achieved through middleware, and it allows granular precision.

In your `app.py` file, import the following to import the CORS middleware:

```
from fastapi.middleware.cors import CORSMiddleware
```

After having imported the middleware, you need to configure it. After instantiating the FastAPI instance with the lifespan, add the middleware:

```
app = FastAPI(lifespan=lifespan)
app.add_middleware(
    CORSMiddleware,
    allow_origins=["*"],
    allow_credentials=True,
    allow_methods=["*"],
    allow_headers=["*"],
)
```

This is a catch-all CORS setup that should be avoided in production, but it will be enough for our purposes and this example backend. The square brackets contain lists of allowed methods (such as POST, GET, and so on), origins, headers, and whether credentials should be allowed.

You can restart the Uvicorn server and check that it works like before. Now, you will deploy the backend on a cloud platform.

# Deployment to Render.com

*Render.com* is one of numerous modern cloud platforms that simplify deploying and managing web applications, APIs, static sites, and other types of software projects. It provides developers with an intuitive and simple interface and powerful automation tools and pipelines.

There are many ways to deploy a FastAPI instance: Vercel (known mainly as the company behind Next.js), Fly.io, Ralway, Heroku, and so on.

In this case, we will choose Render.com as it provides a simple, fast, streamlined deployment procedure, and has a free tier and excellent documentation.

The deployment process can be broken into steps, and you will review each one of them briefly; it is also useful to visit their FastAPI-dedicated page if you wish to get up to speed: https://docs.render.com/deploy-fastapi.

Here are the steps:

1.  Set up a GitHub repo for your backend.

    Again, make sure that your .gitignore file contains entries for the .env file, as well as the env/ directory for the Python environment—you do not want to accidentally commit the secrets and passwords to a public repository, nor do you want to upload the entire virtual environment content.

    If you haven't committed the last changes to your backend, do it now with the following commands:

    ```
    git add .
    git commit -m "ready for deployment"
    ```

Now head to `github.com`, use your credentials to log in, and create a new repository. Name it however you see fit; in this example, we will use the name `FastAPIbackendCh7`.

2. Set up a Render.com account.

Now, head over to `render.com` and create a free account. You can log in with your GitHub account and then navigate to the dashboard link: `dashboard.render.com`.

Locate the **New +** button and select **Web Service**. On the next prompt, select **Build and deploy from a Git repository** and click **Next**.

3. Select the GitHub repository.

In the right-hand menu, select the **GitHub Configure** account and you will be taken to GitHub asking you to install Render. Choose your account, the one you used for the backend repository origin, and proceed to select the repo. This will allow Render to know which repository to pull.

4. Configure the web service.

This is the most important and complex step of the process. Render is informed which repository is involved, and now it has to get all the data necessary for the web service to be deployed. We will examine them one by one:

- **Name**: The name of the service, and it needs to be unique. This name will be part of the deployed service URL.

- **Region**: You should select the region nearest to you in order to reduce latency.

- **Branch**: This tells Render which branch to pull. It will probably be `main`, especially if it is the only branch, as in our case.

- **Root directory**: The directory that contains the main FastAPI instance. In our case, you can leave it blank and it will default to the root `/`.

- **Runtime**: You will be using Python 3; it should be picked up automatically by Render.

- **Build command**: The command that sets up the environment – in your case, the Python 3 virtual environment, so it should be the following:

```
pip install -r requirements.txt
```

- **Start command**: The command that will start the web service once it is installed. Since we are using Uvicorn in production as well, you can refer to Uvicorn's documentation: `https://www.uvicorn.org/settings/`. To allow the service to run on the default port (`80`), the command should be as follows:

```
uvicorn app:app --host 0.0.0.0 --port 80
```

- **Instance type**: You can select the free one, bearing in mind that free instances spin down after periods of inactivity; however, it is more than enough for testing the service.

- **Environment variables**: In these fields, you can now insert your environment variables from the `.env` file, one by one: `DB_URL` and `DB_NAME` for MongoDB, and three Cloudinary variables.

After checking that you have entered all the settings and variables, you can finally click the blue **Create Web Service** button.

The final settings page will look similar to the following images. The settings page is quite long and you will have to scroll a bit, but the first thing that has to be specified are the name of the service and the region:

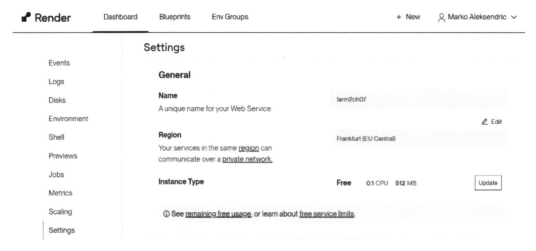

Figure 7.1: The Render web service general settings page

After setting the name and the region, you will see your selected repository and the branch to be deployed (**main**, in your case). You can leave the root directory empty by default.

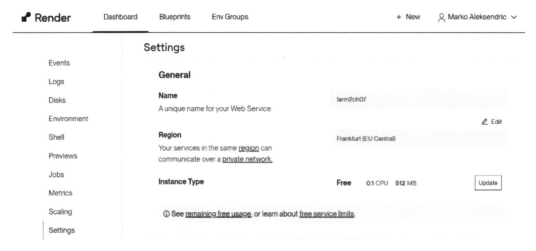

Figure 7.2: The repository and the branch settings

Next, you will specify the build and the start command. The build command is the one that installs your Python environment, while the start command starts the web service – your API.

Figure 7.3: The build and start commands

The last step before starting the actual deployment command is to pass the environment variables to Render.com:

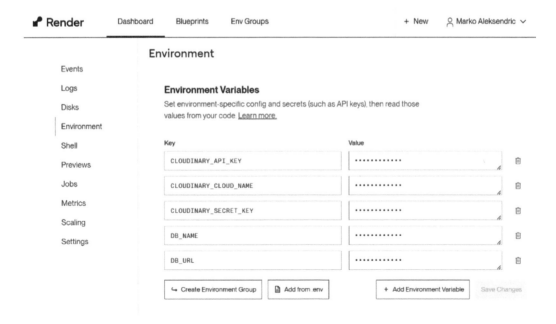

Figure 7.4: The environment variables

After initiating the deployment procedure, you will have to wait a bit—the service will have to create a new Python environment, install all the required dependencies, and start the service. After the process is complete, you can click on the URL on the page (in your case, it will be `https://farm2ch7.onrender.com` you will have to use another address) and you can check your API online.

Your API is now live on the internet and ready to receive requests. It is worth mentioning that due to the recent rise of FastAPI's popularity, more and more hosting and **software-as-a-service** (**SaaS**) providers are providing detailed instructions for hosting FastAPI services. They all share a similar logic—you will have to provide a requirements file to let the platform know what your app needs to be functional, and you will have to provide a GitHub repo with the code. A particularly important step is the handling of the environment variables. They are usually provided manually, although some providers accept entire `.env` files.

## Summary

In this chapter, you have taken a simple business requirement and turned it into a fully functional API deployed on the internet.

You have created the Pydantic models and applied some constraints on the data structure, learned how to connect to a MongoDB Atlas instance, and developed a basic, yet fully functional, CRUD functionality FASTAPI service.

You have learned how to model entities (in your case, cars and users) through Pydantic and how to make the data flow seamlessly to and from your database of choice – MongoDB – through simple pythonic FastAPI endpoints.

You have managed the secret keys – for connecting to MongoDB Atlas and Cloudinary – through `pydantic_settings` and you have crafted simple, yet flexible models that can easily accommodate more requirements, be expanded or include more functionality.

The service is now ready to be used in the frontend – ultimately, giving life to a full-stack web application.

In the next chapter, you will add a simple user model to this same API and build a React frontend that will consume the FastAPI backend.

# 8

# Building the Frontend of the Application

In the previous chapter, you explored how to build your FastAPI backend and connect to MongoDB. This will be used by a React frontend that you will be building in this chapter. The application will be simple and feature-rich and, most importantly, will allow you to see the parts of the stack working together.

In this chapter, you will build the frontend of a full-stack FARM application. You will learn how to set up a React Vite application and install and set up React Router, as well as various ways of loading content. The application will enable authenticated users to insert new items (cars), while there will be several pages for displaying cars.

You will develop a website that will list used cars for sale and allow only logged-in users to post new car ads. You will begin by creating a React application with Vite, then you will lay out the page structure with React Router and gradually introduce features such as authentication, protected pages, and data loading. After this chapter, you will be able to comfortably leverage React Router for your **single-page-applications (SPAs)** and use the powerful **React Hook Form (RHF)** for granular form control.

This chapter will cover the following topics:

- Creating a new React application using Vite
- Setting up the React Router for SPA page navigation
- Managing data with data loaders
- Introduction to RHF and Zod for data validation
- Authentication and authorization with the Context API
- Protecting routes and displaying data with React Router pages

## Technical requirements

The technical requirements for this chapter are similar to the ones listed in *Chapter 4, Getting Started with FastAPI*. You will need the following:

- Node version 18.14
- A good code editor, such as Visual Studio Code
- The Node package manager

## Creating a Vite React application

In this section you will scaffold a Vite React application and set up Tailwind CSS for styling. This procedure has already been covered in *Chapter 5, Setting Up a React workflow,*, so you can refer to it. Make sure to complete the brief tutorial in *Chapter 5*, as the following guide is heavily based on the concepts presented therein.

You are going to use the `create vite` command with the Node package manager to create your project through the following steps:

1. Open your terminal client in a project directory containing the previously created backend folder, and issue the following command for creating a Vite React project:

```
npm create vite@latest frontend-app -- --template react
```

2. Now, change the directory to the newly created `frontend-app` folder and install the dependencies and Tailwind:

```
npm install -D tailwindcss postcss autoprefixer
```

3. Initialize the Tailwind configuration—the following command creates a blank Tailwind configuration file:

```
npx tailwindcss init -p
```

4. Finally, configure the generated `tailwind.config.js` and React's `index.css` files according to the latest documentation at `https://tailwindcss.com/docs/guides/vite`.

Your index.css should now include only the Tailwind imports:

```
@tailwind base;
@tailwind components;
@tailwind utilities;
```

To test that Tailwind has been properly configured, change the `App.jsx` file and start the development server:

```
export default function App() {
  return ( <
    h1 className = "text-3xl font-bold" >
    Cars FARM <
    /h1>
  )
}
```

When you refresh your app, you should see a white page with the text **Cars FARM**.

After setting up a functional React application and Tailwind, it is time to introduce probably the most important third-party React package—React Router.

## React Router

Up to this point, all of your components have fit onto a single page because you were building SPAs. To enable your application to display completely different pages based on the provided route, you will use a package called React Router—the de facto standard when it comes to page routing in React.

While there are some very good and robust alternatives, such as TanStack Router (`https://tanstack.com/router/`), React Router is widely adopted, and getting to know its basic mechanisms will greatly benefit you, as a developer, as you are bound to run into code based on it.

Version 6.4 of React Router has some major changes while retaining previous basic principles, which you will use to build your frontend. However, as of May 2024, even more drastic changes have been announced—**React Remix**, an entire full-stack framework (with functionalities comparable to Next.js), which is based on React Router, and React Router itself should be merged into a single project. In this section, you will learn about the most important components that will allow you to create a single-page experience without page reloading or having knowledge of React Router 6.4, which will be very useful later, as it is the most widely adopted React routing solution.

The basic underlying principle of React Router is to listen to URL path changes (such as `/about` or `/login`) and conditionally display components in a layout. The displayed components can be thought of as "pages," while the layout keeps some parts of the pages that should always be displayed—such as a footer and navigation.

Before looking at React Router, review the pages that you will have in your application:

- **Home page**: This will contain some generic information, corresponding to the root (`/`) path
- **A car list page**: This will display all the cars in the database (`/cars`)
- **An individual car page**: This will provide additional details about the cars (`/cars/car_id`)
- **A login page**: This allows users (in your case administrators) to log in (`/login`)
- **An "insert new car" page**: This will provide a form for the authenticated user only

For simplicity, you will not include a registration route (since there will only be a couple of authenticated employees) and there will not be a deleting or updating functionality on the frontend. In the following section, you will install and configure React Router and make it the basis of your application.

## Installing and setting up React Router

React Router is just a Node.js package, so the installation process is easy. The setting up of the router inside the application, however, includes lots of features and different options. You will be using the most powerful and recommended data router, which provides data loading and is the suggested option by the React Router team.

Working with the router generally involves two steps:

1. Using one of the provided methods for generating the desired routes (`https://reactrouter.com/en/main/routers/picking-a-router`).

2. Creating components, often called **pages**, that will correspond to different routes, such as `Login.jsx` and `Home.jsx`. Additionally, you will almost always create one or more layouts that will contain common components such as the navigation or the footer.

Now, you will perform the steps necessary to install React Router into your application:

1. The first step, as with any third-party package, is to install the `router` package:

   ```
   npm i react-router-dom@6.23.1
   ```

   The version number corresponds to the latest version at the time of writing, so you can reproduce the exact functionality.

   In this chapter, the CSS styling of the application will intentionally be kept to a bare minimum—just enough to distinguish between components.

2. Start by creating a new directory called `/pages` inside the `/src` folder and scaffolding all your pages. The page names will be `Home`, `Cars`, `Login`, `NewCar`, `NotFound`, and `SingleCar`, all with the `.jsx` extensions and you will perform the scaffolding of these other pages the same way as the `Home.jsx` page.

The first component, located at `/src/pages/Home.jsx`, will look like this:

```
const Home = () => {
    return (
        <div>Home</div>
    )
}
export default Home
```

Although they are often referred to as pages when speaking about React Router, these pages are nothing more than regular React components. The distinction, and the fact that they are often grouped together in a directory called `pages`, is based purely on the fact that these components correspond to the pages structure of a SPA and are generally not meant to be reused elsewhere.

3.   After scaffolding the desired pages, implement the router. This procedure consists of creating the router and inserting it into a top-level React component. You will use the `App.jsx` component, which loads and inserts the entire React application in the DOM.

Since version 6.4, React Router has introduced the possibility of fetching data before the route (or page) that needs the said data is loaded, through simple functions called **data loaders**. To highlight this functionality that has become fundamental to the entire ecosystem, you will need to create the router through `createBrowserRouter` (`https://reactrouter.com/en/main/routers/create-browser-router`) since it is *the recommended router for all React Router web projects*, as stated in the documentation.

After selecting `createBrowserRouter` as the desired method of creating the router, it is time to integrate it into your application.

### Integrating the router with the application

In the following steps, you will integrate the router into your application, create a `Layout` component, and plug in the components (pages) that will be loaded on each defined URI:

1.   To properly configure the router, you will need another component—the `Layout` component—in which the previously created pages will be rendered. Inside the `/src` folder, create a `/layouts` folder and create a `RootLayout.jsx` file inside it:

```
const RootLayout = () => {
  return (
    <div>RootLayout</div>
  )
}
export default RootLayout
```

The React router that you will be using and the one that supports data loading is based on three imports from the `react-router-dom` package: `createBrowserRouter`, `createRoutesFromElements`, and `Route`.

2.   Open the `App.jsx` file and import the packages and the previously created pages:

```
import {
  createBrowserRouter,
  Route,
  createRoutesFromElements,
  RouterProvider
} from "react-router-dom"

import RootLayout from "./layouts/RootLayout"

import Cars from "./pages/Cars"
import Home from "./pages/Home"
import Login from "./pages/Login"
import NewCar from "./pages/NewCar"
import SingleCar from "./pages/SingleCar"
```

3.   Now, continuing with the same `App.jsx` file, hook up the router created from the elements that you just imported and defined:

```
const router = createBrowserRouter(
  createRoutesFromElements(
    <Route path="/" element={<RootLayout />}>
      <Route index element={<Home />} />
      <Route path="cars" element={<Cars />} />
      <Route path="login" element={<Login />} />
      <Route path="new-car" element={<NewCar />} />
      <Route path="cars/:id" element={<SingleCar />} />
    </Route>
  )
)

export default function App() {
  return (
    <RouterProvider router={router} />
  )
}
```

There are a few important things to note in the preceding code. After creating the router, you invoked the React Router function called `createRoutesFromElements`, which creates the actual routes. A route is used to define an individual path that corresponds and maps to a component; it can be a self-closing tag (such as the ones used for the pages) or it can enclose other routes—such as the home page path, which in turn corresponds to `RootLayout`.

If you start the React server again and visit the page `http://localhost:5173`, you will see only the text `RootLayout`. Try navigating to any of the routes defined in the router: `/cars`, `/cars/333`, or `/login`. You will see the same `RootLayout` text, but if you enter a path that is not defined, such as `/about`, React will inform you that the page doesn't exist with a message similar to this: `Unexpected Application Error! 404 Not Found`.

This means that the router is indeed working; it is not set up to handle cases in which the user navigates to an undefined route and it does not display the contents of the pages. Now you will fix both problems.

### Creating the layout and the NotFound page

In order to work properly, the router needs a place to display the content of pages— remember that "pages" are just React components. Now you will create `Layout.jsx` and also handle cases in which a user hits a URI that doesn't exist, resulting in a `Page Not Found` error:

1.  First, create a new page in the `/src/pages` directory and name it `NotFound.jsx`, with the following content:

    ```
    const NotFound = () => {
      return (
        <div>This page does not exist yet!</div>
      )
    }
    export default NotFound
    ```

    Now, create a catch-all route that will display the *Not Found* page in cases where the path doesn't match any defined route. Remember that the order of routes is important—React Router will attempt to match routes sequentially, so it makes sense to use the * symbol to catch all previously undefined routes and associate them with the `NotFound` component.

2.  Update the `App.jsx` file to display the `NotFound` route as the last route in the `RootLayout` route:

    ```
    createRoutesFromElements(
      <Route path="/" element={<RootLayout />}>
        <Route index element={<Home />} />
        // more routes here…
        <Route path="*" element={<NotFound />} />
      </Route>
    )
    ```

    To achieve the main functionality of the router—displaying other components/pages in the layout component—you will use the `Outlet` component, which is a special React Router component that is used to nest routes inside routes. Your router currently has one parent route—the one defined with the following:

    ```
    <Route path="/" element={<RootLayout />}>
    ```

All the other pages are nested. You will need to modify RootLayout (which will always be loaded, even for non-existing routes!) and provide the Outlet component for rendering page-specific components.

3.  Open RootLayout.jsx and modify it:

```
import { Outlet } from "react-router-dom"
const RootLayout = () => {
    return (
        <div className=" bg-blue-200 min-h-screen p-2">
            <h2>RootLayout</h2>
            <main className="p-8 flex flex-col flex-1 bg-white ">
                <Outlet />
            </main>
        </div>
    )
}
export default RootLayout
```

With the Outlet component now in place, you have achieved routing. If you try to navigate to the pages defined in the router, you should see the page update with the component content, in which the layout is displayed as before, but the Outlet component changes and displays the content of the page selected in the URL.

The whole point of using the router is to achieve navigation through "pages" without having to reload the page.

4.  Now, to finalize the RootLayout component, you will update the component and add some links, using the provided NavLink component from React Router:

```
import {
  Outlet,
  NavLink
} from "react-router-dom"
const RootLayout = () => {
  return (
    <div className=" bg-blue-200 min-h-screen p-2">
      <h2>RootLayout</h2>
      <header className="p-8 w-full">
        <nav className="flex flex-row
          justify-between">
          <div className="flex flex-row space-x-3">
            <NavLink to="/">Home</NavLink>
            <NavLink to="/cars">Cars</NavLink>
            <NavLink to="/login">Login</NavLink>
            <NavLink to="/new-car">New Car</NavLink>
```

```
                </div>
               </nav>
           </header>
           <main className="p-8 flex flex-col flex-1
              bg-white ">
              <Outlet />
           </main>
         </div>
      )
   }
   export default RootLayout
```

Now you have a simple navigation in place and the NotFound page loads when needed. The router also provides navigation history, so the browser's back and forward buttons are functional. The app styling is intentionally minimalistic and used only to underline the different components.

So far, you have only one layout, but there could potentially be more—one for the cars list page and the individual car pages—embedded into the main layout. Just like APIRouters from FastAPI, React routes and layouts can be nested. React Router's nesting is a powerful feature that enables the construction of layered websites that load or update only the necessary components.

After having set up the React Router, let's explore an important feature that is available only when using data routers, such as the one you used—data loaders—special functions that allow developers to access data in a more efficient way.

## React Router loaders

Loaders are simply functions that can provide data to the route before it loads (https://reactrouter.com/en/main/route/loader) through a simple React hook.

In order to use some data, first create a new .env file and add the address of your Python backend:

```
VITE_API_URL=http://127.0.0.1:8000
```

If you restart the server now, Vite will be able to pick up the address in your code and the URI will be available at import.meta.env.VITE_API_URL.

> **Note**
> To learn more about how Vite handles environment variables, head over to their documentation: https://vitejs.dev/guide/env-and-mode.

Now you will learn how React Router manages data loading and prefetching. Perform the following steps to load data from your backend into the React application and learn how to use the powerful and simple useLoader Hook.

First, work on the `/src/pages/Cars.jsx` component to see how data loaders can help you manage component data:

1.  Create a `src/components` folder and inside, create a simple static React component in the `CarCard.jsx` file for displaying a single car:

```
const CarCard = ({ car }) => {
  return (
    <div className="flex flex-col p-3 text-black
      bg-white rounded-xl overflow-hidden shadow-md
      hover:scale-105 transition-transform
      duration-200">
      <div>{car.brand} {car.make} {car.year} {car.cm3}
        {car.price} {car.km}
      </div>
      <img src={car.picture_url} alt={car.make}
        className="w-full h-64 object-cover
        object-center" />
    </div>
  )
}
export default CarCard
```

With the `Card` component out of the way, you can now see how the data loader works.

Loaders are functions that provide data to the components in the router before they are rendered. These functions are usually defined and exported from the same component, although this is not mandatory.

2.  Open `Cars.jsx` and update it accordingly:

```
import { useLoaderData } from "react-router-dom"
import CarCard from "../components/CarCard"
const Cars = () => {
  const cars = useLoaderData()
  return (
    <div>
      <h1>Available cars</h1>
      <div className="md:grid md:grid-cols-3 sm:grid
        sm:grid-cols-2 gap-5">
        {cars.map(car => (
          <CarCard key={car.id} car={car} />
        ))}
      </div>
    </div>
  )
```

```
    }
    export default Cars
```

The component imports useLoaderData—a custom hook provided by React Router whose sole purpose is to provide the data from the loader function to the component that needs it. This paradigm is at the heart of React Remix and similar to some Next.js functionalities, so it is useful to get acquainted with. The useLoader function will contain the data from the server, usually in JSON format.

3. Now, export the carsLoader function as well in the same file:

```
    export const carsLoader = async () => {
      const res = await fetch(
        `${import.meta.env.VITE_API_URL}/cars?limit=30`
        )
      const response = await res.json()
      if (!res.ok){
        throw new Error(response.message)
      }
      return response['cars']
    }
```

> **Note**
>
> These two pieces—the component and the function—are not connected. This connection must happen in the router and allow preloading of data at the router level.

4. Now you will connect the component and the loader through the router. Open the App.jsx file and modify the code by providing the loader argument to the /cars route:

```
    import Cars, { carsLoader } from "./pages/Cars"
    // continues
      <Route path="/" element={<RootLayout />}>
        <Route index element={<Home />} />
        <Route path="cars" element={<Cars />}
          loader={carsLoader} />
          <Route path="login" element={<Login />} />
          <Route path="new-car" element={<NewCar />} />
          <Route path="cars/:id"
            element={<SingleCar />} />
          <Route path="*" element={<NotFound />} />
      </Route>
```

With the loader now in place, you are ready to test your /cars page, which should be displaying the cars saved in the collection so far.

The next few sections will explore the implementation of another piece of functionality that you will likely encounter in every React (or Next.js, or web development in general) project—handling forms with React with RHF. You will implement the login functionality with the help of the most popular third-party package for handling forms with React, and also perform data validation with the Zod package.

# React Hook Form and Zod

There are many ways of handling forms with React, and one of the most common patterns was shown in *Chapter 5, Setting Up a React Workflow*. State variables are created with the useState Hook, the form is prevented from submitting and is intercepted, and, finally, the data is passed through JSON or as form data. While this workflow is acceptable when working with simple data and a couple of fields, it can quickly become difficult to manage in cases where you have to keep track of dozens of fields, their constraints, and their possible states.

RHF is a mature project with a thriving community and is distinguished from other similar libraries by its speed, minimal amount of rendering, and deep integration with the most popular data validation libraries for TypeScript and JavaScript, such as Zod and Yup. In this case, you will learn the basics of Zod.

## Performing data validation with Zod

The JavaScript and TypeScript ecosystem currently has several validation libraries—with Zod and Yup arguably being the most popular ones. Zod is a TypeScript-first schema declaration and validation library that provides data validation of data structures. Zod provides a simple and intuitive object-based syntax for creating complex validation rules for objects and values in JavaScript applications and greatly facilitates the process of ensuring data integrity across the application.

The basic idea of these packages is to provide them with a prototype of the desired data structure and to perform a validation of the data against said defined data structure:

1.  First, install the package:

    ```
    npm i react-hook-form@7.51.5
    ```

    Since the version number at the time of writing and used in the book's repository is 7.51.5, use the preceding command if you want to reproduce the exact code from the repository.

2.  Update the Login.jsx component and make it display LoginForm, which you will create shortly:

    ```
    import LoginForm from "../components/LoginForm"
    const Login = () => {
      return (
      <div>
        <h1>Login</h1>
        <LoginForm />
      </div>
      )
    ```

```
    }
    export default Login
```

3.  Now, the `/src/components/LoginForm.jsx` file will contain all the form functionality as well as the data validation with Zod:

```
import { useForm } from "react-hook-form"
import { z } from 'zod';
import { zodResolver } from '@hookform/resolvers/zod';

const schema = z.object({
  username: z.string().min(4, 'Username must be at least 4 characters
long').max(10, 'Username cannot exceed 10 characters'),
  password: z.string().min(4, 'Password must be at least 4 characters
long').max(10, 'Password cannot exceed 10 characters'),
});
```

The component begins with the imports—the `useForm` hook and Zod, as well as the Zod resolver for integration with the form hook. Data validation in Zod is similar to how it is in Pydantic—you define an object and set the desired properties on various fields. In this case, we set that the username and password is between 4 and 10 characters long, but Zod allows for some very complex validation, as you can see on their website (`https://zod.dev/`).

The `useForm` Hook provides several useful functions:

-   `register` is used to register single-form fields with the hook

-   `handleSubmit` is the function that will be called upon submission

-   `formState` contains different information about the form state (`https://react-hook-form.com/docs/useform/formstate`)

4.  Now, set up the `form` Hook:

```
const LoginForm = () => {
  const { register, handleSubmit,
    formState: { errors } } = useForm({
      resolver: zodResolver(schema),
    });
  const onSubmitForm = (data) => {
      console.log(data)
    }
```

In this case, you will only track the errors (tied to the validation defined previously with Zod), but this object tracks much more. In your code, you'll just output the data to the console once it is validated.

5.  Now, build the form's JSX and add some styling to see what's happening:

```
return (
  <div className="flex items-center justify-center">
    <div className="w-full max-w-xs">
      <form className="bg-white shadow-md rounded
        px-8 pt-6 pb-8 mb-4"
        onSubmit={handleSubmit(onSubmitForm)}>
```

The component will output some mildly styled JSX containing the form and the form onSubmit event is bound to the handle. This process is quite simple: the form has an onSubmit method that you handed over to the handleSubmit method of RHF. This handleSubmit method is destructured from the hook itself, along with the register function (for mapping input fields) and the errors that reside in the form state. After establishing the connection, the handleSubmit method needs to know which function should process the form and its data. In this case, it should pass the handling to the onSubmitForm function.

The two form fields, for the username and the password, are nearly identical:

```
<div className="mb-4">
  <label htmlFor="username" className="block
    text-gray-700 text-sm font-bold mb-2">
    Username
  </label>
  <input id="username" type="text"
    placeholder="Username" required
    {...register('username')}
    className="shadow appearance-none border
      rounded w-full py-2 px-3 text-gray-700
      leading-tight focus:outline-none
      focus:shadow-outline"/>
    {errors.username && <p className="text-red-500
      text-xs italic">{errors.username.message}</p>}
</div>
```

The highlighted parts of the code are the registration of the fields with the useForm Hook—a way of letting the form know which fields to expect and the errors (if they are present) that are related to their respective fields.

This way, the fields are registered to the hook form through this spread operator syntax. Since the errors provided by the form are bound to the fields, take this opportunity and show them next to the fields that report errors for a more pleasing user experience.

The rest of the component is intuitive and covers the `password` field and the `submit` button:

```
<div className="mb-6">
  <label htmlFor="password" className="block text-gray-700
    text-sm font-bold mb-2">Password</label>
  <input id="password" type="password" placeholder="****"
    required
    {...register('password')}
    className="shadow appearance-none border rounded w-full
    py-2 px-3 text-gray-700 mb-3 leading-tight
    focus:outline-none focus:shadow-outline" />
  {errors.password && <p className="text-red-500 text-xs
    italic">{errors.password.message}</p>}
</div>
<div className="flex items-center justify-between">
        <button type="submit">Sign In</button>
      </div>
    </form>
  </div>
</div>
  )
}
export default LoginForm
```

The complete code from the book is available in the book repository.

The form is now ready and is handled completely by the hook form with a Zod validation. If you try to input data that doesn't meet the validation criteria (username or password shorter than four characters, for instance) you will get an error message next to the fields. After setting up the form for logging in, you will create an authentication context that will allow the user to stay logged in. The authentication process—the creation of a React context and storing the JWT—will be very similar to the one covered in *Chapter 6, Authentication and Authorization*, so this next section only covers and highlights the important parts of the code.

## Authentication context and storing the JWT

In this section, you will use your brand-new form, powered by RHF, and connect it to the Context API. The procedure for defining a React Context API was covered in detail in *Chapter 4, Getting Started with FastAPI* and in this chapter, you will apply that knowledge and create a similar context for keeping track of the authentication state of the application:

1.  Create a new folder in the `/src` directory and name it `contexts`. Inside this folder, create a new file called `AuthContext.jsx` and create the provider:

    ```
    import { createContext, useState, useEffect } from 'react';
    import { Navigate } from 'react-router-dom';

    export const AuthContext = createContext();
    export const AuthProvider = ({ children }) => {
      const [user, setUser] = useState(null);
      const [jwt, setJwt] =  useState(localStorage.getItem('jwt')||null);
      const [message, setMessage] = useState(
        "Please log in"
      );
    ```

    The context that you are creating is rather simple and contains a couple of state variables and setters that will be needed for the authentication flow: the username (whose presence or absence thereof will indicate whether the user is authenticated), the JWT, and a helper message that, in this case, is only useful for debugging and illustration.

    The initial values are set to `null` and a generic message through the `useState` hook—the username is set to `null`, the JWT to an empty string, and the message to `Please log in`.

2.  Next, add a `useEffect` hook that will fire once the context is loaded or when the page is reloaded:

    ```
    useEffect(() => {
      const storedJwt = localStorage
        .getItem('jwt');
      if(storedJwt) {
        setJwt(storedJwt);
        fetch(
          `${import.meta.env.VITE_API_URL}/users/me`, {
          headers: {
          Authorization: `Bearer ${storedJwt}`,
          },
            })
        .then(res => res.json())
    ```

The first part of the useEffect hook checks whether there is a JWT present in the local storage. If it is present, the useEffect hook performs an API call to the FastAPI server to determine whether the JWT is able to return a valid user:

```
.then(data => {
  if(data.username) {
    setUser({user: data.username});
    setMessage(`Welcome back, ${data.username}!`);
  } else {
```

If the token is invalid or it has been tampered with or has expired, the useEffect hook removes it from local storage, sets the context state variables to null, and sets an appropriate message to the users:

```
localStorage.removeItem(
  'jwt');
setJwt(null);
setUser(null);
setMessage(data.message)

}
})
.catch(() => {
  localStorage
    .removeItem(
      'jwt');
  setJwt(null);
  setUser(null);
  setMessage(
    'Please log in or register'
  );
});
}
else {
  setJwt(null);
  setUser(null);
  setMessage(
    'Please log in or register'
  );
}
}, []); };
```

To sum it up, the `useEffect` hook performs a cycle. First, it checks for the local storage and if it doesn't find a JWT, it deletes the JWT from the context, sets the username to `null`, and prompts the user to log in. The same result is obtained if the API call to the `/me` route, with the existing JWT, does not yield a valid username. This means that the token is present, but invalid or expired. If the JWT is indeed present and it can be used in order to obtain a valid username, the username is then set and the JWT is stored in the *Context*. Since the dependency array is empty, this hook will run only once on the first render.

## Implementing the login functionality

The login function will reside again inside the context for simplicity, although it could be in a separate file. Following is the login flow:

1.  The user provides their username and password.

2.  A fetch call to the backend is performed.

3.  If the response has an HTTP status of `200` and the JWT is returned, `localStorage` is set, as well as the context, and the user is authenticated.

4.  If the response doesn't return an HTTP status of `200`, it means that the login information was not accepted and, in that case, both the JWT and the username values are set to `null` in the context and effectively invalidated.

To implement the login functionality, perform these steps:

1.  First, the `login` function needs to call the login API route with the provided username and password. Paste the following code into the end of the `AuthContext.jsx` file:

```
const login = async (username,
  password) => {  const response = await fetch(`${import.meta.env.
VITE_API_URL}/users/login`, {
      method: 'POST',
      headers: {
        'Content-Type': 'application/json',
      },
      body: JSON.stringify({
        username,
        password
      }),
    });
```

2.  Next, depending on the response, the function will set the state variables in the context accordingly:

```
const data = await response
  .json();
if (response.ok) {
  setJwt(data.token);
  localStorage.setItem('jwt', data
    .token);
  setUser(data.username);
  setMessage(
    `Login successful: welcome  ${data.username}`
  );
} else {
  setMessage('Login failed: ' +
    data.detail);
  setUser(null)
  setJwt(null);
  localStorage.removeItem('jwt');
}
return data
};
```

The logic is similar to the one applied in the useEffect hook—if a valid user is found, the context state variables (username and JWT) are set; otherwise, they are set to null.

3.  The final part is just the logout function and the returning of the context provider. The following logout function is defined inside AuthProvider:

```
const logout = () => {
  setUser(null);
  setJwt(null);
  localStorage.removeItem('jwt');
  setMessage('Logout successful');
};

return ( <
  AuthContext.Provider value = {
```

```
      {
        username,
        jwt,
        login,
        logout,
        message,
        setMessage
      }
    } > {
      children
    } <
    /AuthContext.Provider>
  );
```

At this point you have accomplished quite a lot: you have set up the context, defined the login and logout functions, and created the context provider. Now, to facilitate the use of the context, you will create a simple custom React hook, based on the useContext built-in hook.

### Creating a custom hook for accessing the context

With the Context API set up, you can now proceed and create a useAuth.jsx file inside a new folder, /src/hooks, which will allow easy access to the context from various places:

1.  Create the useAuth.jsx file inside the new folder:

```
import {
  useContext
} from "react";
import {
  AuthContext
} from "../contexts/AuthContext";

export const useAuth = () => {
  const context = useContext(
    AuthContext)

  if (!context) {
    throw new Error(
      'Must be used within an AuthProvider'
      )
  }

    return context
  }
```

The useAuth hook contains an error message in case the hook is accessed outside of the context—but your context will enclose the entire application.

The final step in using a React context is to wrap the components that will need to access it; in your case, this will be `App.jsx`—the root component.

2.  Open the `App.jsx` file and wrap the only component that it is currently returning— `RouterProvider`—**inside** `AuthProvider`:

```
import { AuthProvider } from "./contexts/AuthContext"
// continues
export default function App() {
  return (
    <AuthProvider>
      <RouterProvider router={router} />
    </AuthProvider>
  )
}
```

Finally, display the context data and the state variables inside the `RootLayout` component that currently hosts all of your pages. This is a useful debugging technique while working with React Context API; you do not need to switch to and from the developer tools constantly.

3.  Open `RootLayout.jsx` and edit the file:

```
import { Outlet, NavLink } from "react-router-dom"
import { useAuth } from "../hooks/useAuth"

const RootLayout = () => {
    const { user, message, logout } = useAuth()
```

4.  After having access to the various state variables and the `logout` function, you can now add a little bit of JSX conditional rendering and create a dynamic menu:

```
const RootLayout = () => {
  const {
    user,
    message,
    logout
  } = useAuth()

  return (
    <div className=" bg-blue-200 min-h-screen p-2">
      <h2>RootLayout</h2>
      <p className="text-red-500 p-2 border">
        {message}
      </p>
      <p>Username: {user}</p>
      <header className="p-3 w-full">
```

```
            <nav className="flex flex-row justify-between
              mx-auto">
            <div className="flex flex-row space-x-3">
              <NavLink to="/">Home</NavLink>
              <NavLink to="/cars">Cars</NavLink>
                {user ? <>
              <NavLink to="/new-car">New Car</NavLink>
                <button onClick={logout}>Logout</button>
              </> : <>
              <NavLink to="/login">Login</NavLink>
              </>}
            </div>
          </nav>
        </header>
        <main className="p-8 flex flex-col flex-1
          bg-white ">
          <Outlet />
        </main>
          </div>
        )
    }
    export default RootLayout
```

The application is rather simple, but it showcases the login/logout process well. As an exercise, you could easily implement the registration page—the API endpoint already exists and you should create the logic for handling the register form.

The following section will focus on completing some more functionality—the route for inserting new cars is still reachable for users who are not logged in and the form doesn't exist yet. Now you will secure the resource creation endpoint and create protected pages with React Router.

## Protecting routes

Protected routes are routes and pages that are not accessible to everyone—they usually require the user to be logged in or to have certain privileges (admin or creator). There are many ways of protecting routes in React Router. One popular pattern is through high-order components—they are wrapper components that wrap routes that require a logged-in user. The new React Router and its Outlet component allow you to easily implement gate logic and redirect the user if they need to be authorized.

Create a basic component that checks for the presence of a user (through the username). If the user is present, the component will use an Outlet component to let the wrapped routes make their way to the browser; otherwise, a redirect to the login page will ensue:

1. Create a new component in the /src/components folder and name it AuthRequired.jsx:

```jsx
import {
  Outlet,
  Navigate
} from "react-router-dom"
import {
  useAuth
} from "../hooks/useAuth"
const AuthRequired = () => {

  const {
    jwt
  } = useAuth()

  return (
    <div>
        <h1>AuthRequired</h1>

        {jwt ? <Outlet /> : <Navigate to="/login" />}

      </div>
  )
}
export default AuthRequired
```

The logic is simple; the component ensures you perform the JWT presence check. It then acts like a semaphore or a simple IF construct that checks for a condition—if a JWT is present, the Outlet component will show the enclosed components (in our case only one: the NewCar page), and if not, React Router's Navigate component is used for programmatic navigation to the home page.

This simple solution will not force the authenticated user to be redirected to the home page if they reload a protected page, since the useEffect hook in Layout.jsx will detect whether the JWT is invalid only after the component loads. If the JWT is indeed invalid, the useEffect hook will invalidate the JWT, thus triggering the redirect.

2. Now, update the `App.jsx` component, import the `AuthRequired` component, and enclose the `NewCar` page:

```
import AuthRequired from "./components/AuthRequired"
import { AuthProvider } from "./contexts/AuthContext"
// code continues
const router = createBrowserRouter(
  createRoutesFromElements(
    <Route path="/" element={<RootLayout />}>
      <Route index element={<Home />} />
      <Route path="cars" element={<Cars />} loader={carsLoader} />
      <Route path="login" element={<Login />} />
      <Route element={<AuthRequired />}>
        <Route path="new-car" element={<NewCar />} />
      </Route>
      <Route path="cars/:id" element={<SingleCar />} />
```

You have learned how to protect routes that need authentication. Now, you will build another form to insert data about new cars and upload images (one image per car, to be precise) to Cloudinary through FastAPI.

## Creating the page for inserting new cars

The page for inserting new cars into the collection—the `NewCar.jsx` component—is protected and can be accessed only by authenticated users. In this section, you will build a more complex form and gradually modularize the code:

1. First, update the `NewCar.jsx` page and add a `CarForm` component, which you will build shortly:

```
import CarForm from "../components/CarForm"
const NewCar = () => {
    return (
        <div>
            <CarForm />
        </div>
    )
}
export default NewCar
```

2. Now, create this component in the `/src/components` folder. In this folder, create a new file and name it `CarForm.jsx`. Before starting to code the form, quickly review what type of data the form needs to collect and send to the API:

   • **Brand**: A string

   • **Make**: A string

- **Year**: An integer

- **Price**: An integer

- **Km**: An integer

- **Cm3**: An integer

- **Picture**: A file object

It would be rather tedious and repetitive to create each field in the form as an individual input and just copy and paste everything across the file. Instead, you can abstract the input field and make it a reusable component. This component will need to accept some props, such as a name and type (number or string), and RHF can register it and associate an error, if any, to said field. So, before starting the form, create another component that will be reused as many times as needed and that will significantly facilitate the process of creating and updating the form should you need to add even more fields later—in a real-life scenario, cars can have hundreds of fields.

3. Create a new file in the `/src/components` folder and name it `InputField.jsx`:

```
const InputField = ({ props }) => {
  const { name, type, error } = props;
  return (
    <div className="mb-4">
      <label
        className="block text-gray-700 text-sm mb-2"
        htmlFor={name}
      >
        {name}
      </label>
      <input
        className="shadow appearance-none border rounded w-full py-2
px-3 text-gray-700 leading-tight focus:outline-none focus:shadow-
outline"
        id={name}
        name={name}
        type={type}
        placeholder={name}
        required
        autoComplete="off"
        {...props}
      />
      {error && <p className="text-red-500 text-xs italic">{error.
message}</p>}
    </div>
  );
};
export default InputField;
```

The field component is simple, yet useful—it abstracts all the functionality and even adds some styling.

4.  Now, go back to the `CarForm` file and start with the imports:

```
import { useForm } from "react-hook-form"
import { z } from 'zod';
import { zodResolver } from '@hookform/resolvers/zod';
import { useNavigate } from "react-router-dom";
import { useAuth } from "../hooks/useAuth";
import InputField from "./InputField";
```

5.  You are going to use Zod again for data validation, so add a schema—it should ideally match the Pydantic validation rules on the backend for consistency:

```
const schema = z.object({
    brand: z.string().min(2, 'Brand must contain at least two
letters').max(20, 'Brand cannot exceed 20 characters'),
    make: z.string().min(1, 'Car model must be at least 1 character
long').max(20, 'Model cannot exceed 20 characters'),
    year: z.coerce.number().gte(1950).lte(2025),
    price: z.coerce.number().gte(100).lte(1000000),
    km: z.coerce.number().gte(0).lte(500000),
    cm3: z.coerce.number().gt(0).lte(5000),
    picture: z.any()
        .refine(file => file[0] && file[0].type.startsWith('image/'),
{ message: 'File must be an image' })
        .refine(file => file[0] && file[0].size <= 1024 * 1024, {
message: 'File size must be less than 1MB' }),

});
```

The Zod schema syntax is rather intuitive, though there might be some aspects that need caution—numbers need to be coerced, as HTML forms send strings by default, and files can be validated through handy functions.

6.  Now, start the actual form component:

```
const CarForm = () => {
    const navigate = useNavigate();
    const { jwt } = useAuth();
    const { register, handleSubmit,
    formState: { errors, isSubmitting } } = useForm({
        resolver: zodResolver(schema),
    });
```

The `useNavigate` hook is used to navigate away from the page once the submission is complete, while `useForm` is similar to the one used for logging users in.

7.  Create a simple JavaScript array containing the data about the fields that are needed for the form:

```javascript
let formArray = [
    {
        name: "brand",
        type: "text",
        error: errors.brand
    },
    {
        name: "make",
        type: "text",
        error: errors.make
    },
    {
        name: "year",
        type: "number",
        error: errors.year
    },
    {
        name: "price",
        type: "number",
        error: errors.price
    },
    {
        name: "km",
        type: "number",
        error: errors.km
    },
    {
        name: "cm3",
        type: "number",
        error: errors.cm3
    },
    {
        name: "picture",
        type: "file",
        error: errors.picture
    }
]
```

8.  With this array, the form code becomes much more manageable. Look at the onSubmit function:

```
const onSubmit = async (data) => {
  const formData = new FormData();
  formArray.forEach((field) => {
    if (field == "picture") {
      formData.append(field, data[field][0]);
    } else {
      formData.append(field.name, data[field.name]);
    }
  });
};
```

Suddenly, the onSubmit function is much more succinct—it loops over the array and adds the fields to the formData object. Keep in mind that the file field is special—it is an array and you want only the first element, that is, the picture.

9.  To complete the onSubmit function, you need to make the POST request to the API:

```
const result = await fetch(`${import.meta.env.VITE_API_URL}/cars/`, {
  method: "POST",
  body: formData,
  headers: {
    Authorization: `Bearer ${jwt}`,
  },
});
const json = await result.json();
if (result.ok) {
  navigate("/cars");
} else if (json.detail) {
  setMessage(JSON.stringify(json));
  navigate("/");
}
```

The fetch call is simple. After you get the result back, you can apply custom logic. In this case, you JSONify—render the error object as a JSON string and set the message to show it—if the error is coming from the server.

10. Finally, the JSX is trivial, thanks to your InputField component and formArray, while you also use the submitting value from the useForm hook:

```
return (
  <div className="flex items-center justify-center">
    <div className="w-full max-w-xs">
      <form
        className="bg-white shadow-md rounded px-8 pt-6 pb-8 mb-4 "
```

```
          encType="multipart/form-data"
          onSubmit={handleSubmit(onSubmit)}
      >
          <h2 className="text-center text-2xl font-bold mb-6">Insert
new car</h2>
          {formArray.map((item, index) => (
            <InputField
              key={index}
              props={{
                name: item.name,
                type: item.type,
                error: item.error,
                ...register(item.name),
              }}
            />
          ))}
          <div className="flex items-center justify-between">
            <button
              className="bg-gray-900 hover:bg-gray-700 text-white w-full
font-bold py-2 px-4 rounded focus:outline-none focus:shadow-outline"
              type="submit"
              disabled={isSubmitting}
            >
              {isSubmitting ? "Saving..." : "Save new car"}
            </button>
          </div>
        </form>
      </div>
    </div>
  );}
export default CarForm
```

The submit button is now reused as a submission indicator—it displays a different message while submitting and is also disabled to prevent multiple requests.

Building a page to update cars would be very similar to the previous endpoint—RHF plays extremely well with initial or default data that can be populated from an existing object, and you can also play with the online form builder: `https://react-hook-form.com/form-builder`. Deleting cars is also relatively simple as the request needs only to be authenticated and contains the car ID.

You have now built a car creation page, which can be extended in numerous ways. You have learned how to modularize your React code and how to provide meaningful messages and logic to your application, depending on the data flow to and from the server. Now you will build a page for displaying single cars and use loaders again.

## Displaying single cars

Now that you have created the pages for displaying multiple items (cars), authenticating, and creating new items, create an individual car page and see how React Router deals with parameters in the URL:

1.  Edit the `SingleCar.jsx` file and introduce the `useLoaderData` hook, already used for preloading data on the cars page:

    ```
    import { useLoaderData } from "react-router-dom";
    import CarCard from "../components/CarCards";

    const SingleCar = () => {
        const car = useLoaderData()
        return (
            <CarCard car={car} />
        );
    };
    export default SingleCar
    ```

    To save space, we reused the `CarCard` function to display data about the car. However, in a realistic scenario, this page would contain possibly an image gallery, much more data, maybe some comments or notes, and so on. The goal here, however, is just to show another way of creating the loader function.

2.  Open the `App.jsx` file that currently hosts the router and update the `cars/:id` route, bearing in mind that the colon denotes a parameter, in this case, the string version of the `ObjectId` component of the car in the MongoDB collection:

    ```
    import fetchCarData from "./utils/fetchCarData"
    // continues
    const router = createBrowserRouter(
      createRoutesFromElements(
        <Route path="/" element={<RootLayout />}>
          <Route index element={<Home />} />
          <Route path="cars" element={<Cars />} loader={carsLoader} />
          <Route path="login" element={<Login />} />
          <Route element={<AuthRequired />}>
            <Route path="new-car" element={<NewCar />} />
          </Route>
          <Route
            path="cars/:id"
            element={<SingleCar />}
            loader={async ({ params }) => {
              return fetchCarData(params.id);
            }}
    ```

```
      errorElement={<NotFound />} />
    <Route path="*" element={<NotFound />} />
  </Route>


  )
)
```

There are just two changes in the route: the `loader` function, which is supplied as a part of an async function that takes in the parameter ID, and `errorElement`. The `NotFound` component will be displayed, in case the `loader` function encounters an error while fetching the data. Here, again, you reuse an existing element, but it could be customized.

3.  The final piece of the puzzle is the `fetchCarData.js` file, which is located in the `/src/utils` folder:

```
export default async function fetchCarData(id) {
    const res = await fetch(`${import.meta.env.VITE_API_URL}/
cars/${id}`)
    const response = await res.json()
    if (!res.ok) {
        throw new Error(response.message)
    }
    return response
}
```

The `async` function just performs a single API call to retrieve the data related to an individual entity and, in case of an error, `errorElement` will be triggered.

Loader functions are extremely handy. By preloading data, they enable the user to have a much better user experience and the application feels faster.

# Summary

In this chapter, you created a React application using a modern Vite setup and implemented the basic functionality—creating new resources and, listing and displaying cars. This chapter also served as a refresher for you on the basic React hooks, such as `useState` and `useEffect`, and the Context API. You also learned the basics of React Router with its powerful loader functions. In this chapter, you created two forms using RHF and learned how to manage various steps and states involved with the use of your API.

The following chapter will explore Next.js version 14—the most powerful and feature-rich React.js-based full-stack framework.

# 9

# Third-Party Services Integration with FastAPI and Beanie

After learning about the tools that compose the FARM stack, you will see them combined in a more complex setting in this chapter. You will build on your knowledge of Pydantic and FastAPI to learn about **Beanie,** one of the most popular MongoDB **Object-Document Mappers (ODMs)**, and how it can make your code more efficient and enhance your developer experience.

Finally, you will see how the stack's flexibility is useful when you need to extend your application with external, third-party functionality. In this chapter, you will add a fully AI-based salesperson assistant that will make use of OpenAI to create catchy car descriptions, and then you will use the **Resend** API service to send automated emails.

These functionalities are becoming more and more central to web application requirements in the modern web, and through this chapter, you will see how the right set of tools can make application development more efficient.

This chapter will walk you through the following tasks:

- Installing and using Beanie – a Python MongoDB ODM
- Learning about the basic Beanie features (connections, CRUD operations, and aggregations)
- Using FastAPI's background tasks to handle long-running processes while maintaining the responsiveness of the application
- Programmatically sending emails from an application
- Integrating OpenAI's ChatGPT (or any other **Large Language Model (LLM)**)

# Technical requirements

The technical requirements for this chapter are similar to the requirements in the chapters in which we created backends with FastAPI, with the addition of a couple of libraries and services for the email-sending functionality and AI integration:

- Python 3.11.7 or higher
- Visual Studio Code with the Python extensions set up (same as in *Chapter 3*)
- An account on MongoDB Atlas
- An account on Render.com (if you wish to deploy the FastAPI backend)
- An OpenAI account with API access, or a free, locally run LLM such as Llama 2 or Llama 3 in case you do not want to deploy the app and incur costs
- A Netlify account (free tier)

We strongly recommend starting with the free (or cheapest) tiers of the previous accounts and making sure that you feel comfortable within these environments.

With the technical requirements out of the way, let's discuss the project you will build throughout this chapter.

# Project outline

Staying with the situation that you operate a (small) used car sales agency, the requirements are somewhat similar to the ones in the previous chapters. You will build a backend for a web app that displays information and pictures of cars that are for sale. Unlike the previous chapters, now you will use an ODM, and you will include email sending and OpenAI integration, which will be handled by FastAPI's background tasks.

The car data model will be handled by Pydantic and Beanie. The application will need authenticated users and, while you will use **JSON Web Tokens (JWTs)** again in the backend, on the frontend, which you will develop in the next chapter, they will be handled by cookies, with the help of a package called `iron-session`.

Finally, you will integrate an LLM API (in this case, OpenAI) to help create useful car model descriptions, list the pros and cons of the newly inserted car model for the marketing pages, and send tailored emails to specified recipients on every new car ad insertion.

---

**Note**

LLMs are machine learning systems designed specifically to generate and understand human language. Trained on huge datasets, they are able to perform efficiently on tasks such as text summarization and generation, translation, and image generation. In the last couple of years, LLMs have gained popularity and adoption, and their fields of implementation will only grow over time.

---

In the next section, you will learn how to create a backend with FastAPI and Beanie and how to integrate OpenAI and email-sending functionality.

# Building the backend with FastAPI and Beanie

For simplicity's sake and to make the application as illustrative as possible, the API that you will build in this chapter will not differ too much from the one built in *Chapter 7, Building a Backend with FastAPI*. This way, you will be able to naturally pick up the main differences in the approaches of using Motor (or PyMongo) directly and the Beanie ODM.

**Object-Relational Mappers** (**ORMs**) and **ODMs** are tools whose main purpose is to abstract the underlying database (whether it's a relational or non-relational database) and facilitate the development process. Some famous Python examples include the **Django ORM** and **SQLAlchemy**—two proven and battle-tested solutions—as well as **SQLModel**, which was created by the creator of FastAPI and tightly integrated into the FastAPI/Pydantic world.

Two modern ODMs that are gaining traction and popularity among the Python and MongoDB community are **Beanie** (`https://beanie-odm.dev/`) and **Odmantic** (`https://art049.github.io/odmantic/`). In this project, you will be working with the more mature and older one of the two—the Beanie ODM.

## Introduction to the Beanie ODM

Beanie is one of the most popular MongoDB ODMs for Python. ODMs are a programming technique that allows developers to work directly with classes (Python classes in our case) representing NoSQL documents. When using Beanie, each MongoDB collection is mapped to a corresponding document class that allows you to retrieve or aggregate data and perform CRUD operations, saving time by removing the necessity of boilerplate code.

Beanie also handles MongoDB's `ObjectId` type elegantly, and since its document class is based on Pydantic, you get to use all of the powerful validation and parsing features of Pydantic right out of the box.

In brief, some of Beanie's salient features include the following:

- Asynchronous, based on the Motor driver and ideal for performant FastAPI apps
- Based on Pydantic and compatible with Pydantic version 2
- Schema-based, with seamless handling of `ObjectId` string conversions
- Simple CRUD operations, as well as support for MongoDB's powerful aggregation framework

In the following section, you will begin creating a Beanie-powered application through which you will learn some features of the ODM.

## Creating the Beanie application

You will learn how to use Beanie by creating a new application and exploring the functionality provided by the ODM—connecting to a database, mapping collections to document classes, and performing CRUD operations on the documents.

To begin the project and scaffold the FastAPI application, perform the following steps:

1. Create a new folder (`chapter9`) and a virtual environment with the following command:

   ```
   python -m venv venv
   ```

2. Activate the virtual environment with the following command (for Linux or Mac):

   ```
   source venv/bin/activate
   ```

   Or, for a Windows system, use the following:

   ```
   venv\Scripts\activate.bat
   ```

3. Activate it and lay out an initial `requirements.txt` file with the following packages:

   ```
   fastapi==0.111.0
   fastapi_cors==0.0.6
   beanie==1.26.00
   bcrypt==4.0.1
   cloudinary==1.40.0
   uvicorn==0.30.1
   pydantic-settings
   PyJWT==2.8.0
   python-multipart==0.0.9
   openai==1.33.0
   resend==2.0.0
   ```

4.  Install the required packages by running the following command:

```
pip install -r requirements.txt
```

If you look closely at the `requirements.txt` file you will notice that you are installing a new package—`fastapi-cors`—that is useful for managing the **Cross-Origin Resource Sharing** (**CORS**) settings through environment variables.

5.  In the same working directory, create an empty `.env` file and then create a `.gitignore` file with the following content:

```
.env
.venv
env/
venv/
```

After getting the basic packages and settings ready, you will now create the models with Beanie.

## Defining the models with Beanie

Before scaffolding the main FastAPI application, you will learn how Beanie handles data models. As mentioned earlier, Beanie's `Document` class represents documents that will eventually be saved into a MongoDB database, and these models inherit Beanie's `Document` class, which itself is a Pydantic's `BaseModel`-based class. As stated on the Beanie website: "The `Document` class in Beanie is responsible for mapping and handling the data from the collection. It is inherited from the `BaseModel` Pydantic class, so it follows the same data typing and parsing behavior." (`https://beanie-odm.dev/ tutorial/defining-a-document/`)

Let's begin creating the models, bearing in mind that the file will also contain several pure Pydantic models for validation of inputs and outputs (not all models will be Beanie-based, only the ones that map documents in collections):

1.  Create a file named `models.py` in the root of the directory, and import the necessary modules:

```
from datetime import datetime
from typing import List, Optional
from beanie import Document, Link, PydanticObjectId
from pydantic import BaseModel, Field
```

The only new import in this code is from Beanie: you are importing the `Document` class—the workhorse of Beanie for working with data—as well as `Link` (needed for referencing data, since you will not be embedding user data in car documents but referencing the users) and `PydanticObjectId`—a field type representing `ObjectId` compatible with Pydantic.

2.  Continue working on the `models.py` file and create the base user model:

```
class User(Document):
    username: str = Field(min_length=3, max_length=50)
    password: str
    email: str
    created: datetime = Field(default_factory=datetime.now)

    class Settings:
        name = "user"
    class Config:
        json_schema_extra = {
            "example": {
                "username": "John",
                "password": "password",
                "email": "john@mail.com",
            }
        }
```

The `User` model inherits from the Beanie `Document` class instead of the `BaseModel` class of Pydantic, but the rest is largely the same. In fact, the `Document` class is based on the `BaseModel` class and inherits its functionality—you were able to use a Pydantic field with the default factory for creating the `datetime` type.

Then, you used the `Settings` class to specify the name of the collection that will be used in MongoDB. This class is quite powerful and allows setting caching, indexing, validations upon saving, and much more, as you can see on the documentation page: `https://beanie-odm.dev/tutorial/defining-a-document/#settings`.

3.  Continuing with the same `models.py` file, you will now provide a couple of Pydantic models used for specific purposes: registering a new user, logging the user in, and providing information about the current user:

```
class RegisterUser(BaseModel):
    username: str
    password: str
    email: str

class LoginUser(BaseModel):
    username: str
    password: str

class CurrentUser(BaseModel):
    username: str
    email: str
    id: PydanticObjectId
```

4. The previous code should feel familiar as it is completely based on Pydantic, so define the document model for the cars:

```
class Car(Document):
    brand: str
    make: str
    year: int
    cm3: int
    price: float
    description: Optional[str] = None
    picture_url: Optional[str] = None
    pros: List[str] = []
    cons: List[str] = []
    date: datetime = datetime.now()
    user: Link[User] = None

    class Settings:
        name = "car"
```

The Beanie document model contains all the fields that you have used throughout the book, and a couple of new ones: two lists of strings that will include small text snippets of pros and cons for each car model—something along the lines of *compact and easy to park*. Also, the car description is intentionally left blank—these fields will be populated later, in a background task, by an OpenAI chat-completion prompt.

The interesting part of this model is the user part: the Link field type provides a direct link to the user. You can check the documentation to see what is possible with Beanie relations and what the current limitations are: https://beanie-odm.dev/tutorial/relations/.

Beanie manages relationships through links in the respective fields, and at the time of writing, only top-level fields are supported. Links to related documents can be links, optional links, and lists of links, as well as backward links.

Backward links are reverse relationships: if an object called House has a link to an owner—a Person object, for instance—then that Person object can have a backward link to all the houses that they own, through a backlink.

5. Finally, add an UpdateCar Pydantic model that will be used for updating cars:

```
class UpdateCar(BaseModel):
    price: Optional[float] = None
    description: Optional[str] = None
    pros: Optional[List[str]] = None
    cons: Optional[List[str]] = None
```

Notice that you haven't defined almost any validation on the fields—this is done only to save some space and simplify the model. Since Beanie is based on Pydantic, it can count on the full functionality of Pydantic and, thus, implement complex and powerful validations.

With the models now defined, you can proceed to connect to the MongoDB database. It is important to have the models defined upfront, as their names will be fed to the Beanie initialization code, as you will see in the next section.

## Connecting to the MongoDB database

The Beanie ODM uses the **Motor** asynchronous driver as its engine. To be able to operate on documents, it needs two things: a Motor database instance, and the list of document models that are going to be used and that can be seen by Beanie. The documentation page describes this process: `https://beanie-odm.dev/tutorial/initialization/`. In order to configure Beanie and the environment variables, you are going to use `pydantic-settings` and its `BasicSettings` class for easy access to the environment variables inside your application.

The process is very similar to the one used in *Chapter 7, Building a Backend with FastAPI*:

- Environment variables are stored in the `.env` file.
- `pydantic-settings` is used to read the environment variables and create a settings object (through the `config.py` file).
- These settings, together with the models, are used to initialize the database connection to Atlas.

To create the database connection and use the models, perform the following steps:

1.  Define the configuration and environment variables by using `pydantic-settings`. Since you need the settings *before* initializing the database connection, and they are read from the environment, populate the `.env` file that will host the environment variables, which are then going to be read through the `config.py` file and instantiated into a settings object.

    The `.env` file should contain the following entries:

    ```
    DB_URL=mongodb://localhost:27017/ or the Atlas address
    CLOUDINARY_SECRET_KEY=<cloudinary.secret.key>
    CLOUDINARY_API_KEY=<cloudinary.api.key>
    CLOUDINARY_CLOUD_NAME=<cloudinary.cloud.name>
    OPENAI_API_KEY=<openai.api.key>
    RESEND_API_KEY=<resend.api.key>
    ```

    You will set up the OpenAI and Resend API keys later, but for now, you can insert the other values for MongoDB Atlas and the **Cloudinary** keys.

2.  Create a file in the root of the same working folder in which you created the models and name it `config.py`. Open the `config.py` file and create the `BaseConfig` class for reading the environment values and easy overriding of these values, based on the desired configuration:

```python
from typing import Optional
from pydantic_settings import BaseSettings, SettingsConfigDict

class BaseConfig(BaseSettings):
    DB_URL: Optional[str]
    CLOUDINARY_SECRET_KEY: Optional[str]
    CLOUDINARY_API_KEY: Optional[str]
    CLOUDINARY_CLOUD_NAME: Optional[str]
    OPENAI_API_KEY: Optional[str]
    RESEND_API_KEY: Optional[str]

    model_config = SettingsConfigDict(
        env_file=".env", extra="ignore"
    )
```

3.  The differences in connecting to a MongoDB database with Beanie compared to plain Motor-based connections become apparent in the database.py file that you will create in the same root directory and populate with the following code:

```python
import motor.motor_asyncio
from beanie import init_beanie
from config import BaseConfig
from models import Car, User

settings = BaseConfig()
async def init_db():
    client = motor.motor_asyncio.AsyncIOMotorClient(
        settings.DB_URL
    )
    await init_beanie(database=client.carAds,
        document_models=[User, Car]
    )
```

The initialization code is highlighted: the async init_beanie function needs the Motor client and the document models.

With the models defined and the database connection in place, you will now begin crafting the FastAPI application and the routers.

## Creating the FastAPI application

All the necessary pieces are ready, and now that you have the connection to the MongoDB database ready, you can start building the application. Use the freshly created database.py file for connecting to your MongoDB instance and wrap it into the lifespan context manager to ensure that the application connects when started and that the connection is deleted on shutdown.

To create the main FastAPI application file (app.py), perform the following steps:

1.  Create the app.py file in the root directory, which will be very similar to the one created in *Chapter 7, Building a Backend with FastAPI*:

    ```
    from contextlib import asynccontextmanager
    from fastapi import FastAPI
    from fastapi_cors import CORS
    from database import init_db

    @asynccontextmanager
    async def lifespan(app: FastAPI):
        await init_db()
        yield
    app = FastAPI(lifespan=lifespan)
    CORS(app)
    ```

    Apart from the init_db function, you imported the fastapi_cors package, which allows easier management of CORS.

    All you need to do now is add one line to the .env file to specify the allowed origins: ALLOW_ORIGINS=*.

    You can explore the documentation of this simple package here: https://pypi.org/project/fastapi-cors/.

2.  The connection initialization code is nested inside a lifespan event, like the previously used solution with Motor, while the rest of the code is just the inclusion of the routers that you will be creating soon and a root endpoint:

    ```
    @app.get("/", tags=["Root"])
    async def read_root() -> dict:
        return {"message": "Welcome to your beanie powered app!"}
    ```

3.  If you have installed a recent version of FastAPI (0.111 or later) that installs the fastapi-cli package, you can now start the development FastAPI server with the following command:

    ```
    fastapi dev
    ```

    Alternatively, you can use the following standard code line:

    ```
    uvicorn app:app --reload
    ```

The preceding code uses the new fastapi-cli package for easier development (https://fastapi.tiangolo.com/fastapi-cli/). fastapi-cors will provide a new endpoint called "health check." If you try it out, you will see the environment variables related to CORS (ALLOWED_CREDENTIALS, ALLOWED_METHODS, ALLOWED_ORIGINS, and others), and they are now settable through the .env file.

The FastAPI main application is now ready, but it needs two routers: one for users and one for cars, as well as the authentication logic. First, you will handle the authentication class along with the users router.

## Creating the APIRouter class for the users and the authentication class

The authentication class will encapsulate the authentication logic, similar to the one shown in *Chapter 6, Authentication and Authorization*, and create the accompanying **APIRouter** for managing users—registration, logging in, and verification.

The authentication.py file will be identical to the previously used one for simplicity's sake. The authentication.py file, located in the root of the project, contains the encoding and decoding JWT logic, the password encryption, and the dependency injection, as shown in *Chapter 7, Building a Backend with FastAPI*.

We provide the file contents here, for your convenience:

```python
import datetime

import jwt
from fastapi import HTTPException, Security
from fastapi.security import HTTPAuthorizationCredentials, HTTPBearer
from passlib.context import CryptContext

class AuthHandler:
    security = HTTPBearer()
    pwd_context = CryptContext(
        schemes=["bcrypt"], deprecated="auto"
        )
    secret = "FARMSTACKsecretString"

    def get_password_hash(self, password):
        return self.pwd_context.hash(password)

    def verify_password(
        self, plain_password, hashed_password
    ):
        return self.pwd_context.verify(
            plain_password, hashed_password
        )

    def encode_token(self, user_id, username):
        payload = {
            "exp": datetime.datetime.now(datetime.timezone.utc)
            + datetime.timedelta(minutes=30),
            "iat": datetime.datetime.now(datetime.timezone.utc),
            "sub": {"user_id": user_id, "username": username},
        }
        return jwt.encode(payload, self.secret, algorithm="HS256")
```

```
def decode_token(self, token):
    try:
        payload = jwt.decode(token, self.secret, algorithms=["HS256"])
        return payload["sub"]
    except jwt.ExpiredSignatureError:
        raise HTTPException(
          status_code=401,
          detail="Signature has expired"
        )
    except jwt.InvalidTokenError:
        raise HTTPException(status_code=401, detail="Invalid token")


def auth_wrapper(self, auth: HTTPAuthorizationCredentials =
Security(security)):
    return self.decode_token(auth.credentials)
```

The user.py router will be placed in the /routers folder, and it will expose three endpoints: for registering new users, for logging users in, and for verifying the user—given a Bearer token in the header. This last route is optional, as you will not use it directly in the next chapter (on Next.js) since we are opting for a simple cookie-based solution.

To create the API router for users, perform the following steps:

1.  Create a routers/user.py file and populate it to create the router for the users. This router is again similar to the Motor version, and it shares the same logic, but some differences are highlighted in the following code:

    ```
    from fastapi import APIRouter, Body, Depends, HTTPException
    from fastapi.responses import JSONResponse

    from authentication import AuthHandler
    from models import CurrentUser, LoginUser, RegisterUser, User

    auth_handler = AuthHandler()
    router = APIRouter()

    @router.post(
        "/register",
        response_description="Register user",
        response_model=CurrentUser
    )
    async def register(
        newUser: RegisterUser = Body(...),
        response_model=User):
        newUser.password = auth_handler.get_password_hash(
            newUser.password)
    ```

```
            query = {
    "$or": [{"username": newUser.username},
        {"email": newUser.email}]}
    existing_user = await User.find_one(query)

    if existing_user is not None:
        raise HTTPException(
            status_code=409,
            detail=f"{newUser.username} or {newUser.email}
            already exists"
        )
    user = await User(**newUser.model_dump()).save()
    return user
```

The router showcases some of Beanie's features: the direct querying of the User model (the users collection) with a MongoDB query, and the simple async creation of a new instance if the checks for existing users pass. In this case, you have two conditions: the username and the email must be available (not present in the collection). The querying syntax of Beanie is very intuitive: https://beanie-odm.dev/tutorial/finding-documents/.

2.  Create the login route in the user.py file:

```
@router.post("/login", response_description="Login user and return
token")
async def login(loginUser: LoginUser = Body(...)) -> str:
    user = await User.find_one(
        User.username == loginUser.username
    )
    if user and auth_handler.verify_password(
        loginUser.password, user.password):
        token = auth_handler.encode_token(
          str(user.id),
          user.username
          )
        response = JSONResponse(
            content={
                "token": token,
                "username": user.username})
        return response
    else:
        raise HTTPException(
            status_code=401,
            detail="Invalid username or password")
```

The login functionality uses the find_one MongoDB method, which is available in Beanie.

3.    Finally, add the /me route, for verifying the logged-in user. This method uses the get method, which accepts an ObjectId:

```
@router.get(
    "/me", response_description="Logged in user data", response_
model=CurrentUser
)
async def me(
    user_data=Depends(auth_handler.auth_wrapper)
):
    currentUser = await User.get(user_data["user_id"])
    return currentUser
```

This completes the users.py APIRouter, which uses several Beanie querying methods. Now, you will create the Car router with Beanie ODM.

## The Car APIRouter

Similar to what you have accomplished in the previous chapters, the Cars router will be in charge of performing some CRUD operations. For simplicity, you will implement only partial updates of the car instances: you will be able to update the fields defined in the UpdateCar model. Since the description and the lists of pros and cons will initially be empty, they need to be able to be updated later (by a call to OpenAI's API).

To create the Cars router, in the /routers folder and the cars.py file, perform the following steps:

1.    Begin by creating a /routers/cars.py file and list the initial imports (there will be some more added later, when you start implementing background tasks):

```
from typing import List
import cloudinary
from beanie import PydanticObjectId, WriteRules
from cloudinary import uploader  # noqa: F401
from fastapi import (APIRouter, Depends, File, Form,
    HTTPException, UploadFile, status)
from authentication import AuthHandler
from config import BaseConfig
from models import Car, UpdateCar, User
```

These imports are similar to the ones used when working with Motor directly; the main difference is the Beanie imports: PydanticObjectId (for handling ObjectIds with Pydantic) and WriteRules, which will enable the relationship of Car and User to be written to the MongoDB database as a reference.

2. Continuing with the file, you can now instantiate the authentication handler (`auth_handler`) class, the settings, and the router, as well as the Cloudinary configuration:

```
auth_handler = AuthHandler()
settings = BaseConfig()
cloudinary.config(
    cloud_name=settings.CLOUDINARY_CLOUD_NAME,
    api_key=settings.CLOUDINARY_API_KEY,
    api_secret=settings.CLOUDINARY_SECRET_KEY,
)
router = APIRouter()
```

3. After having the necessary settings and authentication ready, you can create the first route—the GET handler, which in this case simply retrieves all the cars in the database:

```
@router.get("/", response_model=List[Car])
async def get_cars():
    return await Car.find_all().to_list()
```

The `find_all()` Beanie method is asynchronous, like all Beanie methods, and it simply returns all the documents in the database. Other querying methods are `.find(search query)` and `.first_or_none()`, which are often used to check for the existence of a certain condition (such as a user with a given username or email). Finally, the `to_list()` method, like with Motor, returns a list of documents, but you could also use the `async for` construct (shown in *Chapter 4, Getting Started with FastAPI*) and generate a list that way.

4. Create the GET method for getting one car instance by its ID:

```
@router.get("/{car_id}", response_model=Car)
async def get_car(car_id: PydanticObjectId):
    car = await Car.get(car_id)
    if not car:
        raise HTTPException(status_code=404, detail="Car not found")
    return car
```

This implementation is also simple—it uses the `get()` shortcut to query the collection by `ObjectId`, which is elegantly handled by Beanie.

5. The method for creating the new car instances is a bit more complex, but not too heavy. Since you are uploading an image (a file), you are using form data instead of JSON and the endpoint must upload the image to Cloudinary, obtain an image URL from Cloudinary, and only then insert it into the MongoDB database along with the other data:

```
@router.post(
    "/",
    response_description="Add new car with picture",
    response_model=Car,
    status_code=status.HTTP_201_CREATED,
)
async def add_car_with_picture(
    brand: str = Form("brand"),
    make: str = Form("make"),
    year: int = Form("year"),
    cm3: int = Form("cm3"),
    km: int = Form("km"),
    price: int = Form("price"),
    picture: UploadFile = File("picture"),
    user_data=Depends(auth_handler.auth_wrapper),
):
    cloudinary_image = cloudinary.uploader.upload(
      picture.file,
      folder="FARM2",
      crop="fill",
      width=800,
      gravity="auto" )
    picture_url = cloudinary_image["url"]
    user = await User.get(user_data["user_id"])

    car = Car(
        brand=brand,
        make=make,
        year=year,
        cm3=cm3,
        km=km,
        price=price,
        picture_url=picture_url,
        user=user,
    )
    return await car.insert(link_rule=WriteRules.WRITE)
```

The route for creating new resources uses the Beanie methods for getting a user by the ID (provided in the Bearer token in the header) and the insert() method for inserting a new car.

Finally, link_rule allows you to save the salesperson's ID (https://beanie-odm.dev/tutorial/relations/).

6.  The `update` method is similar to its Motor counterpart, and it could be easily incorporated into a dashboard to update or delete car model adverts:

```
@router.put("/{car_id}", response_model=Car)
async def update_car(
    car_id: PydanticObjectId,
    cardata: UpdateCar):
    car = await Car.get(car_id)
    if not car:
        raise HTTPException(
            status_code=404,
            detail="Car not found")
    updated_car = {
        k: v for k, v in cardata.model_dump().items()    if v is not
None}
    return await car.set(updated_car)
```

Once again, you only update the fields that are provided in the request, using the Pydantic `model_dump` method to verify which fields are actually provided, leaving the other ones (which are `null` or None, in Python terminology) unaltered.

7.  In the `delete` method, you only need to provide the selected document and invoke the `delete()` method:

```
@router.delete("/{car_id}")
async def delete_car(car_id: PydanticObjectId):
    car = await Car.get(car_id)
    if not car:
        raise HTTPException(status_code=404, detail="Car not found")
    await car.delete()
```

You have now completed your API routers, and you are ready to implement some more advanced functionality, which FastAPI and the FARM stack in general make a quick and fun task. Before being able to use the routers, however, you will need to import them into the `app.py` file. Open the `app.py` file and modify the imports at the top, adding the routers and aliasing them as cars and users:

```
from contextlib import asynccontextmanager
from fastapi import FastAPI
from database import init_db
from routers import cars as cars_router
from routers import user as user_router
from fastapi_cors import CORS
```

Finally, integrate them in the application by modifying the same app.py file:

```
@asynccontextmanager
async def lifespan(app: FastAPI):
    await init_db()
    yield
app = FastAPI(lifespan=lifespan)

CORS(app)

app.include_router(
    cars_router.router,
    prefix="/cars",
    tags=["Cars"]
)

app.include_router(
    user_router.router,
    prefix="/users",
    tags=["Users"]
)

@app.get("/", tags=["Root"])
async def read_root() -> dict:
    return {"message": "Welcome to your beanie powered app!"}
```

With the routers hooked up, you will integrate a simple, yet functional, AI assistant that will provide marketing information about the newly inserted cars, and automatically send emails to the salespersons, to a list of customers, or to a group of subscribers.

## Background tasks with FastAPI

One of the most interesting features of FastAPI is how it handles background tasks—functions that should be run asynchronously after the response has already been sent to the client.

There are many use cases for background tasks. Any operation that could potentially take some time, such as waiting for an external API call to return a response, sending emails, or creating a complex document based on data processing in the endpoint, is a potential candidate for a background task. In all these cases, it would be bad practice and lead to a horrible user experience to just let the application hang while waiting for the result. Instead, these tasks are handed to the background to be processed while the response is returned immediately.

While very useful for simple tasks, background tasks shouldn't be used for processes that require significant processing power and/or multitasking. In this case, a more robust tool such as **Celery** (https://docs.celeryq.dev/) might be the best solution. Celery is a Python task queue framework that distributes work across threads or different machines.

FastAPI defines a class called BackgroundTasks, inherited from the **Starlette** web framework, which works simply and intuitively, as you will see in the following section when you use it to plug external services into your FastAPI application.

Before using background tasks for interfacing with third-party services, create a very simple task for demonstration purposes:

1.  Create a file called background.py in the root of the project and populate it with the following code:

    ```
    from time import sleep
    def delayed_task(username: str) -> None:
        sleep(5)
        print(
            f"User just logged in: {username}"
        )
    ```

    This function is very simple—it sleeps for five seconds and then prints a message on the console.

    The syntax for integrating the task into an endpoint will be shown in the following API router.

2.  Open the /routers/user.py file because you will attach this simple background task to the login function.

    This function could also perform some logging or some more complex and time-consuming operations that would block the response until completion, but in this case, a simple print statement will be used.

3.  At the top of the file, import the background tasks and modify only the login endpoint in the following way:

    ```
    from fastapi import APIRouter, BackgroundTasks, Body, Depends,
    HTTPException
    from background import delayed_task
    # code continues …
    @router.post("/login", response_description="Login user and return
    token")
    async def login(
        background_tasks: BackgroundTasks,
        loginUser: LoginUser = Body(...)
    ) -> str:
        user = await User.find_one(
            User.username == loginUser.username
        )
    ```

```
if user and auth_handler.verify_password(
    loginUser.password, user.password
):
    token = auth_handler.encode_token(
        str(user.id), user.username
    )
    background_tasks.add_task(
        delayed_task,
        username=user.username
    )
    response = JSONResponse(
        content={
            "token": token,
            "username": user.username
        }
    )
    return response
else:
    raise HTTPException(
            status_code=401,
            detail="Invalid username or password"
    )
```

The background tasks syntax is as follows: the first argument is the name of the function to be invoked, and the next arguments are the arguments passed to this function.

Now, run the development server with the following line of code:

```
fastapi dev
```

You can navigate to the address of the interactive documentation (127.0.0.1:8000/docs) and try to log in.

4.  If you have also installed HTTPie, you can leave one terminal running the FastAPI application in development mode, open another terminal, and issue a login POST request, making sure to use the correct username and password of a user that you have created before. For example, the following command tests logging in for the user tanja:

```
http POST 127.0.0.1:8000/users/login username=tanja password=tanja123
```

If you look at the first terminal, you will see the following message after five seconds:

```
User just logged in: tanja
```

You have just created a straightforward, but potentially useful, background task and learned the syntax.

In the next section, you will create two background tasks that will create a new car description using OpenAI's API and email the logged-in user—the user that inserted the car—with the description and the car data.

## Integrating OpenAI with FastAPI

LLMs have been the buzzword in the last couple of years and they have been dominating the web development discourse, and it is becoming hard to find successful applications that aren't using some form of LLM integration. Modern applications make use of image, text, and audio processing, and they might provide an edge to your next web application as well.

In your car-selling and advertising application, you are going to use one of the simplest features of a behemoth such as OpenAI—the task at hand is to make things a bit easier on the salespersons and provide them a baseline marketing line for each new car that gets put on sale:

1.  After having obtained the OpenAI key and setting your environment variable, modify the `background.py` file:

    ```python
    import json
    from openai import OpenAI
    from config import BaseConfig
    from models import Car

    settings = BaseConfig()
    client = OpenAI(api_key=settings.OPENAI_API_KEY)
    ```

    In the previous code, you imported a couple of necessary libraries: `json` for decoding the OpenAI response, the `openai` module, as well as the `config` module for reading the API keys. After instantiating the settings and the OpenAI client, you will create a helper function that will generate the prompt for OpenAI.

    Although these tasks are handled much more elegantly with a library called LangChain—the de facto standard when working with LLMs in Python—for simplicity's sake, you will use a simple Python `f-string` to regenerate the prompt on each request.

    Remember, the prompt needs to provide a text description and two arrays—one for the positive aspects and one for the negative aspects of the car.

    > **Note**
    > You can easily swap OpenAI for another LLM, such as **Google Gemini**.

2.  The following is one way to create a prompt for generating car data, but you will probably want to get more creative or conservative in the descriptions provided by OpenAI, depending on your case:

    ```python
    def generate_prompt(brand: str, model: str, year: int) -> str:
        return f"""
        You are a helpful car sales assistant. Describe the {brand}
    {model} from {year} in a playful manner.
    ```

Also, provide five pros and five cons of the model, but formulate the cons in a not overly negative way.

You will respond with a JSON format consisting of the following:

a brief description of the {brand} {model}, playful and positive, but not over the top.

This will be called *description*. Make it at least 350 characters.

an array of 5 brief *pros* of the car model, short and concise, maximum 12 words, slightly positive and playful

an array of 5 brief *cons* drawbacks of the car model, short and concise, maximum 12 words, not too negative, but in a slightly negative tone

make the *pros* sound very positive and the *cons* sound negative, but not too much

""""

3.  Now that the prompt is ready to be generated, it is time to perform a call to the OpenAI API. Please always refer to the latest OpenAI API documentation (`https://platform.openai.com/docs/overview`), as it is subject to frequent modifications. Currently, at the time of writing, the following code demonstrates the way to communicate with the API, which you should paste into your background.py file:

```
async def create_description(
    brand,
    make,
    year,
    picture_url):
    prompt = generate_prompt(brand, make, year)
    try:
        response = client.chat.completions.create(
            model="gpt-4",
            messages=[{"role": "user", "content": prompt}],
            max_tokens=500,
            temperature=0.2,
        )
        content = response.choices[0].message.content
        car_info = json.loads(content)
        await Car.find(
            Car.brand == brand,
            Car.make == make,
            Car.year == year
        ).set(
```

```
                   {
                       "description": car_info["description"],
                       "pros": car_info["pros"],
                       "cons": car_info["cons"],
                   }
               )
       except Exception as e:
           print(e)
```

The preceding code makes a call to the OpenAI client through the chat completion method. You have selected a model (`gpt-4`), started the `messages` array, and set `max_tokens` and `temperature`. Again, for all the parameter settings, refer to the latest OpenAI documentation. In this case, you are limiting the number of tokens to 500 and setting the temperature to `0.2` (this quantity impacts the "creativity" and the "conservativeness" of the responses).

After receiving the response from OpenAI, you parsed the JSON content (`car_info`) into a Python dictionary containing the desired keys: description (text) and two arrays of strings (pros and cons). Armed with this newly generated data, you performed a MongoDB update (through Beanie) that selects all the cars that match the brand, the make, and the production year, and you set their description, pros, and cons to the data returned by OpenAI. In case of an error, we simply display the error.

4.  Now plug the background task into the `POST` endpoint. Open the `/routers/cars.py` file and import the newly created background function at the top:

    ```
    from background import create_description
    ```

5.  The rest of the code will remain unaltered; you are only modifying the `POST` endpoint:

    ```
    @router.post(
        "/",
        response_description="Add new car with picture",
        response_model=Car,
        status_code=status.HTTP_201_CREATED,
    )
    async def add_car_with_picture(
        background_tasks: BackgroundTasks,
        brand: str = Form("brand"),
        make: str = Form("make"),
        year: int = Form("year"),
        cm3: int = Form("cm3"),
        km: int = Form("km"),
        price: int = Form("price"),
        picture: UploadFile = File("picture"),
        user_data=Depends(auth_handler.auth_wrapper),
    ):
    ```

```
cloudinary_image = cloudinary.uploader.upload(
    picture.file,
    folder="FARM2",
    crop="fill",
    width=800,
    height=600,
    gravity="auto"
)
picture_url = cloudinary_image["url"]
user = await User.get(user_data["user_id"])
car = Car(
    brand=brand,
    make=make,
    year=year,
    cm3=cm3,
    km=km,
    price=price,
    picture_url=picture_url,
    user=user,
)
background_tasks.add_task(
    create_description, brand=brand, make=make,
    year=year, picture_url=picture_url
)
return await car.insert(link_rule=WriteRules.WRITE)
```

This could be performed in a much more granular way: you could await the generated ID of the newly inserted car and update only that particular instance. The function also lacks some basic validation for cases in which the provided car brand and make don't exist, or in cases in which OpenAI doesn't provide a valid response. The point is that the endpoint function returns the response immediately—that is, almost immediately, after performing the MongoDB insertion, and the description and the two arrays are updated later.

If you try to rerun the development server and insert a car, you should see the newly created document (in Compass or Atlas) and, after a couple of seconds, the document will be updated with the initially empty fields: description, pros, and cons.

You can imagine different scenarios that could be covered by this functionality: maybe the car description needs to be approved by a human being and then the advert is set to be published (by adding a published Boolean variable), maybe you want to send the email to all the registered users, and so on.

The next section will take this background job a bit further and show you how you can quickly integrate emails into your application.

## Integrating emails into FastAPI

One of the most frequent requirements of modern web applications is sending automated emails. Today, there are numerous options for sending emails, and two of the most popular options are **Mailgun** and **SendGrid** by Twilio.

Through this application, you will learn how to set up email functionality using a relatively new service called **Resend**. Their API-centric approach is very developer-friendly and easy to start with.

Navigate to the Resend home page (`https://resend.com`) and create a free account. After logging in, navigate to the **API keys** page (`https://resend.com/api-keys`), generate a key, and give it a memorable name, such as `FARMstack`. The key will be visible only once, so make sure to copy it and store it in the `.env` file.

Perform the following steps to add Resend functionality to your application:

1.  Install the `resend` package:

    ```
    pip install resend==2.0.0
    ```

2.  After installing the `resend` package, update the `background.py` file:

    ```python
    import json
    import resend
    from openai import OpenAI
    from config import BaseConfig
    from models import Car

    settings = BaseConfig()
    client = OpenAI(api_key=settings.OPENAI_API_KEY)
    resend.api_key = settings.RESEND_API_KEY
    # code continues …
    ```

3.  Update the `create_description` function to send a message once the response is returned from OpenAI:

    ```python
    async def create_description(brand, make, year, picture_url):
        prompt = generate_prompt(brand, make, year)
        try:
            response = client.chat.completions.create(
                model="gpt-4",
                messages=[
                    {"role": "user", "content": prompt}],
                max_tokens=500,
                temperature=0.2,
            )
    ```

```
        content = response.choices[0].message.content
        car_info = json.loads(content)
        await Car.find(
            Car.brand == brand,
            Car.make == make,
             Car.year == year).set(
            {
                "description": car_info["description"],
                "pros": car_info["pros"],
                "cons": car_info["cons"],
            }
        )
    def generate_email():
            pros_list = "<br>".join([f"- {pro}" for pro in
car_info["pros"]])
            cons_list = "<br>".join([f"- {con}" for con in
car_info["cons"]])

            return f"""
            Hello,
            We have a new car for you: {brand} {make} from
{year}.
            <p><img src="{picture_url}"/></p>
            {car_info['description']}
            <h3>Pros</h3>
            {pros_list}
            <h3>Cons</h3>
            {cons_list}
            """

    params: resend.Emails.SendParams = {
        "from":"FARM Cars <onboarding@resend.dev>",
        "to": ["youremail@gmail.com"],
        "subject": "New Car On Sale!",
        "html": generate_email(),
    }

    resend.Emails.send(params)
except Exception as e:
    print(e)
```

The recipient email should be the same email that you have signed up with Resend as it will be the only option until you register and verify your domain, but more than enough for development and testing purposes: https://resend.com/docs/knowledge-base/.

The `resend` package makes sending emails simple—you just perform a single call to the `resend.Emails.Send` function and define the parameters. In your case, the parameters are the following:

- `to` – a list of recipient emails.
- `from` – the email address of the sender. In this case, you will leave the default provided by Resend, but later on, you will replace it with your own domain address.
- `subject` – the subject of the email.
- `html` – the HTML content of the email.

The parameters are fed to the `resend.Email.send()` function as a dictionary.

The email HTML in this app is constructed directly from an `f-string` in Python, but you could always resort to more sophisticated and complex solutions with **Jinja2** (for a purely Python solution, since the backend is written in Python) or use React Email by Resend (`https://react.email/`). Jinja2 is arguably the most popular Python HTML templating engine, and it is used by the Flask web framework, while React Email provides React-based email templates.

> **Note**
>
> Please refer to *Chapter 7, Building a Backend with FastAPI,* on deploying your backend to Render. com. The procedure will remain largely unchanged: just keep track of the environment variables and make sure to add the newly created ones (the OpenAI and Render keys). Alternatively, you can run the backend from this chapter in order to use it in the next chapter.

# Summary

In this chapter, you learned the basics of Beanie, a popular ODM library for MongoDB, built on top of Motor and Pydantic. You learned how to define models and define Beanie documents that map to MongoDB collections and how to query and perform CRUD operations with the ODM.

You built another FastAPI application in which you integrated third-party services with the help of background tasks, which is a FastAPI feature that allows slow- and long-running tasks to be executed in the background, while maintaining the app's responsiveness.

This chapter also covered integrating the most popular AI service, ChatGPT, into your applications, providing intelligent additional data about your newly inserted entities. Finally, you learned how to implement a simple email-sending solution, which is common in many web applications.

In the next chapter, you will dive into the most popular and advanced web framework based on React. js: **Next.js.** You will learn the basics of the latest version of Next.js (14) and discover the most important features that set it apart from other frontend or even full stack solutions.

# 10

# Web Development with Next.js 14

Next.js is a React framework for building full stack web applications. While React is a library for building user interfaces (web or native), Next.js is a full-blown framework, built on React, that provides dozens of features and, most importantly, a structure for projects ranging from simple websites (like the one you are going to build in this chapter) to incredibly complex applications.

While React.js is an unopinionated declarative library for building UIs, as a framework, Next.js provides configurations, tooling, bundling, compiling, and much more, enabling the developer to focus solely on building the application.

This chapter will cover the following topics:

- How to create a Next.js project and deploy it
- The newest Next.js App Router and its features
- The different types of page rendering: dynamic, server-side, static
- Next.js useful tools: the `Image` component and the `Head` component
- Server Actions along with cookie-based authentication

# Technical requirements

To create the sample application in this chapter, you should have the following:

- Node.js version 18.17 or later
- Python 3.11.7 for running the backend from the previous chapter (either locally or from a deployment, such as Render)

The requirements are identical to those in the previous chapters, and the new packages you will install will be described as they are introduced.

# Introduction to Next.js

Next.js 14 is the latest version of the popular React-based framework for creating full-stack and production-ready web applications.

Next.js goes as far as providing even the possibility of creating the backend server through a new Next.js feature named **Route Handlers** (`https://nextjs.org/docs/app/building-your-application/routing/route-handlers`). This feature provides functions that allow you to create custom HTTP request handlers and create full-fledged APIs by using the Web Request and Response APIs.

These route handlers expose HTTP methods similarly to FastAPI (`GET`, `POST`, and so on) and allow building complex APIs that support middleware, caching, dynamic functions, setting and getting cookies and headers, and much more.

In the next few sections, you'll be able to plug in your own, Python-based server and have that server run independently, maybe serving other applications simultaneously (a mobile application, for instance). You will be able to unleash the power of Python's ecosystem for integrating some data science or AI libraries and work quickly to have a great developer experience with Python.

> **Note**
>
> For more detailed instructions on a particular topic, you can refer to the following website: `https://nextjs.org/docs`.

# Creating a Next.js 14 project

In this project-oriented section, you will learn how to create and deploy your project using your React knowledge. You will create a brand new Next.js app by performing a series of simple steps. The project will use Tailwind CSS (integrated into Next.js) and JavaScript instead of TypeScript.

The frontend that you will be building in this chapter requires a running backend—from the previous chapter. It can run either on your local machine or, in case you performed the deployment, from

**Render**.com. During development, running the background from the previous chapter locally in a separate terminal will be easier and faster, with the virtual environment activated.

To create a brand new Next.js project and set it up the way we have specified (JavaScript instead of Typescript, the new App Router, and so on), perform the following steps:

1.  Open the terminal in the folder of your choice and enter the following command:

    ```
    npx create-next-app@latest
    ```

    The prompt will ask you if you wish to install the latest `create-next-app` package, which at the time of writing is *version 14.2.4*. Confirm the installation.

    After the installation of the `create-next-app` package and starting it with the previous command, the CLI tool will pose a series of questions (`https://nextjs.org/docs/getting-started/installation`). For your project, you should choose the following:

    -   What is your project named? **farm**

    -   Would you like to use TypeScript? **No**

    -   Would you like to use ESLint? **Yes**

    -   Would you like to use Tailwind CSS? **Yes**

    -   Would you like to use the `src/` directory? **Yes**

    -   Would you like to use App Router? (recommended) **Yes**

    -   Would you like to customize the default import alias (@/*)? **No**

2.  Change the directory through the terminal with the `cd FARM` command and run the development server:

    ```
    npm run dev
    ```

    The CLI will inform you that the server is running on the URL `http://127.0.0.1:3000`. If you visit this page in your browser, the first render of the page could be a bit delayed, which is normal, because Next.js would be compiling the first and currently only page.

3.  The page currently displays a lot of Next.js-specific styles, so to start with a clean slate, open the only automatically defined page in `/src/app/page.js` and make it an empty React component (you can use the `rafce` shortcut from the React Snippets extension):

    ```
    const Home = () => {
      return (
        <div>Home</div>
      )
    }
    export default Home
    ```

4.  Also, delete the Next-specific styles from the `/src/app/globals.css` file and leave just the three Tailwind imports at the top:

```
@tailwind base;
@tailwind components;
@tailwind utilities;
```

Now you have a blank Next.js application running, and you are ready to define the application pages. Next.js uses a different type of routing system than React Router. In the next section, you will learn how to use the most important features of the Next.js framework as you need them. Before proceeding, you will briefly observe the Next.js project structure and get acquainted with the main folders and files in the next section.

## Next.js project structure

While the documentation goes into great detail explaining each file and folder's function (`https://nextjs.org/docs/getting-started/project-structure`), it is good to know where you started. The `/app` folder is the center of the application. Its structure will determine the application routing that will be covered in the following section.

The most important files and folders that define a Next.js project structure are the following:

- The `/public` folder in the root project directory can be used for serving static files, and they are referenced by the base URL.

- The `next.config.js` file is a Node.js module used for configuring your Next.js application—prefixing assets, `gzip` compression, managing custom headers, allowing remote image hosts, logging, and much more can be configured from this file (`https://nextjs.org/docs/app/api-reference/next-config-js`).

- The `globals.css` file is the global CSS style imported into every route. In your application, you are keeping it minimal and importing only the Tailwind directives.

- Optionally, you can create a `middleware.js` function that will contain middleware that will be applied on every or only selected requests. See the documentation on middleware to learn more: `https://nextjs.org/docs/app/building-your-application/routing/middleware`

- Optionally, you can create a `/components` directory outside the `/app` folder (which has the special routing role) and create your React components inside it.

Now that you've gone through the brief project structure, you will create the pages for your application and learn the basics of the Next.js App Router along the way. You will keep styling intentionally to a minimum in order to showcase the functionalities and component boundaries.

## Routing with Next.js 14

The latest and recommended routing system in Next.js relies on the **App Router**, which you chose to implement while creating the project. The App Router is based on a file structure that resides inside the `src/App` folder—generally, every URL has a corresponding folder with the appropriate name and a `page.js` file inside of it. This structure allows you to even replace the `page.js` file with a `route.js` file, which is then treated as an API endpoint. You will create a simple route handler for demonstration purposes, but you will not use route handlers in the project.

> **Note**
> A detailed introduction to the App Router is available on the Next.js documentation website (`https://nextjs.org/docs/pages/building-your-application/routing`).

You will now build the basic page structure: a home page, a page for displaying all the cars as well as an individual car, a private page for inserting new cars (for authorized users only), and a login page.

### Creating the pages structure with the App Router

You already have a `page.js` file in the root of the App directory; it maps to the `/root` URL of the website.

Now, you will build the routes for the remaining pages:

1.  To create a route for displaying the cars (at `/cars` in the URL), create a new folder and name it `cars` in the `/app` directory, with a simple `page.js` file inside (the name `page.js` is mandatory):

    ```
    const Cars = () => {
        return (
            <div>Cars</div>
        )
    }
    export default Cars
    ```

2.  While inside the `/src/app/cars` directory, create a nested folder for displaying the individual cars based on the ID of the car. Create another folder inside the `cars` directory and name it `[id]`. This will tell the router that the route should map to `/cars/someID`. The `/cars/` part is based on the fact that the folder is inside the `/cars` directory, while the brackets syntax notifies Next.js of the presence of a dynamic parameter (`id`, in this case). Inside the `[id]` folder create a `page.js` file and name the component inside `CarDetails`.

3.  Repeat the same procedure and create a `/app/login/page.js` file and a `/app/private/page.js` file with the corresponding file structure. Run the `rafce` command and create a simple component corresponding to each page.

Now, you have the defined pages, and you can test their functionality by manually visiting the various URLs: `/`, `/cars`, `/private`, and `/login`.

This is a good moment to compare the App Router to other solutions that we used in the previous chapters—namely, React Router.

## Layouts in Next.js

Similar to React Router and its `Slot` component, the Next.js App Router provides a powerful `Layout` component that blends into the directory structure concept. `Layout` is a user interface that is shared among routes; it preserves state, remains interactive, and does not re-render. Instead of a `Slot` component used in React Router, the Next.js layout accepts a `children` prop that will render inside the base page—practically the entire application will be loaded inside this layout component.

You can inspect the mandatory root layout that is used throughout the entire Next.js application and is located in `/app/layout.js`. Try adding an element inside the body and before the `{{children}}` component and inspect on which pages the element is visible—it should be visible on every page. The root layout isn't the only layout that you can use; in fact, you can and you should create layouts for related routes that encapsulate common functionality or user interface elements.

To create a simple layout that will be used for the cars list page and the individual cars (so it will be located inside the `/app/cars` folder), create a file named `layout.js` inside the `/app/cars` directory:

```
const layout = ({ children }) => {
    return (
        <div className="p-4 bg-slate-300 border-2
            border-black">
            <h2>Cars Layout</h2>
            <p>More common cars functionality here.</p>
            {children}
        </div>
    )
}
export default layout
```

You will notice that the layout affects the `/cars` and `/cars/id` routes, but not the other ones; it is the location of the layout file that defines when it will be loaded. This functionality enables you to create different nested routes and keep reusable UI functionality based on your application logic.

Before moving on, there are a couple of features of the Next.js router that need to be mentioned:

- **Templates** are defined with a file named `template.js` that wraps the entire child layout or page but does not persist across requests. It can be used, for instance, with Framer Motion to add page transitions and animations between different pages.

- **Catch-all segments** are routes defined with an ellipsis inside the brackets, such as `[...folderName]`. These segments will match more additional path parameters. The Next.js documentation on route segments is available at `https://nextjs.org/docs/app/building-your-application/routing/dynamic-routes#catch-all-segments`.

- **Route groups** are useful when you want to prevent a folder from being included in the route's URL path, while retaining the layout functionality. Route groups are documented at `https://nextjs.org/docs/app/building-your-application/routing/route-groups`.

After having created the necessary pages and learned about the main features of the App Router, in the next section, you will learn about Next.js components and how to leverage layouts in your application structure.

## Next.js components

One of the main new concepts of Next.js is the distinction between **server** and **client** components. The most important difference is that *server components* allow you to create user interfaces that will be rendered and cached on the server, while *client components* can be prerendered on the server and then can use client JavaScript code for browser and user interactivity (React Hooks, browser APIs such as `localstorage`, and so on).

> **Note**
>
> The Next.js documentation explains the major but also the more subtle differences here: `https://nextjs.org/docs/app/building-your-application/rendering/composition-patterns`.

Generally speaking, since server components can access data on the server directly, they are preferred for tasks such as data fetching and working with sensitive information (access tokens, API keys, and so on). Client components are a better fit for classic React **single-page application (SPA)** tasks: adding interactivity, using React hooks, custom hooks that depend on the state, interfacing with the browser, geolocation, and so on.

By default, Next.js components are *server* components. To turn them into client components, you must add the `"use client"` directive as the first line. This directive defines a boundary between a server and a client component module.

## Creating the navigation component

To begin crafting Next.js components, now you will create a simple navigation component and learn about the `Link` component in Next.js.

To create a navigation component, implement the following steps:

1. Create a folder called `/src/components/` alongside the `/app` folder (not inside it, since these will not be user-navigable pages) and create the `NavBar.js` file inside it:

   ```
   import Link from "next/link"

   const Navbar = async () => {
       return (
           <nav className="flex justify-between
   ```

```
                    items-center bg-gray-800 p-4">
                    <h1 className="text-white">Farm Cars</h1>
                    <div className="flex space-x-4 text-white
                        child-hover:text-yellow-400">
                        <Link href="/">Home</Link>
                        <Link href="/cars">Cars</Link>
                        <Link href="/private">Private</Link>
                        <Link href="/login">Login</Link>
                    </div>
                </nav>
        )
    }
    export default Navbar
```

The NavBar.js component is very similar to the ones created in previous chapters. However, here, you have imported the Link component—the Next.js component that extends the <a> element (the native HTML link component) and provides data pre-fetching (https://nextjs. org/docs/app/api-reference/components/link).

2.  The previous code utilizes a Tailwind plugin that enables developers to target descendent selectors directly. To use it, open the tailwind.config.js file and edit the content by changing the plugins array value:

```
plugins: [
  function ({ addVariant }) {
    addVariant('child', '& > *');
    addVariant('child-hover', '& > *:hover');
  }
],
```

3.  Now open the root layout, located at /src/app/layout.js, and insert the NavBar.js component before the children props by replacing the existing RootLayout function with the following code:

```
import Navbar from "@/components/NavBar";
...
export default function RootLayout({ children }) {
  return (
    <html lang="en">
      <body>
        <Navbar />
        {children}
      </body>
    </html>
  );
}
```

In this step, you added the newly created component to the root layout since it will be displayed on every page.

You now have defined the routes, scaffolded the basic pages of the application, and created a simple navigation menu. In the next section, you will see how Next.js simplifies data loading through server components.

## Data loading with server components

The following process will help you learn how to load data from your FastAPI server into the /cars page without resorting to hooks and states, and see how Next.js extends the native fetch functionality.

To load data from your FastAPI server into the /cars page without hooks, implement the following steps:

1. Before creating the page that should display information about all the cars that are currently present in your cars collection, create a .env file in the root of the Next.js project (parallel to the /src folder) and use it to map the address of your API:

   ```
   API_URL=http://127.0.0.1:8000
   ```

   This value will have to change once you deploy and wish to use your Render.com API URL, or whatever backend deployment solution you might choose.

2. Once it has been set in the environment, the address will be available in your code:

   ```
   process.env.API_URL
   ```

   It is important to remember that in order to be visible in the browser, the environment variables need to be prepended by the NEXT_PUBLIC_ string. In this case, however, you are doing data fetching on the server, in a server component, so it is perfectly fine to hide the API address.

   Now you are ready to perform the first server-side fetch. Make sure that your backend server is running on the specified port 8000.

3. Open the /app/cars/page.js file and edit it:

   ```
   import Link from "next/link"
   const Cars = async () => {
       const data = await fetch(
           `${process.env.API_URL}/cars/`, {
           next: {
               revalidate: 10
           }
       }
       )
       const cars = await data.json()

       return (
           <>
   ```

```
                    <h1>Cars</h1>
                    <div>
                        {cars.map((car) => (
                            <div key={car._id} className="m-4 bg-white p-2">
                                <Link href={`/cars/${car._id}`}>
                                    <p>{car.brand} {car.make} from {car.
year}</p>
                                </Link>
                            </div>
                        ))}
                    </div>

                </>
            )
        }
        export default Cars
```

The previous code might seem simple, but it represents a completely new paradigm in React-based development.

You used the Next.js `fetch` function, which extends the native Web API `fetch` method and provides some additional functionalities. It is an `async` function, so the entire component is asynchronous, and the call is awaited.

> **Note**
>
> This fetch functionality is explained in great detail on the Next.js website: `https://nextjs.org/docs/app/building-your-application/data-fetching/fetching-caching-and-revalidating`.

While providing various features such as access to headers and cookies, the `fetch` function allows granular control over caching and revalidating the received data. Revalidation in this context means the cache invalidation and re-fetching of the latest data. Your cars page might have very frequent updates, and you can set a time limit on the content. In the preceding code, the content is revalidated every 10 seconds. In some cases, it might make sense to revalidate the data after a couple of hours or even days.

Before moving on to specialized components provided by the framework, you will learn about the `error.js` file, which is used for catching errors while staying within the boundaries of a layout and route group.

## Error pages in Next.js

To catch unexpected errors that might arise in server components and client components, and to display a fallback user interface, you can create a file called `error.js` (the name is mandatory) inside the desired folder:

1.  Create a file, `/src/app/cars/error.js`, with the following simple content:

```
"use client"
const error = () => {
  return (
    <div className="bg-red-800 text-white p-3">
      There was an error while fetching car data!
    </div>
  )
}
export default error
```

The component must use the `"use client"` directive as per the documentation.

2.  You can test the error handling page by throwing a generic error inside `[id]/page.js`:

```
const SingleCar = () => {
  throw new Error('Error')
}
export default SingleCar
```

If you now try to navigate to any car details page, you will see that the page is loaded—the navigation is present, and the main layout and the cars layout are rendered. Only the inside of the innermost route group, which contains the `error.js` file, displays the error message.

After learning how to get data inside the page directly from the server, in the following section, you will create a statically generated single-car page and learn about the powerful Next.js `Image` component.

## Static page generation and the Image component

Next.js provides yet another way of generating pages—*static rendering*. In this case, pages are rendered at build time (instead of at request time), or, in case of data revalidation, in the background. The resulting page is then cached and pushed to the content delivery network, for efficient and fast serving. This makes Next.js effectively behave like a static site generator, much like Gatsby.js or Hugo, and achieve maximum performance in terms of website speed.

However, not all routes are suitable for static rendering; pages that are personalized and contain user-specific data are examples of pages that shouldn't be statically generated. Blog posts, documentation pages, or even car ads, however, are not pages that should display different features to different users.

In this section, you will first generate individual car pages as server-side rendered pages, like the cars page before, and afterward, you will modify the page(s) to be statically rendered.

Before you begin working with the `Image` component, modify the `next.js.mjs` file—the Next.js configuration file—and let Next.js know that it should allow images from an external domain—in your case, Cloudinary—since this is where our car images are hosted.

Perform the following steps:

1.  Open the `next.config.mjs` file and edit the configuration:

    ```
    /** @type {import('next').NextConfig} */
    const nextConfig = {
      images: {
        remotePatterns: [
          {
            hostname: 'res.cloudinary.com',
          },
        ]
      }
    };
    export default nextConfig;
    ```

2.  After this modification, restart the Next.js development server manually:

    ```
    npm run dev
    ```

    Now you will create the server-side rendered version of the cars page.

3.  Open `/app/cars/[id]/page.js` and modify it accordingly:

    ```
    import {
      redirect
    } from "next/navigation"
    import Image from "next/image"
    const CarDetails = async ({
      params
    }) => {
      const carId = params.id
      const res = await fetch(
        `${process.env.API_URL}/cars/${carId}`, {
          next: {
            revalidate: 10
          }
        }
      )
      if(!res.ok) {
        redirect("/error")
      }
      const data = await res.json()
    ```

In the preceding code, you imported the `next/image` component and you destructured the parameters as `params` from the URL. Then, you performed a similar `fetch` request and checked the result status. In case of an error, you used the Next.js `redirect` function to redirect the user to the error page, which is yet to be created.

4.  Now, continue editing the component and return some basic JSX:

```
return (
  <div className="p-4 flex flex-col justify-center
    items-center min-h-full bg-white">
    <h1>{data.brand} {data.make} ({data.year})</h1>
    <p>{data.description}</p>
    <div className="p-2 shadow-md bg-white">
      <Image src={data.picture_url}
        alt={`${data.brand} ${data.make}`}
        width={600} height={400}
        className="object-cover w-full" />
    </div>
    <div className="grid grid-cols-2 gap-3 my-3">
      {data.pros && <div className="bg-green-200
        p-5 flex flex-col justify-center
        items-center">
        <h2>Pros</h2>
        <ol className="list-decimal">
          {data.pros.map((pro, index) => (
            <li key={index}>{pro}</li>
          ))}
        </ol>
      </div>}
      {data.cons && <div className="bg-red-200 p-5
        flex flex-col justify-center items-center">
        <h2>Cons</h2>
        <ol className="list-decimal">
          {data.cons.map((con, index) => (
            <li key={index}>{con}</li>
          ))}
        </ol>
      </div>}
    </div>
  </div >
  )
}
export default CarDetails
```

The rest of the functional component is rather simple. You have used the Image component and provided the mandatory data, such as the width, height, and alt text. The Image component has a rich API that is documented on the Next.js website (https://nextjs.org/docs/app/api-reference/components/image), and it should be used whenever possible because it vastly improves your site's performance.

The redirect function is imported from next/navigation (https://nextjs.org/docs/app/building-your-application/routing/redirecting).

The statically generated version of the page(s) includes providing a generateStaticParams() function to the page and exporting it; Next.js uses this function to know which pages to generate at build time.

5. For your /app/cars/[id]/page.js file, this function will need to loop over all the cars that need a static page (all cars in this case) and provide an array of IDs:

```
export async function generateStaticParams() {
  const cars = await fetch(
    `${process.env.API_URL}/cars/`).then((res) =>
    res.json())
  return cars.map((car) => ({id: car._id,}))
}
```

If you add the preceding generateStaticParams() function to the component, stop the development server and run another Next.js command:

```
npm run build
```

Next.js will produce an optimized build of the entire site, rendering the individual car pages at build time as static HTML pages. If you inspect the console, you will see the list of routes and a legend that shows which pages were rendered at build time.

Running the production build is possible with the following command:

```
npm run start
```

Before closing this section, let's take care of the cases in which the user hits the wrong URL, resulting in a nonexistent car. To handle these 404 Page Not Found errors, create a new file called /src/app/not-found.js and populate it:

```
import Link from "next/link"
const NotFoundPage = () => {
  return (
    <div className="min-h-screen flex flex-col
      justify-center items-center">
      <h1>Custom Not Found Page</h1>
      <p>take a look at <Link href="/cars"
        className="text-blue-500">our cars</Link>
      </p>
    </div>
  )
}
export default NotFoundPage
```

This route will cover all the route groups, in a similar way to the $\star$ route in the React Router package.

After having created the dynamic server-side and statically generated pages and exploring some of the most important features of Next.js, you will learn how to authenticate users with the existing API in the next section.

# Authentication and Server Actions in Next.js

You have learned about quite a few Next.js features that make it stand out as the premier web framework, but the list of the most important functionalities wouldn't be complete without a very brief introduction to **Server Actions**.

Server Actions are simply asynchronous functions executed only on the server and designed to handle data fetching and mutations (through `POST`, `PUT`, and `DELETE` methods), and they can be called through plain form submissions (the default browser form handling method), but also through event handlers (a React-y approach) or by third-party libraries such as Axios.

The benefits of such an approach are numerous. Performance is improved because the client-side JavaScript is significantly reduced, and since the actions run only on the server, the overall security of the application is enhanced and applications can even run with JavaScript disabled, much like the old-school applications of a couple of decades ago.

You will now create your first server action that will be used for logging users in, with the help of a package called **Iron Session**—a stateless session utility based on cookies that takes care of all the work that you implemented earlier with `localStorage`: signing and encrypting cookies. The usage is quite simple, and it is documented here: `https://github.com/vvo/iron-session`.

1.  Install the Iron Session package with the following command:

    ```
    npm i iron-session
    ```

2.  To use the `iron-session` functionality, create a `sessionOptions` object in a file called `/src/lib.js`:

    ```
    export const sessionOptions = {
      password:
        "complex_password_at_least_32_characters_long",
      cookieName: "farmcars_session",
      cookieOptions: {
        httpOnly: true,
        secure: false,
        maxAge: 60 * 60,
      }
    };
    ```

The configuration object defines the options necessary for the cookie encryption and decryption and you should use a strong, computer-generated random password.

The Iron Session API is very simple as the session object allows for setting and getting dictionary-like values. You will use it to set two simple values: the currently logged-in username as well as the `jwt` itself, necessary for performing calls to your FastAPI endpoints.

Now you will begin creating the server actions needed for the application, beginning from the login action for authenticating users:

1.  Create a `/src/actions.js` file and import the necessary packages:

    ```
    "use server";

    import { cookies } from "next/headers"
    import { getIronSession } from "iron-session"
    import { sessionOptions } from "./lib"
    import { redirect } from "next/navigation"

    export const getSession = async () => {
      const session = await getIronSession(
        cookies(), sessionOptions)
        return session
    }
    ```

    The previous code imports the cookies from Next.js and the `getIronSession()` function from Iron Session, as well as the `sessionOptions` class you defined earlier. You then created a simple function for getting the current session and the data within.

2.  Now, in the same file, handle the login functionality:

    ```
    export const login = async (status, formData) => {
      const username = formData.get("username")
      const password = formData.get("password")
      const result = await fetch(
        `${process.env.API_URL}/users/login`, {
          method: "POST",
          headers: {
            "Content-Type": "application/json"
          },
          body: JSON.stringify({ username, password })
        })
      const data = await result.json()
      const session = await getSession()
      if (result.ok) {
        session.username = data.username
        session.jwt = data.token
        await session.save()
        redirect("/private")
        } else {
    ```

```
            session.destroy()
            return { error: data.detail }
    }
  }
```

The code is straightforward and not unlike the code you saw in the React Router and `localStorage` solution. The important parts are the ones related to the session object—if the `fetch` call returns a successful response, it means that a valid user was found, and the session is set with the username and the corresponding `jwt`. If not, the session is destroyed.

A redirect to the `/private` page is performed only when the user logs in and the session is successfully set.

Now that you have created your first Server Action, you are ready to create a Next.js client component—the login form that will be used on the login page.

3. Create a new component file, `/src/app/components/LoginForm.js`:

```
"use client"
import {login} from "@/actions"
import { useFormState } from "react-dom";

const LoginForm = () => {
  const [state, formAction] = useFormState(login, {})
```

`LoginForm` is, unlike the previously created `NavBar` component, a client component, which means that it will get rendered on the client and thus needs to begin with the `"use client"` directive.

The `useFormState` hook is one of the newest additions to the React ecosystem (it is, in fact, imported from the React-Dom package, and not Next.js) and it allows you to update the state based on the form action (`https://pl.react.dev/reference/react-dom/hooks/useFormState`).

4. Continue building the `LoginForm` component:

```
return (
    <div className="flex flex-col items-center justify-center max-w-sm
mx-auto mt-10">

        <form className="bg-white shadow-md rounded px-8 pt-6 pb-8
mb-4" action={formAction}>
            <div className="mb-4">
                <label className="block text-gray-700 text-sm font-
bold mb-2" htmlFor="username">
                    Username
                </label>
                <input
                    className="shadow appearance-none border rounded
```

```
                            w-full py-2 px-3 text-gray-700 leading-tight focus:outline-none
                            focus:shadow-outline" id="username" name="username" type="text"
                            placeholder="Username" required />
                    </div>
                    <div className="mb-6">
                            <label className="block text-gray-700 text-sm font-
                    bold mb-2" htmlFor="password">
                                    Password
                            </label>
                            <input className="shadow appearance-none border
                    rounded w-full py-2 px-3 text-gray-700 mb-3 leading-tight
                    focus:outline-none focus:shadow-outline" id="password" name="password"
                    type="password" placeholder="*****************" required />

                    </div>
                    <div className="flex items-center justify-between">
                            <button className="bg-blue-500 hover:bg-blue-700
                    text-white font-bold py-2 px-4 w-full rounded focus:outline-none
                    focus:shadow-outline" type="submit">
                                    Sign In
                            </button>
                    </div>
                    <pre>{JSON.stringify(state, null, 2)}</pre>
                </form>
            </div >
        )
    }
export default LoginForm
```

This login form uses the `useFormState` hook, which provides the state—essentially the error object, and `formAction`. In the form, you are displaying the state as a stringified JSON object, but in a realistic scenario, you can access all the individual errors provided by the server (FastAPI in your case) and display them accordingly.

5.  After updating the `/src/app/login/page.js` page and simply adding the `LoginForm` component, you will have the following:

```
import LoginForm from "@/components/LoginForm"
const page = () => {
  return (
    <div>
      <h2>Login Page</h2>
      <LoginForm />
    </div>
  )
}
export default page
```

Now, if you try to navigate to the /login route and insert some invalid credentials, the error will be printed below the form in a stringified JSON format. If the credentials are valid, you should be redirected to the /private route, and in the **Application** tab of the Chrome or Firefox developer tools, you will be able to see a secure cookie with the encrypted data—the username and jwt, available across the entire application.

You have added the authentication functionality through the use of the iron-session package and with the Next.js Server Actions.

In the next section, you will create a protected page that is visible only to authenticated users. Although there are different ways of protecting pages in Next.js, including the use of Next.js middleware, you are going to protect just one page with a simple session verification.

## Creating protected pages

In this section, you will create one protected page—the page for inserting new cars into the MongoDB database collection. Use Iron Session to check the validity of the cookie and to pass the value of the logged-in user's username and jwt across pages.

You will create a protected page by verifying the data from the session. If the session is present (and includes a username and jwt), the user will be able to navigate to it and perform an action to create new cars through the form and an associated Server Action. If not, the user will be redirected to the login page.

The only authenticated page that you will need in this application is the one for inserting new cars, and Iron Session makes this job very easy:

1.  Open /src/app/private/page.js and edit the file:

```
import { getSession } from "@/actions"
import { redirect } from "next/navigation"

const page = async () => {
  const session = await getSession()
  if (!session?.jwt) {
    redirect("/login")
  }
  return (
    <div className="p-4">
      <h1>Private Page</h1>
      <pre>{JSON.stringify(session, null, 2)}</pre>
    </div>
  )
}
export default page
```

The previous code uses the Iron Session object: if `jwt` in the session is present, the user is able to see the page that currently contains the session data. If the session is invalid, the user is redirected to the `/login` page.

2.  To add logout functionality with the session, add another action to the `/src/actions.js` file:

    ```
    export const logout = async () => {
      const session = await getSession()
      session.destroy()
      redirect("/")
    }
    ```

    This action can now be invoked from the `NavBar` component, and the session object can be used to show or hide the login and logout links accordingly.

3.  To incorporate the logout functionality into the website, create a simple one-button form for logging the user out in a new `LogoutForm.js` file:

    ```
    import { logout } from "@/actions"

    const LogoutForm = () => {
      return (
        <form action={logout}>
          <button className="bg-blue-500
              hover:bg-blue-700" type="submit">
            Logout
          </button>
        </form>
      )
    }
    export default LogoutForm
    ```

    `LogoutForm` consists of only one button that invokes the logout action defined earlier. Let's add it to the navigation (`NavBar.js`) component with some conditional logic.

4.  Open the `src/components/Navbar.js` file and edit the navigation component:

    ```
    import Link from "next/link"
    import { getSession } from "@/actions";
    import LogoutForm from "./LogoutForm";
    ```

    After importing the `getSession` function—to track whether the user is logged in or not—and the `LogoutForm` button, you can define the component:

    ```
    const Navbar = async () => {
      const session = await getSession()
      return (
        <nav className="flex justify-between items-center
    ```

```
            bg-gray-800 p-4">
            <h1 className="text-white">Farm Cars</h1>
            <div className="flex space-x-4 text-white
              child-hover:text-yellow-400">
              <Link href="/">Home</Link>
              <Link href="/cars">Cars</Link>
              <Link href="/private">Private</Link>
              {!session?.jwt && <Link
                href="/login">Login</Link>}
              {session?.jwt && <LogoutForm />}
            </div>
          </nav>
      )
  }
  export default Navbar
```

The component now keeps track of the logged user and displays conditionally the login or logout link depending on the user's logged-in status. The private link is deliberately always visible, but you can test it out; if you are not logged in, you will not be able to visit the page and you will get redirected to the login page.

You have now completely implemented the login functionality. There are a couple of factors to consider, starting with the duration of the cookie—set through the `maxAge` property in the file `/src/lib.js`—which should match the duration of `jwt` provided by FastAPI from the backend. The application intentionally lacks user registration functionality since the idea is to have a couple of employees—users who can be created through the API directly. As an exercise, you could write the page for registering users and using the FastAPI `/users/register` endpoint.

In the next section, you will finalize the application by creating a private page that's visible only to authenticated users and will allow only salespeople to insert new cars.

## Implementing the new car page

In this section, you will create the form for inserting new cars. You will not use a form validation library, since that was covered in *Chapter 8, Building the Frontend of the Application*, with the Zod library. In a realistic application, the form would definitely have a similar type of validation. You will create a new Server Action for performing the POST API call and again use `useFormState`—the same pattern that you used for logging the users in.

As the form for inserting cars contains a lot of fields (and there could be many, many more), you will start by abstracting the form field into a separate component. The implementation of the new car advert creation will be broken into the following steps:

1.  Create a new `Field` component in a file named `/src/components/InputField.js`:

```
const InputField = ({ props }) => {
  // eslint-disable-next-line react/prop-types
  const { name, type } = props
  return (
    <div className="mb-4">
      <label className="block text-gray-700
        text-sm font-bold mb-2" htmlFor={name}>
          {name}
      </label>
      <input className="shadow appearance-none
        border rounded w-full py-2 px-3
        text-gray-700 leading-tight
        focus:outline-none focus:shadow-outline"
        id={name}
        name={name}
        type={type}
        placeholder={name}
        required
        autoComplete="off"
      />
    </div>
  )
}
export default InputField
```

With `InputField` now out of the way, create `CarForm`.

2.  Create a new component in the `/src/components/CarForm.js` file and begin with the imports and the array of fields that will be needed:

```
"use client"
import { createCar } from "@/actions"
import { useFormState } from "react-dom"
import InputField from "./InputField"

const CarForm = () => {
  let formArray = [
    {
      name: "brand",
      type: "text"
    },
    {
      name: "make",
```

```
      type: "text"
    },
    {
      name: "year",
      type: "number"
    },
    {
      name: "price",
      type: "number"
    },
    {
      name: "km",
      type: "number"
    },
    {
      name: "cm3",
      type: "number"
    },
    {
      name: "picture",
      type: "file"
    }
  ]
```

The component uses the `useFormState` hook; you already know that it needs to be a client component.

3.  The rest of the component is just a mapping over the `fields` array and the implementation of the hook:

```
const [state, formAction] = useFormState(
  createCar, {})
return (
  <div className="flex items-center justify-center">
    <pre>{JSON.stringify(state, null, 2)}</pre>
      <div className="w-full max-w-xs">
        <form className="bg-white shadow-md rounded
          px-8 pt-6 pb-8 mb-4"
          action={formAction}>
            <h2 className="text-center text-2xl
              font-bold mb-6">Insert new car
            </h2>
            {formArray.map((item, index) => (
            <InputField key={index}
              props={{
```

```
                     name: item.name, type: item.type
                   }} />
                 ))}
                 <div className="flex items-center
                   justify-between">
                   <button className="bg-gray-900
                     hover:bg-gray-700 text-white w-full
                     font-bold py-2 px-4 rounded
                     focus:outline-none
                     focus:shadow-outline"
                     type="submit">Save new car
                   </button>
                 </div>
               </form>
             </div>
           </div>
         )
     }
     export default CarForm
```

The form uses the `createCar` action that you will be defining in the `actions.js` file in a future step.

4.  The form needs to be displayed on the private page, so edit the `/src/app/private/page.js` file:

```
import CarForm from "@/components/CarForm"
import {getSession} from "@/actions"
import { redirect } from "next/navigation"
const page = async () => {
  const session = await getSession()
  if (!session?.jwt) {
    redirect("/login")
    }
  return (
    <div className="p-4">
      <h1>Private Page</h1>
      <CarForm />
    </div>
    )
}
export default page
```

The form is created, and it is displayed on the `/private` page. The only thing that is missing is the corresponding action, which you will create in the next step.

5. Open the `/src/actions.js` file and add the following action to the end of the file for creating a new car:

```
export const createCar = async (state, formData) => {
  const session = await getSession()
  const jwt = session.jwt

  const result = await fetch(`${
    process.env.API_URL}/cars/`,
    {
      method: "POST",
      headers: {
        Authorization: `Bearer ${jwt}`,
        },
        body: formData
    })
    const data = await result.json()
    if (result.ok) {
      redirect("/")
    } else {
      return { error: data.detail }
    }
}
```

The action is straightforward—that is the beauty of Server Actions. It is just a function that checks the session and `jwt` and performs the `API POST` request. The function should also include an earlier redirect to the login page in case `jwt` is not found, but this way, you let the `useFormState` hook display any errors coming from the backend.

You have implemented the website specification—users are able to log in and insert new cars and, after the period of revalidation (15-20 seconds), the cars are displayed on the `/car` page as well as on the dedicated page for the newly inserted car.

In the next section, you will deploy your application to Netlify and learn how to streamline the process, while providing environment variables and configuring settings for a deployment.

## Providing metadata

One of the main features of Next.js is the ability to provide better **search engine optimization (SEO)** than SPAs. While generating static content that is easily picked up by crawlers is important, providing useful page metadata is essential.

Metadata is an important feature of every web application or site, and Next.js solves this problem in an elegant way with the `Metadata` component. Metadata enables direct communication with search engines (such as Google), providing precise information about the site's content, title, and description, as well as page-specific information.

In this brief section, you will learn how to set the title tags of pages. The Next.js documentation is very detailed (`https://nextjs.org/docs/app/building-your-application/optimizing/metadata`) and explains the various pieces of information that can be set, but in this case, you are only going to set the page titles:

1.  Open the `src/app/layout.js` page and edit the `metadata` part:

    ```
    export const metadata = {
      title: "Farm Cars App",
      description: "Next.js + FastAPI + MongoDB App",
    };
    ```

    This simple change will cause all the pages within the layout to have the newly set title and description. Since you have edited the `Root` layout, which encloses all the pages, this means that every page on the website will be affected. These can be overridden on a per-page basis.

2.  Open `/src/app/cars/[id]/page.js` for the individual cars page and add the following export:

    ```
    export async function generateMetadata({ params }, parent) {
        const carId = params.id
        const car = await fetch(`${process.env.API_URL}/cars/${carId}`).
    then((res) => res.json())
        const title = `FARM Cars App - ${car.brand} ${car.make} (${car.
    year})`
        return { title }
    }
    ```

The preceding export signals to Next.js that only these pages should have the title that is returned from the function, while the other pages will have the unaltered title.

You have successfully edited the pages' metadata, and now it is time to deploy the application on the internet, which the next section will detail.

## Deployment on Netlify

Next.js is arguably the most popular full-stack and frontend framework, and there is a plethora of deployment options.

In this section, you will learn how to deploy your Next.js application on Netlify—one of the most popular web platforms for deployment, content orchestration, continuous integration, and much more.

In order to deploy your website on Netlify, you will need to deploy the FastAPI backend. If you haven't already done so, please refer to *Chapter 7, Building a Backend with FastAPI*, on how to do that. Once you have the backend address (in your example, the URL of the deployed FastAPI application is `https://chapter9backend2ed.onrender.com`), it will be used as the API URL for the Next.js frontend.

In order to perform the deployment to Netlify, perform the following steps:

- **Create a Netlify account**: Log in with your GitHub account and create a free Netlify account, since Netlify will pick your code from the repository that you will make for the Next.js app.
- **Create a GitHub repository**: In order to be able to deploy to Netlify (or Vercel for that matter), you will need to create a GitHub repository for your Next.js project.

To create a GitHub repository, implement the following steps:

1.  In your terminal, enter the project folder and type the following:

    ```
    git add .
    ```

    This command adds the modified and newly created files to the repository.

2.  Next, commit the changes:

    ```
    git commit -m "Next.js project"
    ```

3.  Now that your project is under version control, create a new repository in your GitHub account and choose an appropriate name. In your case, the repository is named `chapter10frontend`.

## Pushing the changes to GitHub

Now you can add the new origin to your local repository. In the same terminal inside the project, type the following commands:

1.  First, set the name of the branch to `main`:

    ```
    git branch -M main
    ```

2.  Then, set the origin to the newly created repository:

    ```
    git remote add origin https://github.com/<your username>/<name_of_
    the_repo>.git
    ```

    Here, you need to replace the name of the repository and your username: (`<username>` and `<name_of_the_repo>`).

3.  Finally, push the project to GitHub:

    ```
    git push -u origin main
    ```

Now, you can deploy the repository on Netlify in the following manner:

1. **Create a new site on Netlify**: After logging in to Netlify, click the **Add new site** button and select **Import an existing project**. You will be prompted to select a provider, and you will select GitHub since that is where you committed your Next.js project. From the list of projects belonging to your account (or the account that you logged in to Netlify with), search for the Next.js project (`chapter10frontend` in your case).

2. **Set up the site settings**: You will be presented with a page that will ask you to fill in some details about the project, which are as follows:

   I. Branch to deploy: Leave it as `main` as that is your only branch

   II. Base directory: Leave empty

   III. Build command: Leave it as `npm run build`

   IV. Publish directory: Leave it as `.next`

   V. Set the only environment variable: Click the **Add environment variables** button and set a new variable where the key (the name) will be `API_URL` and the value will be the FastAPI backend URL. If you followed the steps from the previous chapter to host your backend on Render, the value will be `https://chapter9backend2ed.onrender.com`.

3. Hit the **Deploy (<name of your repo>)** button!

After a while, you should have your website deployed to the address indicated on the page. Bear in mind, however, that the API must be working, and since the free tier of Render.com, for instance (if you used Render as your backend deployment option), can take up to a minute to wake up after going stale, be prepared to wake up the API. The recommendation is to wait until the backend is responsive—you can check it by simply visiting the API address—and then begin the deployment process. This way, you will prevent potential deployment and page generation errors.

This is a good moment to analyze the command that you provided to Netlify to build the site—the `build` command. If you run `npm run build` in your Next.js command line, Next.js performs a series of operations and produces an optimized build.

These operations include code optimizations (such as minification and code splitting), the creation of a `.next` directory that contains the optimized, production-ready code, and the directory that actually gets served on the internet.

The `build` command also generates the static pages and the route handlers. You can test the build after it successfully completes, with the following command:

```
npm run start
```

You have now successfully deployed an optimized FastAPI MongoDB-powered Next.js website and you are ready to tackle a host of web development tasks with an incredibly powerful and flexible stack.

# Summary

In this chapter, you have learned the basics of Next.js, a popular React-based full-stack framework that, coupled with FastAPI and MongoDB, allows you to build any virtually any type of web application.

You have learned how to create a new Next.js project, how to implement routing with the new App Router, and how to fetch data with server components.

Important Next.js concepts, such as Server Actions, form handling, and cookies were also introduced and implemented. Apart from this, you explored some of the Next.js optimizations such as the `Image` component for serving optimized images, the `Metadata` tags, and how to create a production build.

Finally, you deployed your Next.js application on Netlify, but the underlying principles of deployment remain the same for other providers.

Next.js is a rich and complex ecosystem in its own right, and you should consider this chapter as a starting point for your next application, which blends the best of the three worlds: FastAPI, MongoDB, and React, with the addition of external third-party services that your application might need.

The next chapter will share some practical advice for you while working with the FARM stack, along with project ideas that can help you get started right away.

# 11

# Useful Resources and Project Ideas

In this final chapter, you will learn about **FastAPI, React, and MongoDB (FARM)** stack components and some recommended actions to understand the technologies that make up this flexible stack.

For building data-driven or data-intensive applications, this chapter provides some practical advice when working with the FARM stack, along with project ideas where the FARM stack, or very similar stacks, could be applicable and helpful. You will also learn how to find your way in the constantly changing web development and analytics fields. This will be helpful for those who come from the most diverse backgrounds, but their jobs or newfound passion drives them to find a path through the data-driven world.

This chapter will cover the following topics:

- MongoDB considerations
- FastAPI and Python considerations
- React practices
- Beginner project ideas

# MongoDB considerations

In *Chapter 2, Setting Up the Database with MongoDB*, you were introduced to MongoDB to get you started with simpler projects. However, MongoDB is a complex ecosystem employed by enterprise-level companies. Therefore, diving deeper into its features and patterns will benefit you as a developer and help you understand the NoSQL paradigm.

One of the first steps in employing MongoDB is understanding data modeling or schema design. Your data model should reflect how your application will see the data and its flow, starting from the queries you make. There are advanced design patterns that apply to MongoDB schemas that are beyond the scope of this book.

*Chapter 2, Setting Up the Database with MongoDB*, covered some popular MongoDB document modeling best practices. The following list provides more tips:

- Objects should be combined in the same document if they are meant to be used together. The quote "*Data that is accessed together, stays together*" might inform your schema.

- When separating objects into different documents, try not to make JOINs necessary, although simple LEFT JOINs are possible through the MongoDB aggregation framework.

- The frequency of the data use cases should dictate the schemas. The most frequent data flows should be the easiest to access.

Coming from the relational database world, modeling relationships often boils down to the choice between **embedding** and **referencing**. In the simple application you worked on in previous chapters that listed used cars, you opted to reference the user ID when you made the CRUD application with users, since it was the simplest thing to do.

However, that could probably apply to a real-world setting as well. There are numerous empirical rules. For example, if the many sides of a *one-to-many* relationship could contain hundreds of items, embedding is probably not the best way to go.

The extensive MongoDB documentation states that **embedding** should be preferred in relationships that are *one-to-one*, *one-to-few*, and *one-to-many*, while **referencing** should be used in *one-to-very-numerous-many* and *many-to-many* cases.

> **Note**
>
> To learn more about the basics of data modeling using real-world examples, check the following documentation: `https://www.mongodb.com/developer/products/mongodb/mongodb-schema- design-best-practices/`.

Additionally, Python drivers such as **PyMongo** and its async counterpart, **Motor**, play seamlessly with MongoDB. With the help of rich data structure system and data-processing capabilities of Python, it is relatively easy to change and mix things up, change schemas, and try out different types of documents until you find the optimal solution for your particular use case.

Here are two interesting projects that could be included in some of your applications:

- **Beanie** (`https://roman-right.github.io/beanie/`) is an Asynchronous Python object-document mapper for MongoDB, based on Motor and Pydantic, that can speed up the creation of CRUD applications. You already learned how to use Beanie for backend development. Please refer to *Chapter 9, Third-Party Services Integration with FastAPI and Beanie*.

- **Mongita** (`https://github.com/scottrogowski/mongita`) can be thought of as SQLite for MongoDB. It could be useful as an embedded database for lighter cases in which you want to keep the data local, or for prototyping even before having to set up MongoDB or Atlas.

# FastAPI and Python considerations

Python encompasses data and text processing, web development, data science, machine learning, numerical computations, visualizations, and virtually every possible aspect of computing.

Best practices in Python are applicable to FastAPI as well. However, since FastAPI translates simple Python functions (or even classes, inspired by the class-based views of Django) into REST API endpoints, you don't have to do anything additional. FastAPI is built in a way that favors the developer, giving you the necessary flexibility and smoothness while writing an API.

The following list provides generic considerations that should be part of your FastAPI development process:

- Use **Git** and **GitHub** and learn a simple workflow. It is easier to learn one workflow and use it until you get used to it and then switch, rather than trying to learn all the commands at once, especially if you're the only developer trying to automate or *REST-ify* a business process.

- Keep your environment variables in `.env` files, but also back them up somewhere (API keys, external services credentials, or elsewhere).

- Learn the type hinting system of Python. It is closely related to Pydantic and adds a layer of robustness to your overall code. It is also an integral part of coding a FastAPI application.

- Structure your application properly. It is very easy and tempting to create a feature-rich application in a single file. This proves true especially if you do not have a clear specification, but you should resist this urge. Refer to the FastAPI documentation on structuring larger applications (`https://fastapi.tiangolo.com/tutorial/bigger-applications`).

The main idea is to break the application into routers and Pydantic models, so that they have separate directories. For example, you have a `/routers` directory in the book, so you should have had a `/models` directory as well. These directories should each have an empty `__init__.py` file, making them Python modules. You can keep the external service utilities either in a separate file or in a `/helpers` directory. You could go granular, depending on the complexity of your app. Remember that you will always end up with an ASGI application that is the only endpoint referenced by your server of choice, such as Uvicorn or another server.

# Testing FastAPI applications

Testing is necessary to ensure that your application behaves the way it is supposed to. This chapter won't cover **test-driven development** (**TDD**), in which tests are written before the actual code. However, there are some specific issues that you may run into when working with the async MongoDB Python driver, called Motor, and FastAPI.

Unit testing your API is essential and simple to set up. Every endpoint should be tested, and each should perform the tasks they are delegated. While unit testing in Python already has several mature frameworks, such as `unittest` and `pytest`, some FastAPI-specific points are worth mentioning.

The FastAPI documentation (`https://fastapi.tiangolo.com/tutorial/testing/`) recommends that you use the `TestClient` class provided by Starlette. Francois Voron, in his excellent book *Building Data Science Applications with FastAPI*, recommends a slightly more advanced setup using `HTTPX` (an async HTTP library similar to `Requests`, developed by the Starlette team) and `pytest-asyncio`, making the whole process completely asynchronous.

The inclusion of Pydantic makes the testing of FastAPI applications a pleasant experience and enforces certain practices that tend to produce more stable software. On the other hand, the automatic documentation of FastAPI is an incredibly helpful tool that saves you time and frequent trips between the code editor and the client.

# React practices

In *Chapter 1*, *Web Development and the FARM Stack*, you chose React for your frontend because of its simplicity and flexibility. If you are a visual learner, try the video course by *Academind GMBH* and its main author, Maximilian Schwarzmüller, called *React – The Complete Guide*.

Solid knowledge of JavaScript and ES6 is the best foundation for becoming a better React developer, but it is also important to dive a bit deeper into some fundamental React concepts and explore the Hooks mechanism, the component life cycle, and the component hierarchy.

You should familiarize yourself with other hooks; in this book, you get a glimpse of two or three of the most popular hooks, but there are many more. Knowing how and why hooks work the way they do will make you a better React developer.

As of 2024, React functional components are generally preferred to older class-based ones as they are more concise, maintainable, and flexible.

# Other topics

This section emphasizes some other important points that would be useful when using the FARM stack. While you can use the FARM stack for virtually any type of web application you choose, the stack might be more suitable for some types of apps and less suitable for others.

## Authentication and authorization

*Chapter 6, Authentication and Authorization*, is dedicated to implementing a JWT-based authentication solution with FastAPI and its consequent application in React. However, as mentioned in that chapter, that might not be the best or a viable solution for certain use cases. You may need to revert to a third-party provider such as Firebase, Auth0, or Cognito. Before committing to a third-party solution, be sure to fully understand the pros and cons, the consequences of a potential lock-in, and the price factor, especially if you are planning to scale the application.

## Data visualization and the FARM stack

*Chapter 1, Web Development and the FARM Stack*, describes some rather simple visualizations, but with properly formatted and granular JSON responses and React as the frontend, almost anything is possible. This possibility to practically mold the data according to your needs gives you a great playground where you can test, tinker, and try out different solutions, perhaps iteratively, until you reach the type of data visualization that you are satisfied with.

There is a broad spectrum of visualization requirements, and it isn't necessary to try and craft a Shirley Wu D3.js piece of art, where a simple two-color stacked run-of-the-mill bar chart could have done the job. However, with the availability of a fast backend and MongoDB accommodating virtually any type of data structure that you might throw at it, you will be ready for any task. The `Observable` wrapper of D3.js has a very interesting interface and abstracts many of the mechanisms of D3.js, so it might be a good place to start.

## Relational databases

If your use case requires the complexity of relational databases, such as SQL, and their strict structure, you don't need to abandon the FARM stack altogether. Given the modularity of FastAPI and some of the deployment options that this book explored, you can plug in a relational database, such as Postgres or MySQL, explore the documentation of SQLAlchemy or some async database Python drivers, and simply add said functionality while managing the users, for instance, through MongoDB.

# Some project ideas to get started

This section lists some project ideas to help you explore the possibilities of the FARM stack and hone your skills, but above all, explore your creativity. These sample project ideas will help you explore some functionalities of the FARM stack, like building document automation pipelines, creating data dashboard applications, and building portfolio sites.

## Old-school portfolio website

This project shows how FastAPI, React, and MongoDB are perfectly capable of handling simple portfolio sites that include content such as an **about** page, service, gallery, contact form, and more.

The following steps outline how you might create an app for this purpose:

1.  Create a nice design (or try to recreate it in Tailwind CSS).
2.  Plug in React-Router or Next.js if you want to make it fast.
3.  Use server-side generation and image optimization.
4.  For the content, define a couple of Pydantic models: a blog post, portfolio item, article and so on. Then, create simple routes for serving them via GET requests.
5.  Since this is a developers' blog, you don't even need to create an authentication system and POST or PUT routes: text-related content will be entered directly into MongoDB (Atlas or Compass) and images will go to separate folders on **Cloudinary**, queried directly through the API.
6.  Incorporate **Markdown**, a powerful text preprocessor that converts simple text (Markdown) into valid HTML. Both Python and ES6/React have excellent libraries for handling Markdown, so you will be able to find a good combination.

## React-admin inventory

Another project idea is to create an inventory system built on top of React-admin (https://marmelab.com/react-admin/), with authentication from Auth0 or Firebase, and a public-facing interface. React-admin provides an admin interface similar to the one used by Django and it is based on CRUD verbs: each resource (or item) that exposes interfaces for POST, PUT, GET, and DELETE operations can be edited, deleted, and read and new instances can be created.

Explore the package and try to think of some type of collection that you may want to manage. There are excellent tools such as **Airtable** that expose REST APIs that can be called from your FastAPI routes.

## Plotly Dash or Streamlit to create exploratory data analysis applications

With Plotly Dash or Streamlit, you can build apps that you can use to play around your data. To see these tools in action, follow these steps:

1. Pick a dataset that you are familiar with.

2. Create an input pipeline that programmatically accepts data and tests it out thoroughly. This data could come from a web or, better, API scraper or from an input file that uploads a JSON or CSV file.

3. Clean the data, preprocess it, and insert it into the MongoDB datastore.

4. Next, based on the structure of the data, figure out some useful filters and controls, not unlike enterprise tools such as Tableau or Looker Studio. If you're already familiar with data like that, you will know what to expect.

5. After that, you can open up a **Jupyter** notebook, install a couple of visualization libraries, and see what types of correlations or groupings can come up.

6. After you have found some interesting pandas-driven data wranglings, you can just extract them into separate functionalities, test them, and incorporate them into FastAPI endpoints, ready to be visualized with D3.js or Chart.js.

7. Finally, you could deploy your application and share it with your friend who manages your team to show them the data backing your draft decisions.

Earlier, you saw how easy it is to embed a machine learning model built with scikit-learn. Next, you can try embedding a neural network model with Keras or try out some simple linear regression.

> **Note**
>
> Knowledge of data visualization and exploration frameworks such as Streamlit (`https://streamlit.io/`) or Dash (`https://dash.plotly.com/`) will help you in building and deploying your data dashboard applications

## A document automation pipeline

Have you always been surrounded by repetitive documents that have the same structure? Here's what you can do:

1.  Try to think of a document server based on the `docx-tpl` package, which allows you to define a Word template, formatted as it should be, and then pass a context containing all the data that needs to be in the document, such as text, images, tables, paragraphs, and titles, all while maintaining the initially defined styles. Similar and even more powerful automation can be achieved with Excel. You can use pandas for complex calculations, pivoting, and merging different documents into one.

2.  After creating the templates, think of some FastAPI endpoints that would perform POST requests and save the posted data to a MongoDB database, along with the data (for instance, the title of the document, the author, the data, or other details), and then trigger a DOCX or XLSX document render.

3.  Save the file with a recognizable name (maybe by adding the current time or the UUID library, for uniqueness) in a directory and ensure this directory is servable, by FastAPI directly (via the static files functionality). If you plan to have a significant number of heavy documents, even an entire Nginx server block could work.

4.  These files could then be accessible to all the team members or even sent directly via mail with the cron command-line utility or something similar.

# Summary

This chapter presented some pointers to help you fortify your FARM stack knowledge, as well as provided some project ideas that you could customize and use as a starting point for your own projects. Using them, you can create numerous simple as well as some complex applications to showcase the capabilities and the flexibility of the stack. With regards to what can easily be achieved with the FARM stack, you can also explore other capabilities such as server-side rendering and image optimization with Next.js, send emails, and perform data visualizations.

FARM stack has a future as the stack of choice for professional development teams and data wranglers or freelancers who just need to tell a story through a web application. By embracing its components, you can build highly interactive and responsive applications tailored to various needs.

With all the knowledge and hands-on examples you performed throughout this book, you should now be confident in your journey to building fully functional applications using the FARM stack. As is true for any technology or tool, the more you practice, the more you get better!

# Index

## A

Aggregation framework: 4-5, 40-42

Angular: 3, 121

Apache: 2-3

APIRouter: 93-94, 128-129, 161-163

asynchronous server gateway interface (ASGI): 7-8, 73-74

Auth0: 149, 281-282

AuthContext: 136-137, 139-141, 143, 146-148, 202, 204-207, 210

AuthHandler: 125-126

AuthProvider: 136, 140, 144-146

## B

Beanie: 129, 219-228, 231-234

## C

cloudinary: 152, 170-174, 226, 233

CORS: 181-182, 223, 228

CRUD: 32-33, 78, 151-152, 161

## D

default_factory: 58, 224

deletedCount: 40

deleteMany: 35, 40

deleteOne: 35, 40

Django: 8, 50, 73

## E

ECMAScript Modules (ESMs): 98

www.packtpub.com

Subscribe to our online digital library for full access to over 7,000 books and videos, as well as industry leading tools to help you plan your personal development and advance your career. For more information, please visit our website.

## Why subscribe?

- Spend less time learning and more time coding with practical eBooks and Videos from over 4,000 industry professionals

- Improve your learning with Skill Plans built especially for you

- Get a free eBook or video every month

- Fully searchable for easy access to vital information

- Copy and paste, print, and bookmark content

Did you know that Packt offers eBook versions of every book published, with PDF and ePub files available? You can upgrade to the eBook version at packtpub.com and as a print book customer, you are entitled to a discount on the eBook copy. Get in touch with us at customercare@packtpub.com for more details.

At www.packtpub.com, you can also read a collection of free technical articles, sign up for a range of free newsletters, and receive exclusive discounts and offers on Packt books and eBooks.

# Other Books You May Enjoy

If you enjoyed this book, you may be interested in these other books by Packt:

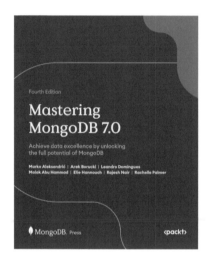

**Mastering MongoDB 7.0 - Fourth Edition**

Elie Hannouch, Leandro Domingues, Malak Abu Hammad, Rajesh Nair, Arek Borucki, Rachelle Palmer, and Marko Aleksendrić, Ph.D.

ISBN: 978-1-83546-047-4

- Execute advanced MongoDB queries for intricate data insights
- Harness the power of aggregation pipelines to transform data
- Optimize query performance using strategic indexing techniques
- Navigate MongoDB Atlas seamlessly for monitoring and backups
- Master RBAC, user management, and data encryption for security

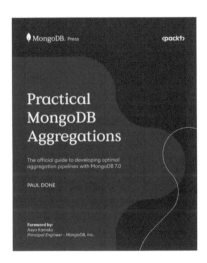

**Practical MongoDB Aggregations**

Paul Done

ISBN: 978-1-83588-436-2

- Develop dynamic aggregation pipelines tailored to changing business requirements
- Master essential techniques to optimize aggregation pipelines for rapid data processing
- Achieve optimal efficiency for applying aggregations to vast datasets with effective sharding strategies
- Eliminate the performance penalties of processing data externally by filtering, grouping, and calculating aggregated values directly within the database
- Use pipelines to help you secure your data access and distribution

## Packt is searching for authors like you

If you're interested in becoming an author for Packt, please visit authors.packtpub.com and apply today. We have worked with thousands of developers and tech professionals, just like you, to help them share their insight with the global tech community. You can make a general application, apply for a specific hot topic that we are recruiting an author for, or submit your own idea.

## Download a free PDF copy of this book

Thanks for purchasing this book!

Do you like to read on the go but are unable to carry your print books everywhere?

Is your eBook purchase not compatible with the device of your choice?

Don't worry, now with every Packt book you get a DRM-free PDF version of that book at no cost.

Read anywhere, any place, on any device. Search, copy, and paste code from your favorite technical books directly into your application.

The perks don't stop there, you can get exclusive access to discounts, newsletters, and great free content in your inbox daily

Follow these simple steps to get the benefits:

1.  Scan the QR code or visit the link below

https://packt.link/free-ebook/9781835886762

2.  Submit your proof of purchase

3.  That's it! We'll send your free PDF and other benefits to your email directly

Milton Keynes UK
Ingram Content Group UK Ltd.
UKHW052309230924
448548UK00001B/1